Byron and the Jews

Byron and the Jews

Sheila A. Spector

WAYNE STATE UNIVERSITY PRESS   DETROIT

© 2010 by Wayne State University Press, Detroit, Michigan 48201. All rights reserved. No part of this book may be reproduced without formal permission. Manufactured in the United States of America.

14 13 12 11 10   5 4 3 2 1

Library of Congress Cataloging-in-Publication Data

Spector, Sheila A., 1946–
  Byron and the Jews / Sheila A. Spector.
    p. cm.
  Includes bibliographical references and index.
  ISBN 978-0-8143-3442-3 (cloth : alk. paper)
  1. Byron, George Gordon Byron, Baron, 1788–1824—Knowledge—Jews. 2. Byron, George Gordon Byron, Baron, 1788–1824—Influence. 3. Byron, George Gordon Byron, Baron, 1788–1824—Translations into Hebrew. 4. Byron, George Gordon Byron, Baron, 1788–1824—Translations into Yiddish. 5. English literature—Jewish authors—History and criticism. 6. Hebrew literature—English influence. 7. Jews—Intellectual life. 8. Jews—Identity. I. Title.
  PR4392.J48S74 2010
  821'.7—dc22

                                                                         2009049309

Typeset by Alpha Design & Composition
Composed in Walbaum and Adobe Garamond Pro

For my cousin, Amy Jean Sussman Scherr

*"She walks in beauty, like the night
Of cloudless climes and starry skies."*

Contents

Acknowledgments ix
A Note on the (Un)Translations xi

Introduction:
Translation and Identity   1

chapter 1.
Byron and English Jews   23

chapter 2.
Byron and the *Maskilim*   54

chapter 3.
Byron and the Yiddishists   94

chapter 4.
Byron and the Zionists   137

Conclusion:
Translation and *Allegoresis*   171

Appendix: Transcriptions   177
Notes   203
Bibliography   223
Index   237

Acknowledgments

As what might be called an "accidental Byronist," that is, as one who found her way to the British Romantic poet through Hebrew and Yiddish translations, I have had to rely a great deal on the kindness of others for help with this study. First, many Byron scholars were essential, not only for their published materials but for their personal generosity as well. In particular, Charles E. Robinson has been a consistent resource, both helping me generate basic research and initiating correspondence with Peter Cochran and Nizhni Novgorod, who helped me locate some of the Russian materials. Frederick Burwick and Paul Douglass commented on early versions of the section on the *Hebrew Melodies;* and Andrew Elfenbein and Emily A. Bernhard Jackson both read portions of the manuscript. Finally, Kari Lokke, Judith W. Page, Donald H. Reiman, Julia L. Scherr, Esther Schor, Reeva S. Simon, and Mike Snell all helped at various stages along the way. Certainly not to be overlooked are the anonymous readers whose critiques enabled me to revise the manuscript into a much stronger study.

I also want to thank the many people who made suggestions when I presented sections of the book at conferences and colloquia. In particular, I appreciate comments from those who attended my panels at the Modern Language Association, the North American Society for the Study of Romanticism, the Joint Conference of the Centro interdiscisplinare di studi romantici and the North American Society for the Study of Romanticism, the International Conference on Romanticism, the American Comparative Literature Association, the Queens College Center for Jewish Studies Faculty Colloquium, and the Eighteenth-Century Group, City University of New York Graduate Center. Discussions following my presentations helped me clarify particular aspects of the relationship between Byron and the Jews.

Needless to say, this study entailed a great deal of archival work, so I have an especially large debt to a number of research institutions and their staffs. In particular, I want to thank the staff at the Dorot Jewish Division,

ACKNOWLEDGMENTS

New York Public Library; Yeshaya Metal at the YIVO Institute for Jewish Research, New York; Linda Stein at the University of Delaware Library, Newark; the staff at the Carl H. Pforzheimer Collection of Shelley and His Circle, the New York Public Library; the Hebraic Section of the Library of Congress, Washington, DC; the Bobst Library of New York University; and the libraries of the City University of New York. I owe special thanks to the National Yiddish Book Center, Amherst, Massachusetts, which, through the Steven Spielberg Digital Yiddish Library, provided me with a reprint of Zilberman's biography of Byron.

Finally, I want to thank Kathryn Peterson Wildfong and the staff at Wayne State University Press for helping me transform my original manuscript into what I hope will be a well-received book.

I apologize for having inevitably omitted some whose contributions also enriched this study. Needless to say, the book's strengths benefited from all those who helped me along the way; the weaknesses, unfortunately, are my own.

A Note on the (Un)Translations

Unless otherwise indicated, all translations, or, to be more precise, "untranslations," are mine. There are several stages involved in the process of translation. Beyond transferring the vocabulary from one language to another, translators must also consider the syntax, the patterns governing how words are put together to make sense; and if translators wish at the very least to be understood by the new audience, they inevitably, at a certain point, must replace the original language's internal logical structures with those of the new. In contrast, the goal of "untranslation" is not to render the text comprehensible to the new audience but rather to reveal the process by which a translator manipulated the original in order to make it conform to the rules of a new language. Therefore, in rendering these Hebrew and Yiddish texts into English, I have tried to work backwards—that is, to expose the means by which the various translators "Judaized" Byron. This includes line numbers, especially of the longer poems where the translators strayed more or less freely from the original. The point was not to adapt the texts for an Anglophone audience. After all, readers already have access to the best English versions—Byron's originals. Instead, I have tried to approximate the version of Byron that Jewish readers would have received.

Placing his argument in the context of Anglophone imperialism, in *The Translator's Invisibility,* Lawrence Venuti asserts:

> The translator's invisibility can now be seen as a mystification of troubling proportions, an amazingly successful concealment of the multiple determinants and effects of English-language translation, the multiple hierarchies and exclusions in which it is implicated. An illusionism fostered by fluent translating, the translator's invisibility at once enacts and masks an insidious domestication of foreign texts, rewriting them in the transparent discourse that prevails. (12–13)

NOTE ON THE (UN)TRANSLATIONS

Although not Anglophone, the Jewish translators, too, strove for "invisibility," and in this study, by exposing the means by which they achieved their "invisibility," I hope to reveal the various agendas behind their translations.

The Hebrew translations are especially problematic. The nineteenth century was part of the transition from Medieval to Modern or Israeli Hebrew. During that period, some *maskilim*, believing that Hebrew had been corrupted by rabbinic use and vernacular influence, attempted to restore the language to what they believed to be its pristine biblical roots. As Angel Sáenz-Badillos, in his *History of the Hebrew Language*, summarizes the results:

> Although some nineteenth-century writers tried to use a fundamentally biblical form of language, they often introduced structures that were alien to its spirit and frequently made grammatical errors, incorrectly employing the article with nouns in the construct state, treating intransitive verbs as transitives, confusing particles, and so on. Also, they frequently had recourse to turgid paraphrase in a desperate attempt not to stray from the limited vocabulary of the Bible for expressing contemporary referents, thus endowing many biblical expressions with new content. (268)

In addition to having a limited vocabulary, biblical Hebrew tends to be parataxic, with grammatical units juxtaposed against each other, often minus the conjunctions or prepositional markers that would indicate relationship. In "untranslating" the Hebrew versions of Byron, I tried to "English" the vocabulary, while retaining, to the extent possible, the translator's use of paraphrase and parataxis. Though the result might seem choppy to an Anglophone ear, it provides, I hope, a more accurate reflection of the "Byron" that Hebrew readers received, certainly more so than would have been possible had I imposed a regularized English syntax on the text.

Yiddish presents the opposite kind of problem. As a fusion language, Yiddish comprises a combination of Hebrew and the various vernaculars used by European Jews, all superimposed onto a medieval German base. Although its syntax is Germanic, and therefore fairly consistent with English, the vocabulary, derived from so many different cultural sources, brings with it a wealth of heteroglossia, to borrow Mikhail Bakhtin's term, making the choice of a particular word resonate with biblical, liturgical, or historical associations that could have a significant cultural, not to mention ideological, impact on the reception of the text. Therefore, although the Yiddish translations tend to be more readable for the Anglophone audience, their Englishing has inevitably reduced their Yiddish plenitude.

Introduction
Translation and Identity

Several years ago, I compiled a bibliography of Hebrew and Yiddish translations of British Romantic literature and to my surprise found that Byron was the most frequently cited writer.[1] Given the unexpected results, I then determined to discover why approximately two dozen Jews, ranging from mid-nineteenth-century Europeans to modern Israelis and Americans, would all be attracted to a gentile poet considered even by his close friends to be "mad, bad, and dangerous to know." My analysis has resulted in this book, the thesis of which is that in their own attempts to define their respective *nations,* Byron and these Jews translated each other in order to develop a sense of identity that was predicated on intellectual elitism and moral integrity, rather than on geographical specificity and religion.[2]

Historically, eighteenth-century rationalism yielded renewed skepticism —not only about revealed religion but also about the role of religious institutions in what were becoming increasingly more diverse states, the result being a competition between religious and secular institutions for dominance over the nation as a whole. It was this kind of conflict that Byron and the roughly two dozen Jews discussed in this book had in common. For his part, Byron, though a citizen of what would become the most expansive colonial power on the globe, felt compelled to leave his geographical homeland in order to escape the restrictive and, in his opinion, hypocritical religious authorities of his nation in order to develop his own identity as a Briton of Scottish ancestry. In contrast, the Jews, who historically had lived in relative isolation in the Diaspora, could not rely on geography to define their nation; so before the Haskalah, their Enlightenment, they had relied on religion to generate their sense of identity, though in so doing, they had ceded to the rabbis an enormous amount of control over their community. Consequently, the more radical reformers, who determined that the religious authorities were out of touch with the realities of the post-Haskalah world, sought a new national identity, one that could replace religion as the central component of the Jewish identity. In their respective quests, Byron and these Jews would turn to each other: Byron to his contemporaries Isaac D'Israeli and Isaac Nathan for both direct and indirect help in crystallizing his identity as the Byronic hero, and later Jews to selected works by Byron for assistance in articulating an alternate Jewish identity.

Given their shared interests, it seems logical that Byron and these Jews would turn to each other.[3] Both wrote about biblical subjects, and, it has been argued, Byron's *Hebrew Melodies* anticipates political Zionism, the movement to be consolidated by Theodor Herzl at the end of the nineteenth century. On a deeper level, though, both Byron and the Jews covered in this study might be considered Spinozans manqué. Most of them shared a skeptical attitude toward organized religion, and they resisted the control institutional authorities attempted to exert over them. However, unlike Spinoza, who left the Jewish community entirely, Byron and this group of Jews all sought, instead, to amend their respective identities to accommodate more capacious views of nationality than those authorized by organized religion; and they all used various forms of translation as the vehicle through which to accomplish that aim.

Translation Theory

On the most basic level, translation is defined as the transfer of information from one mode of expression into another.[4] A number of commonly held misconceptions obscure the full implications of translation, however. Most obviously, the truism that a translation must be an accurate reflection of the author's intention is nugatory. Despite the fact that different languages may have specific words for the same concept—bread, *leḥem* (Hebrew), *breut* (Yiddish)—translation more precisely revolves around the context, not the word, so that, according to the cliché, there can be no exact translations. In fact, if one wants an accurate reading of a text—assuming the validity of the concept of an accurate reading—one works with the original. In contrast, a translation is an interpretation of a text, produced at a different time and place from the original; consequently, a translation is more appropriately evaluated from the perspective of cultural history. Similarly, the belief that translation is about one culture's gaining understanding of another is equally simplistic, for a translation can be no more than a second culture's interpretation of and appropriation from the first; consequently, it is inherently biased.

More precisely, translation should be viewed as an act of transplantation in which the original soil is abandoned so that a text can flourish in an entirely different garden.[5] Therefore, the primary focus of translation study should not be on the intention of the author or the reception by his or her culture, ties with both of which are severed in the act of translation; instead, the interest is shifted to the attitude of the translator toward his or her culture.[6] Regardless of the stated reason for translating a particular text, the act of translation is inevitably a tacit recognition of a lack in the importing culture. For some reason, that culture has not produced, or cannot produce, a given text, and a translation is required to supplement what already exists. There can be many reasons why one translates, rather than producing an indigenous text. The most obvious has to do with national identity. It is possible that the governing structure of a culture is so rigid that it is impossible to think certain thoughts or, if they can be thought, to articulate them intelligibly: hence the need to introduce an alien text. It is also possible that the governing authorities, who interpret their job as perpetuating the culture's current sense of identity, might censor a text that—or punish an author who—threatens to undermine their hegemony. In this case, a popular work from a different, frequently admired culture, could fool censors, who are so impressed with its high-cultural value that they fail to recognize its potentially subversive nature. Finally, it is also possible that the culture lacks an indigenous voice strong enough to produce its own text.[7] Given the control exercised over the mind by the system, especially within a minor culture, it is possible that no one has the ability to articulate, or the power to sustain, what might be perceived as an attack on the cultural structure.[8]

Despite its superficially felicitous reputation, translation is fundamentally an act of cultural subversion, the translator importing into an already existing structure elements that inevitably challenge its validity;[9] and once that alien text has been introduced, the system's configuration will be altered as it adapts to accommodate the new text, for the very act of accommodation compromises the system's own integrity as, bit by bit, elements from other cultures are absorbed until, potentially, the system merges with a universal Culture that threatens to subsume each individual culture. In this way, the act of translation represents a move toward intellectual cosmopolitanism, the inverse of nationalism.[10]

INTRODUCTION

This study applies the theory to the ways the Jews discussed in this book and Byron translated each other.[11] Of Byron's contemporaries, his and Isaac D'Israeli's use of translation was *intralingual*, involving the transfer of a text from one set of signs into a second set of signs, both from the same language. In this case, Byron and D'Israeli translated the *illuy*, the Jewish concept of genius, from D'Israeli's English to Byron's, and then back again to D'Israeli's, through their indirect correspondence. Byron's relationship with his other Jewish contemporary, Isaac Nathan, relied on *intersemiotic* translation to transfer a text from verbal into nonverbal signs; specifically, Nathan translated Byron's verbal lyrics into music, and conversely, Byron translated some of the music into lyrics. Finally, the later Jewish Byronists all practiced *interlingual* translation, transferring the Byronic materials that originated in English into Hebrew or Yiddish.[12]

Byronic Identity

Many of the Jews discussed in this study felt an affinity with what they knew of Byron's biography. As Thomas Babington Macaulay describes him:

> [T]here was a strange union of opposite extremes. He was born to all that men covet and admire. But in every one of those eminent advantages which he possessed over others was mingled something of misery and debasement. He was sprung from a house, ancient indeed and noble, but degraded and impoverished by a series of crimes and follies which had attained a scandalous publicity. The kinsman whom he succeeded had died poor, and, but for merciful judges, would have died upon the gallows. The young peer had great intellectual powers; yet there was an unsound part in his mind. He had naturally a generous and feeling heart: but his temper was wayward and irritable. He had a head which statuaries loved to copy, and a foot the deformity of which the beggars in the streets mimicked. Distinguished at once by the strength and by the weakness of his intellect, affectionate yet perverse, a poor lord and a handsome cripple, he required, if ever man required, the firmest and the most judicious training. But, capriciously as nature had dealt with him, the parent to whom the office of forming his character was intrusted was more capricious still. She passed from paroxysms of rage to paroxysms of tenderness. At one time she stifled him with her caresses: at another time she insulted his deformity. He came into the world; and the world treated him as his mother had treated him, sometimes with fondness, sometimes with cruelty, never

with justice. It indulged him without discrimination, and punished him without discrimination. He was truly a spoiled child, not merely the spoiled child of his parent, but the spoiled child of nature, the spoiled child of fortune, the spoiled child of fame, the spoiled child of society. His first poems were received with a contempt which, feeble as they were, they did not absolutely deserve. The poem which he published on his return from his travels was, on the other hand, extolled far above its merit.[13]

The total effect of these contradictory details has been a kind of cultural chameleon, reflecting back to others that which they wished to see.[14] Not a passive participant in the process, Byron actively exploited the inconsistencies and notoriety to fashion a quasi-fictional persona, one that remained unaffiliated with any particular Christian sect or doctrine.[15] The result was a figure that could be easily adapted into a reflection of the Jewish self-image: a man of integrity, tormented by religious hypocrites.[16]

To summarize very briefly what is generally considered to have been his dysfunctional life, Byron was born in 1788, with a deformed foot. He was raised by an unstable single mother who was a strict Calvinist; and he became sexually active at an early age. At ten, when he unexpectedly inherited the title Lord Byron, his life changed. He attended better schools, later went to Cambridge, and then traveled across war-torn Europe to the Levant, writing about his experiences in the first two cantos of *Childe Harold*, at whose publication, in 1811, he became an overnight sensation. He returned to London, where he enjoyed the perquisites of celebrity, sexual and otherwise. In 1815, he married Annabella Milbank, who left him in 1816. By then, public reaction to his notoriety had grown so vociferous that he felt compelled to leave Great Britain for self-exile in Europe. Eventually, he joined the Greek struggle for independence against the Turks, caught a fever, received poor medical treatment, and died in 1824.

Without distorting the facts too radically, the Byron of this brief sketch can easily be transformed into a Jewish symbol. His physical disability can be read as a metaphor for the political and social disabilities that had been imposed on the Jews; and the public outcry of Christians against what many considered to have been Byron's immoral behavior parallels the anti-Semitic slanders that have been leveled against the Jews throughout history. Finally, his exile from Great Britain made Byron, like them, a diasporean; and his fight for Greek independence prefigured their own struggles, originally for emancipation, and eventually for their own homeland.

INTRODUCTION

Given the figurative correspondences between the Byronic persona and the Jewish self-image, it should not be surprising that none of the Hebrew or Yiddish materials refers to any of Byron's anti-Semitic comments, such as those found in the letters, *Don Juan,* or *The Age of Bronze.*[17]

Consistent with the pared-down version of Byron's life, the Hebrew and Yiddish audiences had access to only a few of Byron's poems. Most notably, there were no translations of the satires—no *Don Juan*. Rather, each translator seems to have chosen those particular works that could be used in the construction of his particular version of the new Jewish identity, consisting primarily of intellectual elitism, moral integrity and, except for the Zionists, a diasporean existence. The specific works include *Childe Harold,* canto 1 (1812), *Hebrew Melodies* (1815), *The Prisoner of Chillon* (1816), *Mazeppa* (1816), *Darkness* (1816), *Manfred* (1817), *Cain* (1821), and *Heaven and Earth* (1821).[18]

Significantly, the only canto of *Childe Harold's Pilgrimage* to be translated into a Jewish language is the first. Although written as Byron's response to war-ravaged Iberia, canto 1 can be interpreted as an emblem of the Jewish Diaspora. Composed between 1809 and 1811, while Byron was on his grand tour, the travelogue recounts his visits to Portugal and Spain, though filtered through the lens of the jaded Harold, whose attitude implied a criticism of war-torn Europe.[19] The protagonist of *Childe Harold,* though distinct from the biographical Byron, was similar enough to generate the kinds of speculations that eventually would consolidate into the mythical Byronic hero: "the highborn, melancholy, vaguely wicked wanderer, the cheerful, sophisticated Epicurean, the doubter, the doer of deeds, the freedom fighter," as he is described by Peter Graham.[20] Probably spurred by a suggestion from John Galt and a reading of Spenser's *Faerie Queene,* it is also likely that the composition was influenced by Isaac D'Israeli's *An Essay on the Manners and Genius of the Literary Character* as well.[21] Unlike the British audience, which read *Childe Harold* like a travelogue of contemporary Portugal and Spain, Jewish readers would associate Byron's descriptions of the war-torn peninsula with their own history, especially the series of expulsions—from England at the end of the thirteenth century, France at the end of the fourteenth, culminating in the expulsion from Iberia at the end of the fifteenth. More contemporaneously to the translator, Childe Harold's travels foreshadowed the pogroms that would lead to mass migrations from Russia at the end of the nineteenth century and the early twentieth.

The *Hebrew Melodies,* the Byronic work most frequently translated by Jews, provides a palimpsest of Jewish history. An aggregate of twenty-nine poems, written on biblical and proto-Zionist as well as secular themes, and placed by composer Isaac Nathan into a Jewish liturgical context, the work provoked anti-Semitic responses in its original audience.[22] Some of the Jewish translators picked up on Byron's religious skepticism, while others, in contrast, presented the lyrics as conventional expressions of Jewish culture. Most seemed to take pride in the fact that Byron would write about what they considered to be explicitly Jewish material, though before the middle of the twentieth century, none of them discussed Nathan's contribution to the song cycle.

If the next poem, *The Prisoner of Chillon*, lacks a direct connection with the Jews, its theme—a man being imprisoned "for [his] father's faith"—implies their concept of moral integrity. The poem was inspired by a visit on June 25, 1816, to Chillon Castle, the site where François Bonivard (b. 1493) was imprisoned between 1530 and 1536 for supporting Protestant Geneva against Catholic Savoy. Although, as Byron indicates in the later "Sonnet on Chillon," Bonivard was an emblem of the struggle for liberty, *The Prisoner of Chillon*, which was written before Byron learned of Bonivard's resistance to oppression, is usually interpreted as a psychological study of the effects of isolation and imprisonment on the human spirit. Still, in "'Making Death a Victory': Victimhood and Power in Byron's *Prometheus* and *The Prisoner of Chillon*," Ian Dennis implies an affinity with the Jewish experience, asserting that Byron's poem demonstrates the power of the minority over the majority: "Abandonment and victimhood are rewarded, as they often are in relations beyond the poem, with a feeling of justification, of righteousness, even of exaltation. Such sentiments are always relative to imagined others: one is justified to or against someone else, exalted over someone else."[23]

Written around the same time as *The Prisoner of Chillon*, *Mazeppa* can be viewed in terms of the stateless diasporean Jew. Based on Voltaire's *History of Charles XII*, *Mazeppa* is about a Polish page in the court of King John Casimir V who, after being banished for adultery with a nobleman's wife, becomes Hetman of the Ukraine under Peter the Great; Mazeppa subsequently defects to Charles XII of Sweden. Framing his account is an encounter in which the king inquires about Mazeppa's past but then falls asleep before the story is over. For eastern European Jews, the connection with the Ukraine would resonate, as would Mazeppa's unappreciated service to various countries that, apparently, took him for granted. With the advent of political Zionism, however, he could also signify the restoration of a long-forgotten component of the Jewish identity, the military hero.

INTRODUCTION

Also included in the volume *The Prisoner of Chillon and Other Poems* is *Darkness*, a poem noted most for anticipating the popular theme of the "last man," an apocalyptic vision that mirrors the uncertainty of Byron's own life, as well as that of Europe as a whole during the period.[24]

The three plays that attracted the Jews—*Manfred, Cain,* and *Heaven and Earth*—all revolve around a combination of the intellectual elitism and moral integrity prized by Byron and post-Enlightenment Jews. The first, *Manfred,* is a three-act "dramatic poem" in which the intellectually superior protagonist (a version of the Byronic hero with elements of Faust and Hamlet), having committed some unspeakable crime, retains his integrity by refusing to bow down to any supernatural or religious authority. The second play, *Cain,* is a three-act "mystery," a term Byron defined as "a tragedy on a sacred subject." Written from the perspective of the biblical Cain, the play had historically been condemned for having subverted religious orthodoxy through a skeptical inquiry predicated on a belief in free will.[25] Critical discussion has also focused on Byron's reading of the Bible.[26] Wolf Z. Hirst, in "Byron's Lapse into Orthodoxy: An Unorthodox Reading of *Cain,*" asserts that "it is not antireligious, that it accepts rather than reverses the Scriptural position, and that the hero's attacks upon God are dramatically invalidated."[27] More recently, Peter A. Schock, in "The 'Satanism' of *Cain* in Context: Byron's Lucifer and the War against Blasphemy," has argued that Byron, like Shelley, followed a "strategy of using the satanic figure to undermine biblical myth."[28] Finally, *Heaven and Earth* indicts what Graham identifies as "the detachment of a Creator who, having filled a world with thinking, feeling creatures, can sweep them away in the sort of catastrophe that is common ground between Genesis and Cuvier's geological theories."[29] To Ray Stevens, though, "The underlying theme, the doctrine of the elect or, more specifically, Byron's attempt to understand the doctrine of the elect, is based on the Genesis record, and supplemented by allusions to other scriptural passages that help to develop that theme and the attendant themes of man's relation to God, prophecy, judgment, and immortality."[30] More than just the biblical resonances, enlightened Jews would appreciate the elements of Spinozan skepticism found in these plays.[31]

Jewish Identity

One reason why these particular works proved so attractive could be that their content can be read as allegorical representations of the cultural struggles experienced by Ashkenazi Jews in the nineteenth and twentieth centuries. As was Byron, the Jews were attempting to reconfigure relationships, first between religious authorities and secularists, later between diasporeans and Zionists.[32] Conventionally, these conflicts are viewed in terms of three overlapping historical movements: (1) the Haskalah, the Jewish Enlightenment that brought the Jewish community into the modern world; (2) *Golus*-Nationalism, the Yiddishist movement that advocated Jewish life in the Diaspora; and (3) Zionism, the political movement that culminated in a separate Jewish homeland.

The initial attempt to modernize the Jewish identity is generally associated with Moses Mendelssohn (1729–86), the philosopher whose 1783 translation of the Bible into German provided the impetus for the Haskalah. Mendelssohn was supported by Naphtali Herz Wesseley (1725–1805), who developed an educational program designed for Austrian Jews.[33] Writing in response to the Austrian Edict of Tolerance, Wesseley urged the Jews to send their children to public schools where they could receive a vocational education in the vernacular. Before this, the Jews had been a *nation* within a *nation*, studying exclusively the traditional rabbinic knowledge, "the Law of God," but not what Wesseley calls *Torat ha-adam*—"the law of man." Through his program, Wesseley hoped the Jews would demonstrate that they merited emancipation—that they could be patriotic citizens who contributed to the commonweal—while at the same time retaining their identity as Jews. The intellectual reforms advocated by Mendelssohn and Wesseley were complemented by the religious reforms of theologians like Abraham Geiger (1810–74), who emphasized rational religion and assimilation, and who advocated a metaphorical interpretation of Zionism. By transforming the literal belief in a return to Jerusalem into the application of the moral principles inherent in Zionism to the actual life in the Diaspora, reformers hoped to demonstrate Jewish patriotism to the host community, while still retaining the Jewish identity.[34]

As poorly as the Haskalah was initially received in the West (Wesseley was excommunicated for his efforts), the response in the East, where the rabbis wielded greater power, was even worse. When the Russian government established a program of state-sponsored education for the Jews, many *maskilim* (adherents of the Haskalah; the singular is *maskil*) accepted teaching positions, believing that they could help eastern Jews assimilate into the dominant community. By the last decades of the nineteenth century, however, *maskilim* were forced to admit that they had been used as pawns in the government's evangelical program designed, ultimately, to convert the Jews, based on the hope that a secular education, especially as delivered by Jewish teachers, would be persuasive. Only gradually did it become clear that those who trusted the government would be left in the cultural limbo of having renounced their own religion but of never really being accepted into the Christian world, either.

During this period, the rabbis did not watch passively as what they considered to be their territory was encroached upon by the *maskilim*. Because the Jews lacked citizenship, the government expected the Jewish community to police itself, giving the rabbis both religious and civil authority over the population. This meant that through their economic and intellectual control, they could threaten the livelihood, and even the freedom, of anyone who, in their opinion, strayed. They denounced secular learning and destroyed *maskilic* texts, so that it became very difficult for Jews in the East to obtain information about the Haskalah, and even harder to embrace its intellectual tenets openly. So, too, with religious reform, it being almost impossible for enlightened rabbis to obtain positions, a necessary prerequisite for modernizing the synagogue service.

The pogroms of 1880–81 effectively ended the Haskalah, a movement whose goal had been assimilation into the dominant community. Instead, *maskilim* were in part replaced by *Golus*-Nationalists, Yiddishists who hoped to establish a homeland in the Diaspora. Starting in the middle of the nineteenth century, the Russian and Austrian empires began granting official recognition to indigenous nations within their hegemony—a status whose primary advantage was the ability to use their own languages for legal purposes. Taking advantage of the possible opportunity, some Jews developed the theory of *Golus*-Nationalism. Etymologically based on the Hebrew term for exile, *Golus*-Nationalism, as distinct from other forms of diasporeanism, refers to voluntary communities whose members choose to remain where they are, rather than seek an idealized homeland from their past. In anticipation of Benedict Anderson's definition of nation as an "imagined political community,"[35] Nathan Birnbaum (1864–1937), architect of *Golus*-Nationalism, explained: "When I found them to be a people with all the signs of a live, separate nation, it became more and more clear to me that a nation that already exists does not have to be created again *de novo*, and that what is of principal importance is preserving its life. Thus I developed my Golus-Nationalism."[36]

Golus-Nationalism occupies the space between two of the most horrific anti-Semitic attacks of the modern era, the pogroms of 1880–81 and the Holocaust.[37] Historically, antecedents for the movement can be traced back to two antithetical trends of the late eighteenth century that were manifested in eastern and central Europe: the Haskalah and Ḥasidism. As noted, the Haskalah originated as a secularizing movement that advocated a vocational education in the vernacular as the means by which Jews would be able to assimilate into the dominant communities. As its polar opposite, Ḥasidism, a mystical, antirationalist movement, opposed assimilation in any form, creating instead self-contained religious communities that adhered to the teachings of particular religious leaders. After the assimilationist aspirations of the *maskilim* had been dashed, a significant bloc of secular Jews turned to *Golus*-Nationalism as an ideology for Jewish progress into the next century. Seizing on the possibility, many thought that they might be able to establish for themselves rights as a Jewish nation within the larger nation-state. However, nationhood would raise another problem for the Jews: which language to use, Yiddish or Hebrew.[38]

The language controversy would dominate Jewish intellectuals for the next half century. At the end of the nineteenth century, neither language was universally viewed as acceptable for general use. Hebrew, the historical language of the Jews, was functionally dead, at that time being used, though with some notable exceptions, primarily for religious purposes. However, Hebraists, including some of the *maskilim* and, later, Zionists, believed that their language could be rejuvenated into a lingua franca for Jews worldwide, especially for what they hoped would be a restored homeland. In contrast, Yiddish was denigrated as a *jargon,* a folk language spoken by the masses who were ignorant of the vernacular, and barely literate in Hebrew, often knowing only enough for prayers. The Ḥasidim, however, used Yiddish for all of their social needs, so while secularists might have rejected the religious orientation of the community, they did recognize the viability of the jargon for a wide variety of purposes. As it progressed, the language debate fragmented into a number of self-contradictory groups. The assimilationists divided into two major factions, those who rejected Yiddish in favor of the vernacular, and those who accepted the reality that the masses could be reached only through their own tongue, even if it was only a jargon. The antiassimilationists, who believed that the Jews must retain their own language, were themselves fragmented. Those who privileged Hebrew were opposed by the religious who felt that the language of the Bible should be reserved strictly for religious use; and the secular Hebraists were seen as *luftmenshen,* people with their heads in the clouds, since not only was Hebrew at that time a dead language, but there was no place where it could be revived. Finally, it should not be surprising that

INTRODUCTION

even among the Yiddishists conflicting ideologies arose, especially those of secularists who, in opposition to the Ḥasidim, hoped to purge the religious terminology as part of the process whereby the jargon was to be transformed into a modern language.

Behind the language controversies was the larger question of *Yiddishkeit,* the Jewish sense of identity. Although they lacked geographical specificity, the Jews had always conceived of themselves as a nation, so the real question, as far as they were concerned, was what constituted their identity. As long as the Jews had their shared religion, they required no other sense of *Yiddishkeit.* But with the post-Enlightenment trend toward secularization, it became apparent that the Jews needed at the very least to supplement their idea of nation. Given the fact that at that time, Yiddish was spoken by the vast majority of Jews in the world, and the reality that, in the period preceding the Balfour Declaration, Zionism was not a viable option, many argued that Yiddish culture could replace the older Hebrew religion as the basis for the Jews' *Golus*-Nationalism.

These controversies came to a head at the Czernowitz Conference of 1908.[39] The official announcement projected modest, almost self-effacing aims for a conference devoted to rehabilitating the language. Ten specific purposes were listed: "(1) Yiddish orthography, (2) Yiddish grammar, (3) foreign and new words, (4) a Yiddish dictionary, (5) Jewish youth and the Yiddish language, (6) the Yiddish press and the Yiddish language, (7) the Yiddish stage and Yiddish actors, (8) the economic situation of the Yiddish writer, (9) the economic situation of Yiddish actors, (10) the recognition of the Yiddish language."[40] Although mentioned last, the most politically significant of the goals was the recognition of Yiddish as what some hoped would be *the* language of the Jews. The extremists at the conference rejected the two mainstays of traditional Jewry, religion and Zionism, instead advocating a secularized diasporeanism that would liberate the community from the control of the traditional establishment. While speakers at the conference ranged from conservative Hebraists to bilingualists advocating the use of both Hebrew and Yiddish, not to mention the antireligious who wished to extirpate Hebrew from Yiddish culture, the result of the conference was less extreme, delegates voting that Yiddish be considered *a,* as opposed to *the,* Jewish language.

In the aftermath of the conference, and leading up to the Holocaust, the Yiddishist movement evolved through three distinct phases. The first, culminating in World World I, entailed the construction of the Yiddishist ideology. The ensuing Russian Revolution and Balfour Declaration led to the second phase, a reconsideration of the extremist ideology that had dominated the initial construction of the Yiddishist identity. Finally, Soviet anti-Semitic purges, along with the rise of Nazism, yielded the collapse of a distinctly Yiddishist identity.

Yiddishist ideology, a social program designed to address the physical needs of the working classes, was buttressed by the cultural theories of the Jewish intelligentsia.[41] Responding both to external developments in Russia and to internal difficulties within the Jewish community, Jewish Socialists organized what would become known as the Bund, the General League [Bund] of Jewish Workingmen in Russia and Poland, in 1897; Lithuania would be added to the name in 1901. Organized during the same period that Lenin founded the national Russian Social-Democratic Labor Party (RSDLP), the Bund joined the larger party as the "sole representative of the Jewish proletariat." Although the original long-range plan was for the Jewish community to assimilate within the larger RSDLP, realities of linguistic, social, and cultural differences required that the Jews join their own organization, leading to the Bund's expulsion from the RSDLP in 1903. As a result, the Jews had their own collective, one that would be used to organize Jewish workers worldwide through the Holocaust and beyond.[42]

The intellectual foundation for the Bund came from Chaim Zhitlowsky (1865–1943).[43] A staunch Yiddishist and Marxist, Zhitlowsky rejected both Zionism and religion in favor of a secularized *Golus*-Nationalism, with the Yiddish language as the unifying principle of the Jewish people. Therefore, he, along with Nathan Birnbaum, organized the Czernowitz Conference with the intention of having Yiddish declared *the* Jewish national language. Ironically, although Zhitlowsky intended Yiddish to provide the means of unifying his people, the Jewish world grew so bifurcated in the early twentieth century that it would take over a decade for an ideology formulated in New York to make its way to Russia, the community from which it had originally derived and for which it was ultimately designed. In the introductory number of his New York periodical *Dos neie leben* (The New Life), published in 1908, Zhitlowsky included a polemical essay, "The Program and Goals of the Monthly *The New Life*," outlining his purpose—to propagate Socialist information in order, ultimately, to buttress the Russian liberation movement:

> To clarify and justify the foundation, on which we built our program; to explain the rejected and erroneous plans and ideas which contradict it; because its basic ideas derive from historical events, which come from

the life of humanity in general and our own people in particular—this is the chief duty of our newspaper. It will issue theoretical articles from all branches of science and culture, which are connected with the fundamental questions that now interest free intellectuals as a whole and the Jews in particular. It will have regular literary chronicles about the events of human progress in philosophy and science, about the development of Socialism and the liberation movement (principally about the revolutionary movement in Russia) and about the historical events in the life of the Jewish people.[44]

Contrary to his expectations, Zhitlowsky's ideology would not reach Russia until after 1917, and by then, what had originated as the fresh ideas of a new Jewish identity had been adapted for the Communist Party's long-range goal of assimilating the Jews.[45] At that point in its history, the Bund was viewed as the Jewish arm of Russian Socialism, providing support for the revolution and then, through Yiddish, acculturating the Jews for massive assimilation in the Soviet era. The policy was doomed to fail for a number of reasons.[46] First, no one could become enthusiastic about a policy specifically designed to be temporary. Second, there was no real content to the program. Because of censorship, little of appeal was being written in Yiddish, the most popular publications being reprints of older Yiddish classics and translations of European literature. Third, the policy of educating Jews in Yiddish schools was impractical, for it handicapped those who wished to pursue higher education in Russian universities. Still, despite these obstacles, the party retained hope throughout the 1920s that Yiddish could be used to acculturate the masses.

In contrast to the Yiddishists, who were staunch diasporeans, the Zionists reintroduced geographical specificity into the Jewish identity. A belief in Zionism has always been an integral part of Judaism, and starting soon after the destruction of the Temple by the Romans in the second century CE, Jews began incorporating into the liturgy prayers for return; still, as the centuries passed, fewer and fewer actually believed that a physical return could be achieved in their own lifetimes. However, with the collapse of *maskilic* hopes that the Jews might be emancipated and assimilated into the dominant communities of Europe, as well as the rise of modern anti-Semitism, some began, in the last decades of the nineteenth century, to explore the possibility of establishing a home of their own.

There was hardly a consensus among Jews about the question of Zionism. A faction of the religious population believed that only God should effect the return, and that any man-made movement would be tantamount to usurping his prerogatives. Those who thought that God might not mind a little help were split between the spiritual and the political Zionists. Spiritual Zionists, who rejected the political approach for both practical and religious reasons, believed that the aspirations for a separate homeland were pipe dreams based on messianic beliefs untenable in the real world. Rather, they thought that the Jews should view Zionism as a spiritual ideal, dependent neither on the geography of nationalism nor on the rituals of religion. In opposition, the political Zionists actively strove to establish a Jewish state, preferably in the Middle East. As formalized by the First Zionist Congress in 1897, the political Zionists pursued diplomatic channels leading, in 1917, to the Balfour Declaration that established the British mandate under which Jews lived until 1948, when, after the Holocaust, the United Nations declared Israel an independent state.

Before Zionism consolidated into a political movement, though, Ḥovevei Ẓion (Lovers of Zion) attempted to establish settlements in the area then called Palestine. Motivated as much by *Ḥibat ẓion* (Lovers of Zion; from the root *ḥavev,* "to love") propaganda as by the pogroms, starting in 1881 young idealists began emigrating to the Middle East—without considering the practical ramifications of their decision. With dreams of fulfilling the religious return to Jerusalem, these *luftmenshen* ignored the geographical, political, social, and economic implications of their move, and were quickly overwhelmed by the difficulties of settling in a completely alien area. As a result, some members of the intelligentsia, concluding that eastern European Jews were not yet prepared for the realities of emigration, advocated an educational program as a prerequisite for an eventual move.

Their intellectual leader was Aḥad Ha'Am.[47] Born Asher Hirsch Ginsberg (1856–1927) in Skvira, Kiev Province in Russia, Aḥad Ha'Am received a traditional Jewish education. Though unable to matriculate at a university, he was an autodidact in secular subjects. As an adult, Aḥad Ha'Am became an advocate for Ḥovevei Ẓion, arguing in his essay "Lo zeh ha-derekh" (This Is Not the Way, 1899) that the consolidation of a Jewish cultural identity was essential before physical communities could be established. Although he would play a role in obtaining the Balfour Declaration, he believed that under Theodor Herzl, political Zionism had lost contact with the Jewish values necessary for generating a Jewish identity.

According to Aḥad Ha'Am, there were two requirements for developing a Jewish identity: the subordination of individual desires to the group's needs, and the support of an intellectual elite. The first principle, to privilege the community, was influenced by the social Darwinists of the day. Believing that the hardships of the Diaspora and the control of rabbinic authorities had deprived the Jewish people of their national spirit, Aḥad Ha'Am insisted that before they could establish physical communities of their own, the Jews required a new sense of community, one more compatible with the exigencies of life in the new century. To that end, he advocated intellectual development, much like that endorsed by Zhitlowsky, though Aḥad Ha'Am believed that Hebrew, not Yiddish, should be the national language. He helped found B'nei Moshe (Sons of Moses), a semisecret society of activists modeled after fraternal groups such as the Masons. He also served as editor of Aḥiasaf, one of the first Hebrew publishing houses. Ideologically, Aḥad Ha'Am thought that religion should be viewed as a manifestation of Jewish culture, and that the national ethic should transcend religion in seeking its moral base.

Without rejecting the diasporean experience, Aḥad Ha'Am believed that a cultural center should be founded in *erez* Israel, "the land of Israel." Replacing the religious establishment that centered around the Temple and Sanhedrin, he envisioned what amounted to an Israeli version of the national academy called for in the first edition of Isaac D'Israeli's *Essay on the Manners and Genius of the Literary Character* of 1795, to include a national library, museum, publishing house, press, and, in Aḥad Ha'Am's words, "a Hebrew academy where fifteen to twenty scholars and writers of the highest level would live and would receive an appropriate salary that would enable them to live simple lives without any concerns." Through the interaction of these cultural institutions, the Jews would be able "to create new forms of collective Jewish consciousness."[48]

As with Zhitlowsky's, Aḥad Ha'Am's idealistic vision of a new Jewish identity would be overtaken by history. The Balfour Declaration hastened what Aḥad Ha'Am believed should have been only a gradual movement; the rise of Nazism increased the need for immigration in the 1930s; and the Holocaust brought about statehood in 1948. Regardless of the plausibility of his ideals in the abstract, they were unviable in the real world.

In contrast to Aḥad Ha'Am, Theodor Herzl (1860–1904), the leading proponent of political Zionism, focused on the most concrete aspect of Zionism: the establishment of a political state for the Jews. Although Herzl is generally viewed as the father of modern Zionism, actually he was more accurately the catalyst of a movement that began years before he developed an interest in what was then known as "the Jewish question,"[49] and culminated, more than a decade after his death, in the British mandate. Born in

Budapest and raised a secular Jew, Herzl worked as a writer and journalist in central and western Europe, where he became concerned about the growing anti-Semitism that he encountered. Eventually, he developed the idea of a Jewish state, and by 1895, he began actively lobbying Jewish philanthropists for contributions, and publishing *Der Judenstaat* (The Jewish State), a pamphlet arguing that the best answer to anti-Semitism would be to give the Jews a state of their own, although Herzl did not specify the precise location of the state—Uganda and Argentina were both considered at different times.

The turning point of the movement came when Herzl, having been rebuffed in his appeals to the western Jewish elite, realized that the eastern Jewish masses were interested in his project, so he called for a World Zionist Congress to respond to the people's desire. Meeting in 1897, in Basel, delegates to the first Zionist Congress represented a cross-section of Jews in terms of age, class, religious affiliation, and national origin. Deciding that the most efficacious location for a Jewish homeland would be Palestine, the congress established a World Zionist Organization whose purpose was to engage in diplomatic negotiations that would facilitate the Jews' return to the Middle East. Not surprisingly, neither the Turkish authorities nor their allies were willing to come to terms with Herzl. In addition, competing factions among the Zionists threatened to undermine the movement. Unfortunately, Herzl suffered a heart attack and died before seeing his work come to fruition.

At the same time that Herzl pursued the diplomatic front, waves of immigrants moved to Palestine, establishing agricultural settlements along with educational and cultural bases. The first *aliyah* (from Hebrew *aliyah*, "going up, ascent"; term used to designate immigration to Israel), beginning in 1882, indicated the initial desire of Jews to return. The second and the third, from 1906 to 1914, and then from 1919 to 1924, reflected more concerted efforts to build a lasting society. Within this context, the Balfour Declaration of 1917, in which the British guaranteed "a national home for the Jewish people," provided the political grounding for the future state.

Cultural development was an essential component of Zionism; and central to culture was language.[50] Starting in 1879, with the publication of an article entitled "She'elah lohatah" (A Burning Question), Eliezer Ben-Yehudah (1858–1922) dedicated himself to transforming Hebrew into a language capable of full use in a modern society.[51] Born Eliezer Yizḥak Perelman in Lithuania, scion of a Ḥasidic family, Ben-Yehudah became interested in secular literature at the age of thirteen, and eventually graduated from the Dvinsk Gymnasium, in 1877. Inspired by the Balkan nations' struggle for liberation, he advocated Jewish liberation, believing that the Jews, too, had a historic homeland and language. Therefore, in 1878, he moved to Paris, where he studied medicine in preparation for a move to the Middle East. After contracting tuberculosis, Ben-Yehuda abandoned his medical studies and settled in Palestine, where he enrolled in the teachers' seminary. There, he began studying Hebrew in preparation for his life's work, the revival of the language through the creation of a simple style and the introduction of neologisms. In 1922, Hebrew was accepted as one of the country's official languages; and by 1948, when Israel gained statehood, Hebrew had been fully consolidated as the national language.

Statehood produced a split in the Jewish sense of identity, the Israeli national identity being in some ways antithetical to the Jewish identity in the Diaspora, especially in the United States.[52] The state was initially founded by Ashkenazi Jews who, upon becoming Israelis, effectively severed their ties with their past, changing their languages and often their names. Considering themselves more authentic than the Jews in the Diaspora, and later, feeling ashamed of those who, in the Holocaust, had passively marched to their death without actively resisting the Nazis, some Israelis overcompensated by inverting the Jewish sense of identity, replacing intellectual elitism with militarism, and moral integrity with pragmatic expediency, all—with the support of the religious parties—for the sake of retaining control over the geographical homeland.[53] This renovated identity, it has been argued, enabled Israel to survive the succession of wars that punctuated its foundational years: the War for Independence, 1947–49; the Kadesh War, 1956; the Six Day War, 1967; and the Yom Kippur War, 1973. Attitudes changed in the early 1980s, however, when in response to what many viewed as a war of choice in Lebanon, a peace movement was generated.[54]

Compounded by Russian immigration at the collapse of the Soviet Union, problems in Israel—including the first Intifada of 1987–93, followed by the Al-Aqsa Intifada of 2000–, and most recently, the second incursion into Lebanon in 2006—have yielded yet another shift in the Jewish identity. Throughout much of the twentieth century, most Jews had acquiesced in the belief that Israeli survival should be a priority; however, once the internal disputes among Israelis surfaced, diasporean Jews began expressing concerns that had been suppressed in the past. In addition, the direction of emigration has begun to shift, with Israelis moving to diasporean communities, primarily those in the United States. As a result, some American Jews have begun questioning Israeli militarism and pragmatism, returning to Aḥad Ha'Am's emphasis on culture as the means of preserving the historical Jewish values of intellectual elitism and moral integrity.[55] In addition, through this new emphasis on cultural values, the American Jewish community has begun reasserting its centrality to Jews worldwide.[56]

Byron and the Jews

Byron and those Jews studied in this volume all used various modes of translation to help expand what they considered to be the more restrictive identity imposed by their respective cultural institutions. For his part, Byron engaged in what might be considered the cultural translation of two contemporary Jews. The first, Isaac D'Israeli, helped Byron consolidate his idea of the Byronic hero through successive editions of a treatise on genius, itself a secularization of the Jewish concept of the *illuy*, or prodigy. Then, Isaac Nathan, composer of the *Hebrew Melodies* worked on during the period when Byron prepared to leave England for the last time, contributed a skeptical view that questioned the validity of religion as a unifying principle.

If these Jews might be said to have influenced Byron through cultural translation, Byron influenced others through the literal translation of selected works, as well as biographical and critical materials. Beginning with the Haskalah, Byron helped individual Jews buttress particular attitudes toward reform. In eastern and central Europe, where the Jewish communities lagged far behind their counterparts in the West, five *maskilim* introduced secular learning in an effort to undermine rabbinic authority and help advance the pursuit of civil rights in the Austrian and Russian empires. The first, one Yaakov Ẓevi, seems to have read Byron's Cain as the figure of a *maskil*, an intellectual posing the kinds of questions that might challenge rabbinic authorities. Contemporaneously, Meir Halevi Letteris used four of the *Hebrew Melodies*, along with *Darkness*, to imply a skeptical attitude toward religion. The next two, translator and author Matisyahu Simḥah Rabener, along with reform rabbi and publisher Eliezer Eliyahu Igel, turned to Byron after the Haskalah had encountered problems with religious authorities, producing a version of the *Hebrew Melodies*, along with an adaptation of *Darkness*, to suggest a compromise between the conservative and enlightened members of their community. Finally, Hebrew poet Judah Leib Gordon translated selected *Hebrew Melodies* to voice his ultimate disillusionment with the Haskalah as a movement.

INTRODUCTION

In the post-Haskalah period, Byron appears to have been used to support opposing positions in the controversy over language within the Jewish community, Yiddish and Hebrew versions of Byron punctuating the progress of these two movements. Among the Yiddishists, at first dominated by secular diasporeans who wanted Yiddish to be declared *the* official language of the Jews, at least seven introduced Byron in the interim between the pogroms of 1880–81 (when the Jews realized that the assimilationist goals of the Haskalah could not be actualized), the Russian Revolution (when Jews questioned the viability of their being assimilated into the new Communist culture), and the Holocaust (when European Yiddish culture effectively ceased to exist). The first three Yiddishists, under the influence of Marxist intellectual Chaim Zhitlowsky, exploited Byron as a means of buttressing their revolutionary ideology. The earliest, Ezekiel Bleicher, used translations to introduce himself into and, finally, exit from the Yiddishist movement, his *Childe Harold,* canto 1 being published in the first issue of Zhitlowsky's leftist journal *Dos neie leben,* and his *Heaven and Earth* being published in Kiev upon his return to the Soviet Union. Ideologically consistent with Bleicher, Elkana Zilberman published a book-length biography of Byron that, absent any reference to the *Hebrew Melodies,* reflects the anti-Zionist stance of some Yiddishists; and Max (Mordechai) Hershman published his translation of *The Prisoner of Chillon* in *Der arbayter fraynd,* at that time an anarchist journal.

By the 1920s, Yiddishists began reconsidering the role of religion in the Jewish identity. In England, Nathan Horowitz, who translated the *Hebrew Melodies, Manfred,* and *Cain* into Yiddish, and then the *Hebrew Melodies* into Hebrew, was the only Jewish Byronist to translate into both languages. In America, Abraham Asen, who translated most of the American and British canons into Yiddish, translated *The Prisoner of Chillon,* the *Hebrew Melodies,* and *Cain,* which included an introduction by well-known satirist Chaim Gutman. In the 1930s, with the rise of anti-Semitism, when the reaction within the Jewish community against the Yiddishist movement set in, Shelomo Simon argued that it was inappropriate to translate *Cain* into Yiddish, the language of the secular masses; and countering the threat of Nazi Germany, Shea Tenenbaum inverted the reading of Byron's character Cain from the freethinking intellectual to the religious apostate whose refusal to accept rabbinic authority threatened the survival of his people. Finally, the last of the Yiddishists, Moisei Khashtshevatski, transformed *The Prisoner of Chillon* into a Communist manifesto, right before he died fighting in the Red Army against the Nazis.

As with the Yiddishists, Zionists also introduced Byronic materials consistent with their beliefs: first in a spiritual Zion; and then, after the Balfour Declaration, in the physical return to mandated Palestine; and most recently, in internal analyses of the direction being taken by the state of Israel. There were three Byronists in the early pre-Balfour period. Solomon Mandelkern, a transitional figure whose initial *maskilic* beliefs were dashed by the pogroms of 1880–81, produced a bilingual translation of the *Hebrew Melodies* that was less ideological than pedagogical, being designed to help English-speaking students learn Hebrew. The most well known of the Byronists, David Frishman, used his Hebrew translations of *Cain, Manfred,* and *Heaven and Earth,* as well as a thirty-seven-page analysis of *Cain,* as building blocks for a nonideological, spiritual Zionist identity. Finally, Isaac Loeb Baruch (born Brocowitz), issued two versions of *The Prisoner of Chillon*—one published while he still lived in eastern Europe and the second after he had moved to the West in preparation for *aliyah*—as well as a translation of the militaristic *Mazeppa,* consistent with the new Israeli national identity.

Finally, four Byronists punctuate the post-Balfour period, as the Jews prepared for statehood and then grappled with the same challenge that had faced Byron: how to develop a national identity that transcended the concepts of geographical specificity and religion. Jacob Orland, an Israeli who served in the British Army during World War II, used his bilingual *Hebrew Melodies* to curb anti-British sentiment in the move for Israeli independence. In 1959–60, during the calm that prevailed after the Kadesh War of 1956, Moshe Giyora's translation of Harold's farewell from the first canto of *Childe Harold* suggests that Israel's rejection of diasporean values might, in the long run, prove counterproductive. Finally, most recently, Shmuel Friedman and Michael Desheh's bilingual edition of the *Hebrew Melodies,* along with a critical afterword, use Byron's life and work to imply questions about the morality of Israeli expansion into Lebanon in 1982.

The four chapters of *Byron and the Jews* trace the use of translation in Byron's and these Jews' quests for their respective identities. Chapter 1, "Byron and English Jews," explores the ways Byron, D'Israeli, and Nathan translated one another. The next three chapters demonstrate how the Byron translations interrelate with the three movements that dominated Jewish culture in the nineteenth and twentieth centuries: chapter 2, "Byron and the *Maskilim*"; chapter 3, "Byron and the Yiddishists"; and chapter 4, "Byron and the Zionists." The conclusion, "Translation and *Allegoresis*," draws the theoretical inference implicit in this study of Hebrew and

INTRODUCTION

Yiddish materials dealing with Byron: that regardless of an author's original intention, the act of translation inevitably produces an allegorical reading of a text. Finally, because few of these Hebrew and Yiddish translations are readily available, the appendix contains transcriptions of many of the texts discussed in this study.

CHAPTER 1

Byron and English Jews

One thing that Byron had in common with Isaac D'Israeli and Isaac Nathan, the Jews discussed in this chapter, was the sense of alienation.[1] Although all three were born in Great Britain, Byron, raised a Scottish Calvinist, and the two English Jews suffered varying degrees of disabilities in a country that identified itself in part through its formally established church, to which none of them belonged. Therefore, it should not be surprising that all three would seek to reconfigure their national identity by replacing geographical specificity and organized religion with intellectual elitism and moral integrity as characteristics more consistent with their own experiences as creative artists who felt inhibited by their respective governing institutions. To that end, Byron can be said to have collaborated with both of them: with D'Israeli, indirectly collaborating to redefine the concept of *genius* in a manner consistent with their attitude toward intellectual elitism; and with Nathan, directly collaborating on the *Hebrew Melodies,* the song cycle that skeptically complicates religion, to imply the need for individuals to develop their own moral integrity.

In their collaborations, D'Israeli, Nathan and Byron performed various acts of translation. In the first instance, D'Israeli shared an *intralingual* relationship with Byron, the two transferring texts from one set of signs into another, both in the same language, English. Specifically, Byron read and annotated D'Israeli's *Essay on the Manners and Genius of the Literary Character,* itself a cultural translation of the Jewish concept of the *illuy,* genius; D'Israeli, in turn, translated Byron's annotations into the second and third editions, with the new title *The Literary Character, Illustrated by the History of Men of Genius, Drawn from Their Own Feelings and Confessions.* For his part, Byron translated the successive editions of D'Israeli's text into his literary persona, the Byronic hero. In the second instance, Nathan shared an *intersemiotic* relationship with Byron, the two of them translating texts back and forth between lyrics and music to produce their song cycle. When viewed together, these acts of translation can be seen to have helped lay the foundation for the use of Byron in the renovation of the Jewish national identity. Significantly, the influence seems to have gone both ways: D'Israeli and Nathan were able to consolidate their Jewish identities in part through their interaction with Byron; and in the process, they helped Byron crystallize his own persona. It should not be surprising, therefore, that later Jews were able to find in Byron echoes of their own culture.

Isaac D'Israeli—Intellectual Elitism

Isaac D'Israeli's attitude toward his Jewishness was always problematic at best.[2] He was born in London on May 11, 1766, but was raised in Middlesex, outside the range of the Anglo-Jewish community, by a mother who regretted being Jewish and a father who wanted him to go into business. As a Jew, D'Israeli was never really comfortable attending English schools, which were Christian, so eventually, in 1780–81, his father sent him to Amsterdam, where he attended what was supposed to have been a superior academy, but was not. To compensate, D'Israeli became an autodidact, developing his own course of study. When he returned home, his parents tried to discourage his literary ambitions, but D'Israeli still attempted, mostly unsuccessfully, to create for himself a place in the literary world. Failing that, at his parents' behest, he returned to Europe, including France, where, in 1788–89, he fell under the influence of the revolutionary philosophers. After returning to England in 1791, D'Israeli inherited his grandmother's fortune, making him financially independent and free to pursue his literary career, without having to worry about parental interference. D'Israeli proved to be extremely prolific, publishing poetry, fiction, literary memorabilia, history, and cultural studies. He was also successful, his work remaining in print long after his death in 1848.

The combination of his relative isolation from the Anglo-Jewish community and his continental education alienated D'Israeli from both the Jewish and the English worlds. As a secularist who rejected any form of revealed religion, he maintained only minimal ties with the Bevis Marks Synagogue; and after his father's death, which coincided with an ongoing quarrel he had with congregational authorities, D'Israeli broke away completely, and even had his children baptized so they would not suffer the legal disabililties that had impeded his own progress. Yet he himself never converted, and to his death he remained concerned about Jewish affairs, in 1833 publishing anonymously *The Genius of Judaism,* and in 1847 endorsing his son Benjamin Disraeli's support for the Jew Bill. Still, D'Israeli was never fully accepted in the English world, either. While he did have personal friendships with Christians, reviews of his work indicate that the British would never forget his Jewish origins, nor would they cede to him a legitimate place in the world of English letters.[3]

D'Israeli resolved these conflicts, in part, through his ongoing analysis of the concept of *genius*. At first, he seems to have believed that the Jews as a people were deficient, if not defective, writing Francis Douce in 1794—"the Jews have no men of Genius or talents to lose. I can count all their men of Genius on my fingers. Ten centuries have not produced Ten great men."[4] Similarly, he states in a footnote to his novel *Vaurien* (1797), "Literary Jews must always be rare . . . their most malignant and powerful enemies will be found among their domestic associates."[5] There were a few exceptions, though. For example, in *Vaurien,* D'Israeli introduces a Mendelssohnian *maskil* engaged in a mock dispute with a Frenchman who tries to persuade the Jewish philosopher to support revolution. Even though D'Israeli's version of the Jewish philosopher criticizes his people's system of education, still he rejects the Frenchman's arguments, concluding: "Let us labour . . . to convince the Christian and the Jew, at the close of the eighteenth century, that 'modes of faith' were never modes of humanity, and that the hour should have already passed, when the Christian should be generous and the Jew grateful."[6] In the following year, he would publish his essay on Mendelssohn, "A Biographical Sketch of the Jewish Socrates." During the same period, perhaps even to help him analyze the reasons why there were so few Jewish geniuses, in 1795 D'Israeli published his *Essay on the Manners and Genius of the Literary Character,* the first of three editions of a study he would revise more than two decades later, with the help of Byron's annotations. As suggested by successive editions of the retitled *The Literary Character, Illustrated by the History of Men of Genius, Drawn from Their Own Feelings and Confessions,* published in 1818 and 1822, and culminating in *The Genius of Judaism* in 1833, D'Israeli's perspective and understanding of the concept evolved from an initial stance that, ironically, incorporated the same Jewish attitudes he would eventually repudiate, into the Byronic hero.

D'Israeli's initial confusion resulted from the numerous conflicting definitions of a concept that itself underwent a radical reconsideration

CHAPTER 1

during his lifetime. Etymologically derived from the Latin "to beget," and the Greek "to be born, come into being," the term *genius* originally signified an early form of national identity, that is, the characteristic by which a society identified itself; and, as indicated by the succession of glosses found in the *Oxford English Dictionary,* the concepts signified by the English term *genius* have evolved in conjunction with cultural history. In its earliest manifestation, the word *genius* referred to a Christianized version of what had originated as a pagan belief in the governing spirit that effectively united the individual with his community through a religious belief:

> The tutelary god or attendant spirit allotted to every person at his birth, to govern his fortunes and determine his character, and finally to conduct him out of the world; also, the tutelary and controlling spirit similarly connected with a place, an institution, etc. . . . (a person's) good, evil genius: the two mutually opposed spirits (in Christian language angels) by whom every person was supposed to be attended throughout his life. Hence applied transf. to a person who powerfully influences for good or evil the character, conduct, or fortunes of another.

The next group of glosses secularizes the concept, associating *genius* on the personal level with the individual's character—"Characteristic disposition; inclination; bent, turn or temper of mind"—with various implications, including social, institutional, and geographical.

In the seventeenth century, the term was inverted so that it no longer signified the ethos that unified the group, but referred to the particular characteristic that distinguished the individual from the general population: "Natural ability or capacity; quality of mind; the special endowments which fit a man for his peculiar work. . . . Natural aptitude." This meaning led eventually to the concept's being associated with the Romantic imagination: "Native intellectual power of an exalted type, such as is attributed to those who are esteemed greatest in any department of art, speculation, or practice; instinctive and extraordinary capacity for imaginative creation, original thought, invention, or discovery. Often contrasted with talent."

By the middle of the eighteenth century, *genius* was used, according to William Bruce Johnson, as a "catch-all term, often with sentimental connotations,"[7] though William Sharpe, along with Alexander Gerard and William Duff, initiated a psychological approach to the subject. As Sharpe delineates the scope of his *Dissertation upon Genius* (1755):

I. By the manner of the acquirement of all our ideas.
II. By the progress of the mind in the improvement of these ideas.
III. By the indispensable equality of the natural faculties.
IV. By reflexions arising from the subject itself, and from the substance of what has been said.
V. By the solution of objections.[8]

The new approach to the concept of *genius* inverts its mode of signification yet again, this time to isolate the individual from the group, his *genius* being the intellectual quality that distinguishes him from the rest of the population. As a result, a term originally associated with the avatar of society now identifies the *other*, the embodiment of that which must be extirpated.[9]

Paralleling the western concept, the Jews, too, developed their own culturally specific concept of *genius,* defining the individual's special talent in terms of the group identity.[10] Known variously as *ḥakham, gaon,* or *illuy,* the Jewish *genius* was historically associated with traditional religious values: the *ḥakham* being the Talmudic scholar, the *gaon* the head of the academies established in the middle of the sixth century, and the *illuy* the young prodigy who was groomed for a position of intellectual leadership in the community. Throughout Jewish history, the *genius* was used as the cultural instrument for maintaining the centrality of religion in the Jewish national identity, his intellectual prowess being defined in terms of his ability to master the Bible and Talmud. Given his importance to Jewish survival, the community frequently supported the *illuy* so that he could mature into a *gaon.*

As a *maskil* who studied both secular and Jewish materials, D'Israeli initially seems to have been oblivious to the historical and cultural confusion about the word *genius,* on the one hand faulting the Jews for not having produced enough geniuses, but on the other advocating the establishment of a Jewish-type academy to support indigenous geniuses. Through the indirect, and initially unintentional, intercession of Byron, however, D'Israeli was able to clarify the distinctions among the different kinds of geniuses so that he could, finally, consolidate his own attitude toward the Jews.

Byron played an instrumental, if accidental, role in the evolution of D'Israeli's attitude toward the concept of genius. During the years 1810 and 1811 (the period, it should be noted, when he began consolidating the Byronic hero in the first cantos of *Childe Harold*), Byron twice read D'Israeli's *Essay on the Manners and Genius of the Literary Character,* annotating the text with often severe criticism of D'Israeli's analysis. Around 1816, John Murray, Byron's publisher, obtained Byron's copy and showed it to D'Israeli who, taking Byron's comments to heart, completely renovated the text he had written some twenty years earlier, publishing it in 1818 as *The Literary Character, Illustrated by the History of Men of Genius, Drawn from Their Own Feelings and Confessions.* In the preface, D'Israeli acknowledges the influence of Byron on the revisions, though without mentioning his name.[11]

Coincidentally, the same thing happened again with the second edition. Byron acquired and annotated a copy that someone then gave to D'Israeli, who again revised the text, incorporating Byron's ideas into what would become an expanded two-volume third edition, published in 1822. This time, D'Israeli sent Byron an inscribed copy which, apparently, was annotated by Teresa Guiccioli, Byron's "last attachment," in Douglass's phraseology, with marginal notations indicating passages purportedly suggested by Byron.[12] In the introduction to yet another edition, the revision published after Byron's death, D'Israeli explained in detail the indirect collaboration as well as including a letter Byron had written to him from Montenero on June 10, 1822, and also publishing a footnote he had suppressed from earlier editions.[13]

D'Israeli's initial purpose for writing his *Essay on the Manners and Genius of the Literary Character* was to complain that the British did not appreciate contemporary writers. As he says in the preface:

> The Literary Character has, in the present day, singularly degenerated in the public mind. The finest compositions appear without exciting any alarm of admiration, they are read, approved, and succeeded by others; nor is the presence of the Author considered, as formerly, as conferring honour on his companions; we pass our evenings sometimes with poets and historians, whom it is probable will be admired by posterity, with hardly any other sensation than we feel from inferior associates.[14]

D'Israeli's solution was to suggest, in effect, that the British become more like the Jews. Using the lives of various purported geniuses who have existed throughout time in order to derive a generalized picture of the type, he concludes that even though the creative writer does not fit into his society, his work does contribute to the country's national identity; therefore, it is incumbent upon his society to create a special niche for him. In other words, English society should emulate the Jewish custom of supporting the literary genius.

In the first three chapters—"Of Literary Men," "Of Authors," and "Men of Letters"—D'Israeli focuses on the social definition of the genius, privileging the gloss that associates the genius with the national ethos. In the first chapter, "Of Literary Men," he introduces literary men in the sense of those who create a national spirit, those "whose particular genius often becomes that of a people; the sovereigns of reason; the legislators of morality; the artificers of our most exquisite pleasures" (1st ed., 1–2). Within that category, he then separates out, in the second chapter, authors: "I shall consider that no Writer, has a just claim to the title of Author, whose CHIEF EMPLOYMENT is not that of STUDY and COMPOSITION" (1st ed., 3). Finally, in chapter 3, "Men of Letters," he subdivides authors into two groups: "[T]he one are induced from many concurring circumstances not to publish their labours; and the other devote their life to communicate their speculations to the world" (1st ed., 11). As thus presented, *authors*—those with a special quality of the mind—seem to be a subcategory of "writers," who are a subcategory of literary men: those who create the distinctive characteristic of a nation. In the rest of the text, he explores how *authors* can develop their special ability in order to articulate the national ideal, a concept to which he returns at the end.

D'Israeli organizes the body of his text from the particular to the general, considering first the personal life of the man of letters, then the professional world, and finally the national implications of his study. On the personal level, he considers, in succession, the childhood and youth of an author, literary solitude, and meditation and conversation. Not to be accused of idealizing his topic, D'Israeli also discusses the limitations of geniuses, with chapters on their artistic and moral shortcomings. He then turns to their professional lives, considering literary friendships and enmities, the degree to which personal character can be inferred from literary works,[15] and the advantages that authors hope to gain from their writing. Finally, D'Israeli concludes with three chapters that focus on how authors contribute to the commonweal. In chapter 13, "Of the Utility of Authors to Individuals," he argues: "[W]herever authors are virtuous and free, their nation partakes most of virtue and of freedom; as on the contrary, where they are dissolute and enslaved, their nations have as little morals as liberty" (1st ed., 165). Because, as D'Israeli quotes Sophocles in chapter 14, "Of the Political Influence of Authors," "OPINION . . . is stronger than Truth"; therefore, he continues, "An author has the singular prerogative of uniting in himself the powers that are proportioned among the higher orders of society. This reflection may appear fanciful to those who are destitute of fancy; and extravagant to those who consider paper and pens as the composition of the manufacturer, and who see nothing in them but rags and feathers" (1st ed., 175). For this reason, in chapter 15, "On an Academy of Polite Literature, Pensions, and Prizes," he calls for national support of authors: "TO deliver any novel observations on an academy for the belles lettres is difficult; but it is more difficult to pass such an object in silent regret" (1st ed., 195). D'Israeli concludes with a plea for universal peace:

> At the present melancholy moment, when Europe appears hostile to Reason, and to Humanity, let us indulge the hope, that this institution may become the ornament of PEACE—of a Peace, that by it's duration may resemble the vision of an admirable philanthropist and a poor politician, the vision of the Abbé de Saint Pierre,—AN UNIVERSAL PEACE. When the principle of Government is VIRTUE, the action of that Government will be PEACE; Governments are, however, always in war. (1st ed., 221–22)

In this first attempt to analyze the concept of genius, D'Israeli transplants for an English context the traditional Jewish construct of *illuy*: the individual who is best able to articulate the national ideal, to be supported by a national academy.[16] With the help of Byron's annotations, however, D'Israeli would then, in subsequent editions, transform what had originated as a Jewish genius into a Romantic hero.

D'Israeli began the process with the revisions for the 1818 edition, as influenced by the Byron of 1810–11, though, likely, affected equally as strongly by both his own and Byron's personal experiences in the interim between 1811 and 1818. During that period, D'Israeli broke with the Bevis Marks Synagogue and had his children baptized. Correspondingly, Byron left England and his young daughter behind to establish residence as a permanent exile on the Continent. Consistent with their changed status, in the next edition, D'Israeli completely eliminated the nationalistic frame he had constructed in the original opening chapters that had situated his analysis specifically within the context of English intellectualism. Instead, D'Israeli refocused the opening chapters from a discussion of the place of the literati within a national context to their supernational literary character. Similarly, he deleted chapter 13, "Of the Utility of Authors to Individuals," which opens with the assertion that "wherever authors are virtuous and free, their nation partakes most of virtue and of freedom; as on the contrary, where they are dissolute and enslaved, their nations have as little morals as liberty"; and he replaced the concluding plea for a national academy with a discussion of the honors other countries accorded their authors. In the body, D'Israeli supplemented his original analysis with seven new chapters: 3, "The First Studies"; 4, "Of the Irritability of Genius";[17] 5, "The Spirit of Literature and the Spirit of Society"; 8, "The Enthusiasm of Genius"; 9, "Literary Jealousy"; 10, "Want of Mutual Esteem";[18] 11, "Self-Praise"; 13, "The Matrimonial State"; and 17, "Literary Old Age." The result is a picture of genius not unlike the Byron of 1818, the cosmopolitan freethinker whose self-conscious genius transcends the more mundane obligations of ordinary people. As Ogden summarizes the changes: "Men of genius are, then, romantic figures. The source of their powers is mysterious. Their contact with their fellow-men is uneasy. They are solitary individuals. Their work is not immediately appreciated, their lives fraught with calamities and quarrels. Yet they are, after all, the unacknowledged legislators of the world."[19] Thus, through Byron's mediation, D'Israeli has replaced the traditional Jewish *illuy* with the isolated Romantic hero who needs to escape the constrictions imposed by the intellectual conservatism of the kind of national academy he had originally advocated.

The third edition reconstructs the relationship between the genius and his nation. Returning to the classification of men that was omitted from the second edition, D'Israeli now reverses the hierarchies upon which he predicates his new analysis. Instead of subordinating authors to the broader category of men of letters, this time, in chapter 2, he redefines the nonwriters as "adversaries of literary men—geniuses and non-geniuses." Also, he adds two chapters: 4, "Of Natural Genius—Minds constitutionally different cannot have an equal aptitude—Genius not the result of habit and education—Originates in peculiar qualities of the mind—The predisposition of genius—The 'white-paper system' enlarged by analogy with the souls of the earth"; and 17, "Poverty, a Relative Quality.—Of the poverty of literary men in what degree desirable.—Extreme poverty.—Task-work.—Of gratuitous works.—A project to provide against the worst state of poverty among literary men." Finally, he expands the section "Conversations of Men of Genius" into a separate chapter.[20]

The effect of these changes is a complete transformation of the text, from what was originally a nationalistic focus into an argument in favor of—to borrow Casanova's title—"the world republic of letters." D'Israeli denationalizes his audience in the beginning of the 1818 edition, explaining, "These literary characters now constitute an important body, diffused over enlightened Europe, connected by the secret links of congenial pursuits, and combining often insensibly to themselves in the same common labours. At London, at Paris, and even at Madrid, these men feel the same thirst, which is allayed at the same fountains; the same authors are read; and the same opinions are formed" (2nd ed., 3). Then, in the beginning of the 1822 edition, he justifies his pan-European perspective: "A new spirit seems to bring them nearer to each other; and as if literary Europe were intent to form but one people out of the populace of mankind, they offer their reciprocal labours; they pledge to each other the same opinions; and that knowledge which, like a small river, takes its source from one spot, at length mingles with that 'ocean-stream' common to them all" (3rd ed., 3). This "order of men" is superior to others, and therefore not bound by the constraints of ordinary morality. Rather, "[t]he LITERARY CHARACTER is a denomination which, however vague, defines the pursuits of the individual, and separates him from other professions, although it frequently occurs that he is himself a member of one. Professional characters are modified by the change of manners, and are usually national; while the literary character, from the objects in which it concerns itself, retains a more permanent, and necessarily a more independent nature" (3rd ed., 5).[21] While acknowledging the importance of the "master-writer" to his nation's identity—"the distinct national character"—D'Israeli emphasizes the isolating, and often alienating, nature of creativity, as well as the inevitable conflict between conventional wisdom and independent thought: "Authors stand between the governors and the governed." Finally, in a passage specifically attributed to Byron:

> There is a consanguinity in the characters of men of genius, and a genealogy may be traced among their races. Men of genius in their different classes, living at distinct periods, or in remote countries, seem to reappear under another name; and in this manner there exists in the literary character an eternal transmigration. In the great march of the human intellect the same individual spirit seems still occupying the same place, and is still carrying on, with the same powers, his great work through a line of centuries. It was on this principle that one great poet has recently hailed his brother as "The Ariosto of the North," and ARIOSTO as "The SCOTT of the South." And can we deny the real existence of the genealogy of genius? Copernicus, Galileo, Kepler, and Newton! this is a single line of descent! (3rd ed., 319–20).

By the third edition, the concept of genius has been completely transformed. D'Israeli had begun by defining the genius as the avatar of a particular culture, his special talent being the ability to articulate the national identity. For this reason, D'Israeli had argued, it was incumbent upon society to support the genius through the establishment of an academy that would support his intellectual efforts. The problem with this definition, as Byron's biography demonstrates, is that national academies almost inevitably solidify into conservative institutions whose function is to maintain the sense of identity characteristic of a given period; and the function of the genius is correspondingly stultified, being used to reinforce the conventional wisdom. In D'Israeli's final version, however, the genius is transformed from the embodiment of the status quo into the revolutionary spirit, the voice of resistance to the conservative institution that constricts thought. This definition of genius not only transcends national bounds but redounds back against the limitations society tries to impose on the human intellect.

This new definition informs D'Israeli's final study of the subject. Neither an apology for nor an attack on Judaism, *The Genius of Judaism* is an evaluation of Judaism from the perspective of the Byronic hero, that is, of the concept of genius he had generated in the process of translating Byron's annotations.[22] D'Israeli establishes the basis for his argument in his first chapter, "With the Israelite Every Thing Is Ancient, and Nothing Is Obsolete," in which he establishes his thesis, that the problem with the Jews is that they have remained mired in a historical moment that has not evolved with time. Rather than arguing against the Jews, he explains in the second chapter, "A More Intimate Knowledge of the Jewish Feelings, and Their History, Required": "If it be permitted by human sagacity to discover the causes which have influenced the singular fate of the Jewish people, it must be sought by a more intimate knowledge of their feelings and their history, than has fallen to the share of ridiculing Polytheists, of hostile Christians, and of doting Rabbins."[23]

Specifying revealed religion as the source of the problem, D'Israeli, in chapter 3, "The Laws of the Jewish People Constitute Their Religion," identifies its origin as the vision of the law on Mount Sinai. That initial experience led to what he defines in the fourth chapter as "the theocracy," which would inevitably decline, as he explains in the fifth. However, in a reference to the Talmudists, D'Israeli claims, as the title of the sixth chapter puts it, that "A Human Supersedes the Divine Code," causing a separation of the Hebrews from the rest of the world. The next four chapters specify four causes for that separation: 7, "Their Written Law Received as of Divine Institution"; 8, "The Sabbatic Institution"; 9, "The Multitude of Their Rites and Their Ceremonial Law"; and 10, "The Prohibition of Partaking of the Food of Whoever Was Not an Israelite."

The problem with the Jews, according to D'Israeli, is their adherence to an obsolete, stultifying national identity, one that prevented, rather than promoted, their acculturation into the modern world. For this reason, as he explains in the eleventh chapter, the "history of Jewish conversions" is a failure. Not only do Christian conversionists themselves rely on revealed religion, but even more important, there are many competing Christian sects, each of which claims its own legitimacy at the expense of the others. For a Jew to choose one is to open himself up to attack by the others. He might as well remain Jewish. Therefore, as D'Israeli continues in chapter 12, "Of the Causes of the Universal Hatred of the Jewish People," the real point of contention is not theological but social. In refusing to assimilate, the Jews set themselves off as a nation within a nation.

Confronting one of the most vociferous accusations of the anti-Semites, that the Jews could not be good citizens because of their divided loyalties, in the next section, "The English Jews," D'Israeli traces the history of Anglo-Judaica, and then argues that the Jews have historically been patriotic to their countries of birth.[24] Having dispelled the imputation that they lacked patriotism, D'Israeli concludes with an exhortation to the English Jews that they make the kinds of internal educational reforms that would enable them to assimilate into English culture:

> I would implore the Jews to begin to educate their youth as the youth of Europe, and not of Palestine; let their Talmud be removed to an elevated shelf, to be consulted as a curiosity of antiquity, and not as a manual of education. Many, indeed, among the higher classes of the Hebrews, have attempted to educate their children in Christian schools, for they have no others; but the conflict of the parental feelings, of their own good sense with the excluding dicta of the Talmudists—the forbidden food and the omitted customs—have scared even the intelligent among them. The civil and political fusion of the Jewish with their fellow-citizens, must commence by rejecting every anti-social principle; let them only separate to hasten to the Church and to the Synagogue. The Hebrew, exulting in his immutable law, has yet to learn that a wise legislature, in accommodating itself to the times, and to the wants of the people, suspends or executes laws as the juncture may require. The chief end of laws is not only their observance, but the good of the people. Salus Populi suprema Lex. Let them remember that their great ancestor, Judas Maccabeus, fought on the Sabbath-day;

for, he said, "It is not as it was heretofore with us!" To free themselves of their superstitions will not be the least difficult conversion of the Jews. The common enjoyments of civil rights will neither endanger the genius of Judaism, nor the genius of Christianity. (265–66)

Echoing the arguments of Mendelssohn and Wesseley, D'Israeli urges the Jews to modernize and assimilate into the mainstream so they can be liberated from the disabilities that had limited his own progress.

By the end of *The Genius of Judaism,* D'Israeli has projected a Judaized form of the Byronic hero. He began his analysis of the concept of genius with a self-contradictory indictment against the Jews for lacking the qualities of a Christian genius, but then, in his *Essay on the Manners and Genius of the Literary Character,* he erroneously, as he would come to believe, encouraged Christians to establish a national academy that, perforce, would replicate the very situation that led to what he would finally conclude was the stagnation of Jewish culture. Through Byron's mediation he was able to recognize that the fault was not with the Jews per se, but with theocracy, and that just as Byron had to transcend the limitations imposed by the Christian establishment, so, too, did the Jews have to transgress the boundaries imposed by the Talmud. He does not advocate conversion; instead, he encourages a secular education that would articulate a new Jewish identity, one that promotes the intellectual elitism of genius over the narrow sectarianism of the old academy.

Isaac Nathan—Religious Skepticism

In contrast to his relationship with D'Israeli, Byron collaborated directly with Isaac Nathan (1790?-1864), and their mode of translation was not *intralingual,* but *intersemiotic,* involving the transfer of the *Hebrew Melodies* back and forth between Byron's verbal and Nathan's musical art.[25] The idea for the song cycle was Nathan's, as was the cultural context, reflecting the composer's conflict between his Jewish and English roots. According to family legend, Nathan's grandfather was the illegitimate child of the Polish king Stanislaus Poniatowski and an unknown Jewish woman. Because of internal Polish problems in the 1770s, when Menahem Mona, Nathan's father, was a child, he and his little brother were sent to Germany. They were soon separated, and Menahem Mona was raised by German Jewish friends until, at the age of twenty, he emigrated to England. Nathan's father married an unidentified Jewish woman, and they had five children, Isaac, born in Canterbury in 1790, being the oldest. Nathan's mother, believed to have run off with an Englishman, deserted the family.

Menahem Mona, himself a cantor, wished his son to be a rabbi and sent Nathan to Solomon Lyon's Anglo-Jewish boarding school in Cambridge to study Latin, Hebrew, and mathematics. But Nathan preferred music, so he persuaded his father to let him abandon theology, and the family moved to London, where Nathan trained with Domenico Corri, student of Nicolo Porpora, Haydn's master. According to his granddaughter, Nathan had all the qualities of a professional and social success:

> Tall, handsome, slightly exotic, his pale face framed with glossy black curls, he was charming in manner and highly educated. His voice was small but beautifully trained, and he could compose sentimental songs by the dozen for his pupils to sing. His Jewish birth was no detriment to him in Regency London, and indeed added to his romantic charm; there are even those who say that the story of the descent from Stanislaus II was invented by him at this time, the better to impress the aristocratic young ladies whose mammas brought them to the studio of the renowned Signor Corri.[26]

If professionally and even socially his religion proved no detriment, personally it created a serious obstacle when Nathan married his student Elizabeth Rosetta Worthington. Mrs. Worthington attempted to sever the relationship, but Isaac, age twenty-two, and Rosetta, seventeen, eloped and, in 1812, they were married twice: first at St. Mary Abbot's, Kensington, and then, three months later, at a London synagogue, where the marriage contract identified Rosetta as a convert to Judaism. Nathan was able to support his family as singing master to Princess Charlotte, only child of the Prince Regent and heiress to the English crown, and also as the Regent's musical librarian, a job he would hold even after 1820, when the Regent became King George IV.

Around this time, collections of what were then called national songs were in vogue, George Thomson having initiated the trend with his publication of *Select Collection of Original Scottish Airs* (1793), followed by, among others, Thomas Preston's *A Selection of Irish Melodies* (1808), Edward Bunting's *General Collection of Ancient Irish Music* (1796), Lady Morgan's *The Lay of an Irish Harp* (1807), James Power's rival *A Selection of Scottish Melodies* (1812), and, of course, Thomas Moore's *Irish Melodies* (1820). Hoping to amplify his income, Nathan advertised a similar project in *Gentleman's Magazine* for May 1813, claiming: "J. Nathan is about to publish 'Hebrew Melodies,' all of them upwards of 1,000 years old and some of them performed by the Antient Hebrews before the destruction of the Temple."

Although his first choice of collaborator was Byron, Nathan believed that the poet, who was then at the height of his popularity, would not consider the project, so he contacted Walter Scott, who declined. Nathan then wrote Byron, on June 13, 1814, sending a musical setting for the lines "This Rose to Calm My Brother's Cares" from the *Bride of Abydos*. Receiving no response, Nathan sent a second letter on June 30, enticing the poet with "a considerable number of very beautiful Hebrew melodies of undoubted antiquity, some of which are proved to have been sung by the Hebrews before the destruction of the Temple of Jerusalem."[27] Likely thanks to the intercession of Douglas Kinnaird, his friend, Byron agreed to write a few songs, though in its final form, the *Hebrew Melodies* contains a total of twenty-nine. The first edition was completed in 1815, and the name of tenor John Braham, who did not work on the songs, was placed on the title page to increase sales. Braham did perform the song cycle, though, and while he received rave reviews, the "Jewish" project, as would be expected, elicited anti-Semitic responses as well.[28] Nathan could not have expected otherwise; yet in neither his biographies nor his own writing are there any references to the anti-Semitism, or even to his attitude toward his Jewish heritage, except for the repeated insistence that his music was authentic.[29] Still, it hardly seems credible that he would have no feelings on the subject. Rather, it seems likely that just as Byron used the lyrics to help articulate his complex attitude toward Christianity, Nathan used the music for the same purpose, to comment on his own complex relationship with Judaism.[30]

The first edition of the *Hebrew Melodies* contained twelve songs, and thus far, liturgical sources have been located for the first nine.[31] Although it is possible to organize and interpret these songs in a number of different ways, when Nathan's juxtaposition of Jewish liturgy and Byronic lyric is placed within the context of post-Enlightenment Anglo-Jewish culture, four general themes emerge: faith versus reason; religious Zionism versus secular nationalism; messianic passivity versus social activism; and, finally, on the personal level, Jewish religion versus English identity. As noted in the introduction, the contemporary debate about faith versus reason, which was central to the Haskalah, originated with Wesseley's proposed educational reforms. Not substantively different from its Christian counterpart, the controversy revolved around the core value of identity, that is, of whether the nation would be defined by its religious or its secular leaders.[32]

The second controversy involves the literal versus metaphorical interpretation of Zionism. Although the political movement would not crystallize until late in the nineteenth century, the religious belief that the Jews would return to Jerusalem has always been a significant element of the liturgy. In the earlier nineteenth century, as noted in the discussion of D'Israeli, Zionism was problematic for diasporean Jews whose quest for emancipation was met with accusations of divided loyalties—between the European nation in which they lived and Jerusalem. In response, reformers advocated the shift from a literal to a metaphorical interpretation of Zionism, in which the idealistic values of Zionism would be actualized through a realistic commitment to the world. A corollary to the controversy over Zionism involved the question of messianism. Although traditionalists believed that the Jews should wait passively for the return of the Messiah to lead them back to Jerusalem, reformers, who thought that the Jews ought to live actively in the present, argued that enhancing their lives in the Diaspora would not contradict belief in a future messianic age. Finally, these abstract conflicts were felt on the personal level, forcing individuals, like Isaac Nathan, to negotiate between the sometimes-conflicting pulls toward their Jewish heritage and British nationality.

Articulating the controversy of faith versus reason, "If That High World" and "The Wild Gazelle" can be read as songs of the Haskalah, the Byronic skepticism of the lyrics creating a counterpoint to the liturgical religiosity of the music. In the first, Nathan places Byron's speculative sonnet "If That High World" in the musical setting of a Kaddish, a juxtaposition that replaces blind faith with rational analysis as the basis for spiritual belief. In general, a Kaddish is a prayer that praises and glorifies God, as it anticipates the establishment of God's kingdom on earth.[33] Written in Aramaic, the Kaddish exists in four forms: the Whole Kaddish, the Half Kaddish, the Kaddish de-Rabbanan ("the scholars' Kaddish"), and the most widely known, the Mourner's Kaddish, which, designed for responsive reading, reads:

> Mourners: Magnified and sanctified be the great name of God throughout the world which He hath created according to His will. May He establish His kingdom during the days of your life and during the life of all the house of Israel, speedily, yea, soon; and say ye, Amen.
> Congregation and Mourners: May His great name be blessed forever and ever.

> Mourners: Exalted and honored be the name of the Holy One, blessed be He, whose glory transcends, yea, is beyond all blessings and hymns, praises and consolations which are uttered in the world; and say ye, Amen.
>
> May there be abundant peace from heaven, and life for us and for all Israel; and say ye, Amen.
>
> May He who establisheth peace in the heavens, grant peace unto us and unto all Israel; and say ye, Amen.[34]

As a mainstay of the Jewish service, the Kaddish has a long history, likely—given the absence of references to the Temple—dating back to biblical times. Musically, it has attracted a wide variety of arrangements, though, of relevance to Nathan's project, in the Ashkenazi rite (that used by Nathan), the music "is distinguished by a striving for sublime melodic expression."[35]

In the poem, Byron exploits the two-part structure of an Italian sonnet for a skeptical analysis of a hypothetical proposition—the question of whether there is an afterlife—the opening octave posing the condition to be fulfilled by the closing sestet. The speaker begins with what could be read as a double hypothetical—"If that high world, which lies beyond / Our own, surviving Love endears" (ll. 1–2)[36]—in which he speculates both about the existence of heaven and about the survival of human emotion after physical death, the former being a prerequisite to the latter. Although there is no verifiable proof of the existence of heaven, still, he would "welcome those untrodden spheres!" (l. 5). Choosing emotion over reason, the speaker prefers "To soar from earth and find all fears / Lost in thy light—Eternity!" (ll. 7–8). After essentially abandoning reason for emotion, the speaker then makes his leap of faith—"It must be so"—the reunion of lovers after death providing the only rationale for existence in this world: "'tis not for self / That we so tremble on the brink" (ll. 9–10). Rather, the only consolation for life is belief in the afterlife:

> Oh! in that future let us think
> To hold each heart the heart that shares,
> With them the immortal waters drink,
> And soul in soul grow deathless theirs!
>   *(ll. 13–16)*

CHAPTER 1

Thus, what opens as a skeptical theological inquiry concludes with an affirmation of spiritual belief. Nathan reports in *Fugitive Pieces,* "In a subsequent conversation, he [Byron] observed to me, 'they accuse me of atheism—an atheist I could never be—no man of reflection, can feel otherwise than doubtful and anxious, when reflecting on futurity. . . . Alas! Nathan, we either know too little, or feel too much on this subject; and if it be criminal to speculate on it (as the gentlemen critics say) I fear I must ever remain an awful offender.'"[37] Both "If That High World" and the Kaddish affirm a spiritual belief, but Byron's lyric makes a conscious choice that redounds back against what, in contrast, appears to be the absolute faith inherent in the liturgy, privileging, by contrast, the active choice to believe, as opposed to passive acceptance of a religious tradition.

The next combination of lyric and liturgy can be viewed as a concrete instantiation of the criticism of blind faith over skepticism, Nathan's choice of the Yigdal, a paraphrase of the Thirteen Articles of Faith, relocating Byron within the context of Jewish skepticism.[38] As formulated by Moses Maimonides (Moses ben Maimon, known as "Rambam," 1135–1204), the Articles of Faith are as follows:

1. The existence of God which is perfect and sufficient unto itself and which is the cause of the existence of all other beings.
2. God's unity which is unlike all other kinds of unity.
3. God must not be conceived in bodily terms, and the anthropomorphic expressions applied to God in Scripture have to be understood in a metaphorical sense.
4. God is eternal.
5. God alone is to be worshiped and obeyed. There are no mediating powers able freely to grant man's petitions, and intermediaries must not be invoked.
6. Prophecy.
7. Moses is unsurpassed by any other prophet.
8. The entire Torah was given to Moses.
9. Moses' Torah will not be abrogated or superseded by another divine law nor will anything be added to, or taken away from it.
10. God knows the actions of men.
11. God rewards those who fulfill the commandments of the Torah, and punishes those who transgress them.

12. The coming of the Messiah.
13. The resurrection of the dead.[39]

In the first half of the fourteenth century, an unknown poet transformed the Articles of Faith into a prayer that begins with the couplet, "The living God O magnify and bless, / Transcending time and here eternally," and concludes:

> Messiah He will send at end of days,
> And all the faithful to salvation lead.
>
> God will the dead again to life restore
> In His abundance of almighty love.
>
> Then blessèd be His name, all names above,
> And let His praise resound forevermore.[40]

As part of the daily liturgy, the Yigdal has been put to music a number of times, all versions sharing "moods of pride and cheerfulness."[41] One of the more popular is the "Leoni *Yidgal,*" attributed to Meyer Leon, cantor at Duke's Place Ashkenazi Synagogue in London. After hearing it sung, Thomas Olivers, a Wesleyan minister, translated "Leoni *Yidgal*" into *The God of Abraham Praise* (published in 1770), a hymn incorporated into the Anglican service.

Although the text is orthodox, its originator was not. Maimonides was a rational philosopher who, though living long before the Haskalah, anticipated many of its reforms: he sought to introduce the study of Greek philosophy into the traditional curriculum; he did not believe in a literal return, but advocated a metaphorical approach to Zionism; and he opposed the control exerted over the Jewish community by biblical exegetes. Though revered, Maimonides remains a controversial figure, having written two apparently contradictory texts: in Hebrew the *Mishnah Torah,* a justification of the Jewish faith, and in Arabic the *Guide for the Perplexed,* a skeptical study of religious orthodoxy.

By superimposing "The Wild Gazelle" onto the Yigdal, Nathan ironizes the liturgical statement of faith. Byron's lyrics can be read as a skeptical interpretation, if not actual parody, of the postexilic Jewish condition. The central symbol of the poem, the wild gazelle, is the opposite of the Jews: it is an uncivilized animal that, though beautiful, is incapable of understanding, much less appreciating the fact that it is permitted to run wild in the Holy Land, and it certainly cannot pray to the God who created the land. As the four stanzas progress, Byron gradually shifts focus from the privileged animal that roams over the still-beautiful hills of Judah to a comparison with the exiled Jews who once far outshone the gazelle, with "an eye more bright," and "statelier maids" (ll. 7, 12). Yet now, vegetation in Jerusalem is "More blest . . . / Than Israel's scattered race" (ll. 13–14). The final stanza contrasts the current state of the Jews with the gazelle:

> But we must wander witheringly,
>   In other lands to die;
> And where our fathers' ashes be,
>   Our own may never lie:
> Our temple hath not left a stone,
> And Mockery sits on Salem's throne.
>   *(ll. 19–24)*

Instead of concluding with a conventional prayer for restoration, Byron replaces the idea of God with a personified Mockery, implying the futility of any messianic hope for the future. When viewed from the context of the musical setting, Byron's lyrics would seem to undermine the Yigdal's joyful articulation of faith. Yet when the words are viewed from the broader perspective of the liturgical history, with its relationship to the Maimonidean controversy, the contemporary debate over the need for Enlightenment and skeptical inquiry emerges. The point, as the combination of "The Wild Gazelle" with the Yigdal seems to imply, is not to abandon faith, but to question the "Mockery" that "sits on Salem's throne."

For the next two songs, "O Snatch'd Away in Beauty's Bloom" and "On Jordan's Banks," Nathan's musical settings seem to undermine the orthodox belief in Zionism, suggesting instead that the Jews might do better to build lives for themselves in the Diaspora. In the first, he uses the traditional song "Eli Zion ve-Areha" ("Wail Zion and Its Cities") to interpret Byron's symbol of lost beauty as the lost Jerusalem, which should be mourned but ultimately forgotten. Choosing a Kinah, an elegy, from a collection of odes to Zion, Nathan places Byron's poem within the context of Zionism. "Eli Zion ve-Areha," anonymously composed in the Middle Ages, consists of twelve stanzas enumerating the cruelties suffered by Judea and its inhabitants during the destruction of the Second Temple. As an elegy, "Eli Zion," which has become for Ashkenazim a symbol of the yearly commemoration of the Destruction, is sung by the congregation while standing.

Byron's lyrics dramatize the emotional conflict created by the loss of a beloved. At death, the first stanza indicates, the mourner gains some degree of solace in the belief that his lost love will become part of the universal life cycle, as "on thy turf shall roses rear," while "the wild cypress wave in tender gloom" (ll. 3, 5). By the second stanza, however, the mourner knows that such consolation is artificial, only a personified Sorrow, "feed[ing] deep thought with many a dream" (l. 8), keeping memory of the beloved alive. Consequently, as the third stanza attempts to assert, the only alternative is to try to forget; "we know that tears are vain" (l. 11). Still, that knowledge does not relieve either the mourner or his consoler: "And thou—who tell'st me to forget, / Thy looks are wan—thine eyes are wet" (ll. 15–16).

Perhaps tellingly, in *Fugitive Pieces*, Nathan says that some time after putting the lyrics to music, he asked Byron about their meaning:

> In submitting this melody to his Lordship's judgment, I once enquired in what manner they might refer to any scriptural subject: he appeared for a moment affected—at last replied, "Every mind must make its own reference: there is scarcely one of us who could not imagine that the affliction belongs to himself, to me it certainly belongs." His Lordship here, with agitation, exclaimed, "She is no more, and perhaps the only vestige of her existence is the feeling I sometimes fondly indulge." (30)

Progressing from the state of mourning, in "On Jordan's Banks" Nathan uses the popular Chanukah song "Ma'oz Zur" to imply an accusation against a God who would deprive the Jews of Jerusalem. Thematically, both Byron's "On Jordan's Banks" and the Hebrew "Ma'oz Zur" can be considered proto-Zionistic; however, the mournful theme and tone of the English lyrics contradict the joyous hopefulness of the traditional song. Probably composed in thirteenth-century Germany by someone named Mordecai (the first letter of each stanza forms an acrostic of his name), "Ma'oz Zur," usually sung at the ceremonial lighting of the candles, contains in its complete form six stanzas, all revolving around the theme of redemption from the loss of Zion. The first stanza, a prayer to restore the biblical Temple worship, is followed successively by stanzas of praise for the delivery from bondage in Egypt, from the Babylonian captivity, from the Persians (as related in the book of Esther), from the Greco-Syrians in the second century BCE (the occasion for the Chanukah celebration) and, finally, from the German emperor Frederic Barbarossa in the twelfth century (this stanza is seldom sung).[42] The tune was so

CHAPTER 1

infectious that Martin Luther adapted it for his chorale "So weiss ich eins was mich erfreut."[43]

Byron's lyrics undermine the tenor of the song. The holiday of Chanukah celebrates the return of the Jews to the Temple after its having been defiled by the Greco-Syrians, the specific miracle being that a small amount of uncontaminated oil lasted for eight days, long enough to keep the lamp lit until more oil could be found. Thematically, each stanza of "Ma'oz Zur" celebrates a return to Zion after a period of exile, bringing the tune to the composer's era. In contrast, Byron approaches the topic from the opposite perspective, focusing on the present loss, rather than the past or future, to question the kind of God who would permit the contamination of his own Holy Land.

The first stanza, depicting the postexilic Middle East, uses the present tense to indict a sleeping God who has permitted the holy sites to be defiled:

> On Jordan's banks the Arabs' camels stray,
> On Sion's hill the False One's votaries pray,
> The Baal-adorer bows on Sinai's steep—
> Yet there—even there—Oh God! thy thunders sleep.
>   (ll. 1–4)

Even more incomprehensible, as the second stanza suggests, is the fact that these were the places where God had revealed himself to the Israelites:

> There—where thy finger scorch'd the tablet stone!
> There—where thy shadow to thy people shone!
> Thy glory shrouded in its garb of fire:
> Thyself—none living see and not expire!
>   (ll. 5–8)

The speaker lays blame not on the people who forgot their God, but the reverse, on a God who, apparently, forgot his obligation to his people. The ultimate question, then, is how long this God will sleep, leaving his people in exile:

> Oh! in the lightning let thy glance appear!
> Sweep from his shiver'd hand the oppressor's spear:
> How long by tyrants shall thy land be trod?
> How long thy temple worshipless, Oh God?
>   (ll. 9–12)

44

By combining Byron's skeptical indictment of Zionism with a celebration of God's delivery of the Jews from exile, Nathan exposes the fundamental question underlying Zionism: should the Jews believe literally in Zionism, or should they transform their belief into a metaphorical interpretation of a return to Jerusalem and actively build a life in the Diaspora?

If Zionism mourns the loss of a golden age in the past, messianism projects its restoration in the future. To Christians, that belief revolves around a spiritual New Jerusalem said to replace the corporeal city. Jews, in contrast, believe in a physical restoration, the Messiah being defined as a human descendant of the House of David who is prophesied to lead the Jews from their exile back to their home in Jerusalem. As with Zionism, enlightened Jews advocated a metaphorical belief in messianism, to be accomplished by transferring the apocalyptic ideals to the reality of their lives in the present. When placed in their musical settings, "She Walks in Beauty" and "Jephtha's Daughter" both can be seen to undermine a literal view of messianism.

"She Walks in Beauty" was the first of the songs Nathan would set to music, but its lyrics predate his collaboration with Byron, who wrote the poem on June 11, 1814, when he first met Anne Beatrix, wife of Byron's second cousin Robert John Wilmot. When they first discussed collaborating, Byron sent to Nathan a few songs, including, among others, "Sun of the Sleepless," "Francisca," "It Is the Hour," and "She Walks in Beauty." Although Nathan assumed that the collaboration would be limited to these few, it seems that Byron was so entranced with how the musical settings deepened and even transformed "She Walks in Beauty" into "an Invocation of the Muse," that he extended the project.[44] For its musical setting, Nathan chose "Lekha Dodi," a celebration of the mystical union between the Messiah and the Shekhinah, the female manifestation of the "divine presence."

Historically, "Lekha Dodi" (Come, my beloved) are the opening words of a poem written by Solomon ha-Levi Alkabez (1505–84), a mystic and poet of the early sixteenth century. Like other Kabbalists of the time, Alkabez literalized and then dramatized what had previously been viewed as metaphorical beliefs. In his song, Alkabez personifies the coming Sabbath as the Shekhinah, kabbalistically interpreted as the female "divine presence," whose union with the Messiah, it is said, will bring about the restoration of the cosmos. Alkabez's poem operates on a number of different levels. As an acrostic consisting of nine stanzas, the initial letters of the first eight spelling out his name, "Lekha Dodi" can be read as a personal

CHAPTER 1

prayer. Mythically, as indicated by its opening line, "Come, my beloved, to meet the bride; let us welcome the presence of the Sabbath," the poem describes the reunification of the Messiah and his Shekhinah, who has been exiled by the Fall. Kabbalists believe that the sexual union of male and female—traditionally occurring on Friday nights—not only fulfills the injunction to be fruitful and multiply but actually assists in the reunification of the Messiah and his Shekhinah. As a celebration of the coming Sabbath, "Lekha Dodi" expresses joy on all of these different levels, from the mundane end of the workweek to the mystical restoration of the cosmos. Soon after its composition, the poem was almost immediately integrated into Friday night services, as Jews worldwide turned to the entrance of the synagogue to welcome the "Sabbath bride."[45]

The musical setting uses only Byron's first stanza, possibly to suggest that a literal belief in messianism creates an artificial stasis that prevents, rather than promotes, progress. When the first stanza is separated from the last two, the repetition of the sentence "She walks in beauty" is transformed from the idealization of a woman to the symbol of man's fallen state, the exile of the Shekhinah:

> She walks in beauty, like the night
>   Of cloudless climes and starry skies;
> And all that's best of dark and bright
>   Meet in her aspect and her eyes:
> Thus mellow'd to that tender light
>   Which heaven to gaudy day denies.
>   She walks in beauty, like the night
>   Of cloudless climes and starry skies.

As an abstract symbol, the Shekhinah lacks the physical characteristics that Byron detailed in the rest of the poem—"the nameless grace" (l. 8), "every raven tress" (l. 9), and the facial expression formed by cheek, and brow, "The smiles that win, the tints that glow" (l. 15). Absent these characteristics, all we know about the woman is that "she walks in beauty"—like the Shekhinah in exile. Without any kind of resolution, the subject of the poem becomes a figure of the contemporary state of the Jewish people, unemancipated in the Diaspora.

Similarly, in "Jephtha's Daughter," the juxtaposition of the biblical trope of willing sacrifice against the melody of the Song of Songs could ironically question the love of God for his people. In the biblical story

(Judges 11:30–40), Jephtha, an illegitimate son of Gilead, is sent from his father's house by his brothers. Soon thereafter, when the Ammonites wage war against Israel, the elders of his tribe ask him to lead them in battle. Jephtha agrees, but only if he can become leader of the tribe. Once back, he attempts to reason with the Ammonites, requesting safe passage through their lands, but they don't trust him. Jephtha then prays for God's assistance, offering as a bargaining chip to sacrifice the first thing he sees when he returns home victorious. It is his only child, his daughter; she does acquiesce to her father's obligation, requesting only that she be permitted to "bewail her virginity" for two months before her death.

Byron's version is written from the daughter's perspective, as she in successive stanzas (1) complies with her father's vow to God for the sake of country; (2) returns from her two months of seclusion; (3) attests to her virginity; (4) agrees to be sacrificed; and (5) prophesies that she will become a symbol. Left out, of course, is the identity of that symbol—the figure of virgin sacrifice to a vengeful God. Hence, according to Nathan, Byron's repeated claim that her blood is not on his hands:

> When these beautiful lines were composed by Lord Byron, I was anxious to ascertain his real sentiments on the subject, hinting my own belief that it might not necessarily mean a positive sacrifice of the daughter's life, but perhaps referred to a sentence of perpetual seclusion, a state held by the Jews as dead indeed to society, and the most severe infliction that could be imposed. With his usual frankness, he observed, "Whatever may be the absolute state of the case, I am innocent of her blood; she has been killed to my hands: besides, you know *such an infliction,* as the world goes, would not be a subject for sentiment or pathos—therefore do not seek to exumate [sic] the lady." On another occasion when Jephtha was the subject of conversation, his lordship with much good humour suddenly put an end to the argument exclaiming, "Well my hands are not imbrued in her blood! I shall not by killing her incur censure from the world, for an attempt to deprive them of the pleasure of thinking a little more on the subject." (10–12)

In his musical setting, Nathan seems not only to proclaim his and Byron's innocence but to direct the blame toward God, who apparently demanded, and certainly accepted, such a sacrifice.

As the most erotic book of the Bible, Shir ha-Shirim, the Song of Songs, is a love poem, attributed to Solomon, in which the lover proclaims his love for his beloved in quite physical terms. Traditionally, the poem is allegorized: by Jews it is seen as the expression of God's love for his people, by Christians as Christ's for his Church. The story of Jephtha and his daughter, however, articulates not love but commerce. Jephtha, a "love child," is banished by his legitimate siblings who do not want to share their inheritance with him; and he is brought back only because they cannot defend themselves. Similarly, he agrees to return only if he can be their leader. Once in power, he attempts to maintain peace but when confronted with war, rather than relying on God's love for his people, he bargains with God, and, finally, insists on fulfilling the bargain, making his daughter the cost of a deal over which she had no say. Thus, the lyrics subvert the idealization of love found in the biblical source of the music.

In addition, when setting the song, Nathan omitted the second stanza, the one expression of the kind of unconditional love represented by Canticles:

> And the voice of my mourning is o'er,
> And the mountains behold me no more:
> If the hand that I love lay me low,
> There cannot be pain in the blow!
>
>   (ll. 5–8)

In this stanza, the daughter describes the only action over which she has control: her choice to sacrifice herself willingly for her father. Minus this stanza, the lyrics focus solely on the economic exchange.

In the last group of songs, Nathan seems to concentrate on the personal question of his identity as an English Jew. In addition to the conflict between his heritage and nationality, Nathan, as a young man, had rejected the rabbinate in favor of secular music. Leaving aside the oedipal implications of how Nathan's choice might relate to the fact that his father was a cantor, the question of his relationship to his religion remains problematic. Although, according to the Jewish marriage contract, his first wife had converted, his children were raised Christian; and his second wife, also a Christian, never signed the Jewish marriage contract at all. The vast majority of Nathan's music was non-Jewish, and after he moved to Australia, he studied indigenous music, ultimately becoming known as the father of Australian music. Yet he himself remained Jewish. These personal conflicts might be revealed through the liturgical settings derived from the Yom Kippur service for lyrics about the theme of music. Specifically, the music for "Oh! Weep for Those" and "My Soul Is Dark" evokes the Kol Nidre prayer that opens the service for the Day of Atonement, and that of "The Harp the Monarch Minstrel Swept" is based on the Ya'aleh, a prayer from the evening service.[46] The juxtaposition of literary theme and musical setting suggests the possibility that on some level, at any rate, these songs might comprise Nathan's own penitence for any sins he feared he might have committed.

While neither "My Soul Is Dark" nor "Oh! Weep for Those" is set to an identifiable tune, motifs in both echo the Kol Nidre, "all vows," a prayer in which the penitent asks to be released from any pledges made rashly to God during the preceding year. Dating back to the eighth century, the prayer developed in response to the fear that rash promises made during times of stress might have been left unfulfilled. Kol Nidre applies solely to vows made to God—those to people cannot be voided through the Kol Nidre prayer—and its purpose is to clear the conscience of the supplicant.[47]

The speaker in "My Soul Is Dark" seems afflicted by the remorse the Kol Nidre prayer is designed to alleviate. According to Nathan, Byron intended this poem, a dramatization of 1 Samuel 16:14–23, to depict madness:

> It was generally conceived, that Lord Byron's reported singularities, approached on some occasions to derangement, and at one period indeed, it was very currently asserted, that his intellects were actually impaired. The report only served to amuse his Lordship. He referred to the circumstance, and declared, that he would try how a *Madman* could write; seizing the pen with eagerness, he for a moment fixed his eyes in majestic wildness on vacancy; when like a flash of inspiration, without erasing a single word, the above verses were the result, which he put into my possession with this remark: "if I am mad who write, be certain that you are so who compose!" (37)

Within the poem, the specific form of madness seems to be that described in the Bible, the torment produced by "an evil spirit of the lord," that which afflicts the penitent before reciting the Kol Nidre prayer. Byron's lyrics contain two stanzas, the first asserting that only David's music will ease Saul's suffering—"My soul is dark—Oh! quickly string / The harp I yet can brook to hear" (ll. 1–2); and second, that the music must be "wild and deep," that is, intense enough to reach the depths of his suffering. Not coincidentally, the poem anticipates Nathan's description from the preface to the first edition: that the music evinces "a certain wildness and pathos, which have at length become the chief characteristic of the Sacred Songs of the Jews."[48]

CHAPTER 1

Although "Oh! Weep for Those" is thematically closer to poems with proto-Zionistic lyrics, its musical setting, with a Kol Nidre motif, shifts the emphasis from a lost Jerusalem to the need for atonement. It is based on Psalms 55:6, "And I say, 'Oh that I had wings like a dove! for then would I fly away, and be at rest,'" but Byron transforms the psalmist's subjunctive into the elegiac, "Oh! weep for those that wept by Babel's stream, / Whose shrines are desolate, whose land a dream" (ll. 1–2). After mourning the loss of Jerusalem in the first stanza, the speaker asks in the second where the New Jerusalem might be—"And where shall Israel lave her bleeding feet?" (l. 5)—only to mourn its impossibility in the third: "Israel but the grave!" (l. 12). Significantly, from Nathan's perspective, while the first two stanzas contain references to music, the third does not. That is, when referring to the loss of Jerusalem, Byron says: "Weep for the harp of Judah's broken shell" (l. 3), and when exploring the possibility of a new home, he asks:

> And when shall Zion's songs again seem sweet?
> And Judah's melody once more rejoice
> The hearts that leaped before its heavenly voice?
>   *(ll. 6–8)*

Yet the last stanza, dealing with the impossibility of a return to Jerusalem, contains no reference to music, as though there can be no music without life—and conversely, no life without music. This requirement, from the composer's perspective, might have suggested the emotional value of the Kol Nidre.

Finally, the last of the lyrics, "The Harp the Monarch Minstrel Swept," is set to Ya'aleh taḥanun. A three-part supplication, the text of the Ya'aleh is designed to span the twenty-four hours of Yom Kippur. Beginning with the lines

> O may our supplications arise at nightfall,
> Our prayers approach Thy presence from the dawn,
> And let our exultation come at dusk
>   *(ll. 1–3),*[49]

Ya'aleh refers, first, to the utterance of the prayer at Kol Nidre, the evening before Yom Kippur; second, to the continuation of prayer, beginning at dawn, on the Day of Atonement; and finally, to the culmination at sunset, by which time, the penitent hopes, the prayer will have been accepted by God.

According to Nathan,

> When his Lordship put the copy into my hand, it terminated thus—
>   Its sound aspired to Heaven, and there abode.
> This, however, did not complete the verse, and I wished him to help out the melody. He replied, "Why I have sent you to Heaven—it would be difficult to go further." My attention for a few moments was called to some other person, and his Lordship, whom I had hardly missed exclaimed—"Here, Nathan, I have brought you down again," and immediately presented me the beautiful and sublime lines which conclude the melody." (33)

While Nathan does not indicate what melody he had in mind when he asked Byron for a fourth verse, the result can be read as a prologue and three-part Ya'aleh taḥanun. The first stanza sets the stage for the Ya'aleh, describing the loss of music, when the harp's "chords are riven!" (l. 5). The speaker then describes how David's music had, in effect, ascended to heaven—"Till David's Lyre grew mightier than his throne!" (l. 10), and in stanza 2, how it arrived before God—"Its sound aspired to Heaven and there abode!" (l. 15), to conclude with the prayer for reconciliation:

> Since then, though heard on earth no more,
>   Devotion and her daughter Love
> Still bid the bursting spirit soar
>   To sounds that seem as from above,
>   In dreams that day's broad light can not remove.
>   *(ll. 16–20)*

The last stanza, like the last part of the Ya'aleh prayer, returns to the uncertainty of everyday life. At the end of the Ya'aleh, the spiritual elevation to the level of God, all one can do is hope that the prayer, "though heard on earth no more," has been accepted: "Still bid the bursting spirit soar."

By definition, liturgy is a public expression of faith, one in which the sounds reinforce the sense of the verbal prayer. By juxtaposing the traditional Jewish music with the Byronic lyrics, Nathan accomplishes two objectives. First, he disconnects what had been a union of sound and sense, leaving each to be analyzed as an independent component. At the same time, by merging the religious music with the secular lyrics, he ironizes both, simultaneously imposing a religious implication onto Byron's lyrics, while, in effect, profaning the sacred, demonstrating that the music could be spiritual, even without its specifically religious content. Embodied in the procedure is an attitude of religious skepticism, a questioning of why organized religion is necessary for spiritual development, and in this mixing of Jewish music and Christian lyrics, both predicated on the Hebrew Bible, a questioning of which is truly the revealed religion. Under the circumstances, the only alternative for both Nathan and Byron was to rely on personal integrity rather than organized religion for their identities, both of them eventually seeking more expansive communities outside of Great Britain, where they would be free to create with less interference from religious authorities.

No consensus has been reached about the value of D'Israeli's and Nathan's contributions to Jewish culture. In the last century, D'Israeli received mixed reviews. Goodman Lipkind, in his article for the older *Jewish Encyclopedia*, claims, "Religiously, Isaac D'Israeli was a man far in advance of his times, and was perhaps the first English Jew who took the modern attitude toward Jewish ceremonial." Of D'Israeli's *Genius of Judaism,* he asserts that "he wrote enthusiastically of Israel's past history, but deplored its social exclusiveness in his own day."[50] Similarly, historian Cecil Roth classified D'Israeli with a group of Spanish and Portuguese Jews "all more highly considered in that day than in ours," who had "begun to play a respectable part in English letters."[51] In contrast, Harold Harel Fisch's one-paragraph entry in the newer *Encyclopaedia Judaica* claims that *The Genius of Judaism* testifies "to his estrangement from Judaism."[52] Most recently, though, Todd M. Endelman has approved of D'Israeli's "attack[ing] the Judaism of his time in a manner similar to that of the radical, post-Mendelssohnian maskilim in Germany."[53]

As for Nathan, his work as a Jewish composer is generally dismissed. Neither Endelman nor Roth mentions him at all. In his entry for the *Jewish Encyclopedia*, Francis L. Cohen denigrates the music as being "very poor; it has deservedly sunk into oblivion, like other music composed by Nathan for Lord Byron's verses."[54] Bathja Bayer's contribution to the *Encyclopaedia Judaica* is barely more complimentary: "Several traditional Jewish melodies are found in his *Musurgia Vocalis*. For some of the *Hebrew Melodies* he also used some traditional tunes, but, except for "Ma'oz Ẓur" (set to Byron's 'On Jordan's Banks'), they are quite transformed by his superficial compositional initiative."[55]

Although it would appear from these comments that neither D'Israeli nor Nathan had much of an impact on subsequent Jewish culture, it is arguable that through their collaboration with Byron each did, indeed, contribute to the consolidation of the post-Enlightenment Jewish indentity. For his part, D'Israeli helped Byron adapt what had originated as a religious concept, the *illuy*, for secular purposes; and for his, Nathan helped Byron consolidate a skeptical mode of thought that would enable subsequent generations of Jews to analyze objectively their own attitudes toward faith, Zionism, and messianism. As will be seen in the following chapters, through later Byronic translations, D'Israeli and Nathan had at least an indirect impact on a number of Jews at key points in modern history.

CHAPTER 2

Byron and the Maskilim

Given the close relationship between intellectual advances and religious reform, presentations of Byron have provided a touchstone for measuring attitudes toward the Haskalah in the East, where development was impeded by both internal and external pressures.[1] Unlike the more progressive West, where, in the nineteenth century, Jews were being more easily integrated into the general population, central and eastern European Jewish communities were defined by the pale of settlement, those areas where, since 1794, the migrating Jewish communities had been confined variously by the Russian, Polish, and Austrian governments. Not only were they isolated from the larger community, but Jews in the pale were also subjected to more stringent control by rabbinic authorities who, having been empowered by the government to maintain order in their communities, resisted Enlightenment for a number of reasons. Most obviously, they believed that a secular education would dislodge Jewish learning from its place of prominence in the Jewish culture. Beyond that, they were concerned that a vocational education might tempt the young away from the Jewish community entirely. Even more serious to some was the possibility that religious reform would diminish the control they had over the communities at large. Finally, the metaphorical transformation of Zionism from the spiritual belief in a return to Jerusalem into the symbolic application of Zionist ideals in the Diaspora threatened to replace communal loyalty with individual action.

Countering the rabbis' opposition to secular education, the Russian government, starting in the 1840s, initiated a program of assimilation, the ultimate goal being conversion. Crucial to these plans were government-sponsored Jewish schools, staffed by Jewish teachers who were hired to provide children with a secular education. Although at first the teachers—characteristically young and enthusiastic *maskilim*—thought that the schools would support the Mendelssohnian goal of acculturating Jews while permitting them to retain their religion, eventually the hidden agenda became evident. Some of the *maskilim* converted, only to find that they would never be fully welcomed in the Christian community; others, realizing that they had been duped by the government, returned to a Jewish community that frequently forced them to recant their enlightened views and even burn their "heretical" books.[2]

All of these positions hinged on attitudes toward Hebrew. On one extreme were those who believed that the language should be reserved for religious purposes; on the other were those who thought that a vernacular education would facilitate assimilation. In the middle, however, many *maskilim* believed that Hebrew should be the everyday language of the Jews. Their problem, besides ideology, was linguistics. Some skeptics thought that Hebrew, having for millennia been reserved for religious use, was incapable of meeting a broad spectrum of needs. Purists believed that Hebrew had been contaminated by the admixture of other vernaculars introduced into postbiblical religious treatises. They thought that the later accretions needed to be removed before Hebrew could be transformed into a functioning modern language. Recognizing the reality that the biblical vocabulary and syntax were inadequate for modern purposes, many *maskilim* dedicated themselves to at least trying to develop Hebrew into a modern language.

The early Jewish Byronists were all committed Hebraists, their translations punctuating major stages in the Haskalah as a movement. The first two, translating contemporaneously in two different communities, evince some of the difficulties that confronted those *maskilim* who attempted to introduce new ideas into the culture. The first, one Yaakov Zevi, is completely unknown except for his translation of *Cain*. The fact that his codex, containing both an introductory essay and a translation of the play, was never published suggests at least the possibility that communal forces made it almost impossible for eastern *maskilim* to introduce non-Jewish material at that place and time. Even though his translation of *Cain* is extant, there is no way of knowing how many other texts were destroyed, or even how many people actually read his. The next Byronist, Meir Halevi Letteris, was more successful at getting published, though he seems to have done so at the expense of his own voice. A respected poet in his own right, Letteris used several of the *Hebrew Melodies*, along with *Darkness,* to introduce skeptical ideas he apparently was able to articulate only through the medium of translation. A decade later, Matisyahu Simḥah Rabener and Eliezer Eliyahu Igel, respectively translator and publisher of a Hebrew version of the *Hebrew Melodies*, were more attuned to the political realities of their community. Working within the system, Hebrew teacher Rabener and reform rabbi Igel couched their translation within conventional preliminary materials, in effect transforming Letteris's skepticism to an optimistic view of the Haskalah. Unfortunately, that optimism would be undermined by history as eastern European Jews grew disillusioned with the belief that the Haskalah would bring about positive change in their status. As the last of the Byronic *maskilim,* Judah Leib Gordon translated selections of the *Hebrew Melodies* to signal the failure of Enlightenment, while also initiating the transition to what he thought should be a delayed Zionism. Although he did believe in a literal return to Zion, Gordon felt that the Jews should first be given a western European education in preparation for governing their own state, and his translation of seven lyrics can be read as an argument for postponing the return to Jerusalem until the Jews were ready.

Yaakov Ẓevi—Youthful Enthusiasm

Regarding one Yaakov Ẓevi, I have been unable to locate any information beyond that contained in his codex. As his name indicates, he retains his identification with the Jewish community, on his title page describing himself as the son of a rabbi and a Levite; and from his dedication, I gather that his uncle, a man named Solomon the Levite, from the city of Boskowitz, in Moravia, had received some sort of censure from religious authorities for espousing enlightened ideas. This information seems to place Yaakov Ẓevi within the context of the later, eastern *maskilim,* as opposed to those of the West, who had initiated the movement. In Germany, the Haskalah, which was directly influenced by the Christian Enlightenment, had originally taken root in a more tolerant climate where the Jews, though denied the full rights of citizenship, were still able to engage in intellectual discourse with the dominant community, and where Moses Mendelssohn could assume that a German translation of the Pentateuch would facilitate Jewish assimilation into the secular culture. Concomitant with the philosophical theory of the Haskalah, the Reform Movement provided a theological basis by which the westernized Jews might develop a form of religion that would enable them to retain their Jewish identities, but without alienating the Christian majority.

In the East, however, the Jews were restricted by a far more repressive national government, giving the rabbinic authorities far more extensive power. Consequently, *maskilim* encountered a great deal of resistance in their attempts at acculturation. Frequently hindered in their academic pursuits, many were forced to use underground libraries for information about the Haskalah. Therefore, it seems not unreasonable to infer that Yaakov Zevi's education might lag around a half century behind that of his western counterparts; and this might be one reason why he chose to structure his analysis of Byron's *Cain* around the same arguments that had been proffered by Wessely at the end of the eighteenth century.[3]

The text itself, surviving in a single codex owned by the Jewish Theological Seminary of America, contains a twenty-two-page introduction, written in Rashi script,[4] and a complete Hebrew translation of Byron's play, in block script.[5] The title page reads:

> *Kayin*
> *Myster nach Lord Byron in 3 Acten.*
> *melitsah bat shalosh ma'arakhot*
> *Ha'atakah hofshit be-mishkol ha-tenu'ot u-mil'el*
> *mi-meni ha-tsa'ir*
> *Yaakov Zevi B[en] R[abi] Avraham ha-Levi L'ev*
>
> ore'aḥ ḥayim pen tefilas
> Na'an Ma'egelatiya lo toda
> me'ale H'V'
>
> Po K'K Unsdorf: Shenat Berit li-f[erat] k[atan]

In English:

> *Cain*
> **A Mystery by Lord Byron in 3 Acts [in German]**
> **Mystery in three acts [in Hebrew]**
> The ancient freedom in the fluctuation of meter and accentuation

CHAPTER 2

**by the young man
Jacob Ẓevi son of Rabbi Abraham the Levite Lev**

A wanderer in life for the sake of balance
If not for his wandering he would not be known
by H.V.

Here in Unsdorf: the year of the covenant [1851–52]

In his introductory essay, Yaakov Ẓevi uses Byron's *Cain* as the vehicle for defending the Haskalah against the kinds of charges that had been leveled against Wessely. Countering the conservative viewpoint that an expansion of the curriculum would dilute the traditional Jewish education, Yaakov Ẓevi asserts that there is nothing subversive about reading secular literature. Acknowledging that "I didn't know if the words would be pleasing in the eyes of my brothers, the sons of Israel, who take pleasure only in Torah and the faith through which it is spread," still, he argues, "Torah and philosophy are perfectly coordinated brothers" (8). Moreover, he continues, Byron's treatment of Cain is consistent with the practices of Jewish exegetes who question the literal reading of the text. Throughout the essay, he cites numerous rabbinic authorities in order to counter, point by point, the more specific charges leveled by opponents of Jewish Enlightenment.

Responding to the accusation that the Haskalah would undermine the religious authority of the rabbis and ultimately lead to apostasy, Yaakov Ẓevi contends that rational thought is necessary for buttressing ethical values and for countering atheism. Throughout history, he argues, the rabbis themselves proffered contradictory interpretations of difficult biblical passages, and the only means of "testing the difference between truth and lies" (16) is reason. From this perspective, Byron's character Cain is the epitome of the *maskil*, being morally superior to his passively obedient family, for he questions, examines, and explores in his effort to comprehend the logical basis of the cosmos. Countering the criticism that Byron's Cain is too much like Job, Yaakov Ẓevi reminds his readers that in the past, Job, too, had been accused of atheism; and in any case, because Cain is a guilty perpetrator, through him "are revealed the warmth of exalted God on an unrighteous man, a murderer who spilled the blood of his righteous brother on the land. And despite all this, God places a sign on his brow saying: Do not kill Cain" (12).

Knowledge, Yaakov Ẓevi insists, regardless of its origin, is the real weapon against atheism. In addition to rabbinic sources, he cites kabbalistic authorities as well as Greek and Christian philosophers. He also reminds his readers that not all biblical texts were originally written in Hebrew, and that even some elements of Job derived from non-Jewish materials. Consequently, there has always been a multicultural tradition in Jewish theology, the rabbis historically having turned to others for knowledge.

Regarding the accusation that the Haskalah will lead to Jewish heresy in particular, Yaakov Ẓevi corrects the misstatements found in the note Byron added to his preface. Byron says:

> The reader will perceive that the author has partly adopted in this poem the notion of Cuvier, that the world had been destroyed several times before the creation of man. This speculation, derived from the different strata and the bones of enormous and unknown animals found in them, is not contrary to the Mosaic account, but rather confirms it; as no human bones have yet been discovered in those strata, although those of many known animals are found near the remains of the unknown. The assertion of Lucifer that the pre-Adamite world was also peopled by rational beings much more intelligent than man and proportionably powerful to the mammoth, etc., etc., is, of course, a poetical fiction to help him to make out his case.[6]

In his note, Byron is at great pains to demonstrate that he is not committing Christian heresy; conversely, Yaakov Ẓevi argues what is tantamount to the opposite: that, in fact, the British poet is conforming to *Jewish* orthodoxy in both the matter of Georges Cuvier's geological studies and the reference to pre-Adamic creation.

Author of *Essay on the Theory of the Earth* (originally published in 1808), Georges Cuvier, a pioneering geologist, concluded from his examination of extant fossils that, scientifically speaking, prehistoric animals antedated the appearance of man. In the English translation, first published in 1813, Robert Jameson presented Cuvier's analysis as a validation of the biblical account of creation.[7] For his part, in 1850, Yaakov Ẓevi completes the circle, using the rabbis to validate Cuvier, and by extension, to support Byron himself. Similarly, Yaakov Ẓevi provides rabbinic support for Byron's fairly obvious disclaimer against accusations that he was a Christian heretic, that is, that Lucifer's reference to pre-Adamic rational creatures is "a poetical fiction." As Yaakov Ẓevi points out, not only is there a fairly extensive Jewish tradition of pre-Adamic life, but an analysis of comparative mythology indicates that most ancient cultures—including the Farsi, Egyptian, Greek, and Roman—had similar traditions. Thus, as the rabbinic authorities have claimed all along, their knowledge conforms to that of other peoples; and conversely, as Yaakov Zevi demonstrates, familiarity with other forms of knowledge will, therefore, inevitably lead back to the rabbis.

Next, Yaakov Zevi counters the accusation that the Haskalah will lead to acculturation, and that the children of the religious elite will be enticed away from the Jewish community. Citing the long tradition of fencing off holy knowledge so that the necessities of daily life can be met, he refers to Genesis, noting that in order to survive, the first family had to learn how to make food, clothing, and shelter, and that as the generations progressed, people made advances in the arts and humanities as well.

Yaakov Zevi concludes by defending his use of Hebrew for secular purposes. Although in 1850, the language lacked the extensive vocabulary and precise syntax that would have made this a cogent argument in favor of the Haskalah, still, he does foreshadow the direction to be taken by Jewish culture in the next half century. As he concludes:

> Thus, I have extended our language. Here she was poor, isolated, solitary, wrapped in a veil of her widowhood.... Yet, her clothing brought her love. Some have denigrated and condemned the existence of her beauty, singling out her archaic nature, absorbing the influence of this or that nation until she is contaminated. But there is good in evil, and evil in good.... Silver will be coined, and wisdom will be mined.... Perhaps, enemies are skeptical that a Hebrew book can be sold, and this is the precious thing that will astonish them. Please, my brother, do not sound the alarm! Here I set out before you, today, the translation with abundant beauty in it. Come, my brother, be nourished by the sweet foundation, because it is our language.... God would want us to cure our holy tongue, so that the stammering language will soon speak smoothly in our days. The speech will pour forth milk and honey. (29–30)

Not coincidentally, in his last sentences, Yaakov Zevi prays that God will endorse the Haskalah. Unfortunately, he personally never witnessed the fulfillment of his prayer—his translation, never having been published, remaining extant only in the single copy, and the introduction's Rashi script deterring most readers today. Still, the many additions, marginal notes, and tipped-in pages indicate at the very least that Yaakov Zevi continued working on the introduction after copying it for the codex; there is also the possibility that he may have shown the text to others as well.

Meir Halevi Letteris—Covert Activism

As one of the more moderate of the eastern *maskilim*, Meir Halevi Letteris (1800?–71), according to Israel Zinberg, "was the epigone of the Galician Haskalah."[8] The son of Gershon ben Ze'ev Letteris, a rhetorician and printer who saw to it that his son studied Hebrew grammar and scripture, Meir was most strongly influenced by philosopher Nahman Krochmal (1785–1840), a leading figure in the Galician Haskalah, under whose influence Letteris developed an interest in secular poetry. At first, Letteris was an autodidact, studying French and Latin on his own, though later, he apparently received a doctorate from the university in Lemberg.[9] Fluent in German, Letteris edited German journals and wrote German poems, receiving for his collection *Sagen aus dem Orient* (1847) a gold medal from the Austrian emperor Franz Joseph. However, his primary medium was Hebrew. A prolific exponent of the Haskalah, Letteris published in a number of different genres, including books of Hebrew poetry, Hebrew literary collections, translations into both Hebrew and German, editions from manuscripts, a treatise on the Bible, a biography of Spinoza, and the first part of his autobiography. His most controversial works were the biography of Spinoza, in which he called for the rehabilitation of the seventeenth-century skeptic among the Jews, and his adaptation of Goethe's *Faust,* in which he recast the Romantic hero as Elisha ben Abuyha, the *tanna* known as *aher,* "the other one," that is, the apostate.[10] His own poetry, however, tended to be rather muted. Possibly because he was never financially secure, Letteris avoided the more strident tones of leading *maskilim,* choosing instead the more conciliatory approach of those who lacked "the courage or the firm conviction to break in enmity with the old world. These were more passive, meditative natures. They lacked partisan, aggressive force, and so felt helpless and weak. From this derived their sentimental, romantic mood."[11]

It is likely that at least in part to compensate for his reluctance to articulate his own skepticism, Letteris used Byron as one vehicle for subverting the communal establishment. His Byron translations are part of a forty-three-page compilation published in Vienna in 1852, with a bilingual title page—the top part in Hebrew, followed by the German. As translated into English:

> **Gold Dust**
> These Are
> Precious Poems from the Great Poets of the World
> Made in Their Image
> And Made Proud in the Hebrew Language
>
> Poems
> by
> **Schiller and Lord Byron**
> in one anthology in Hebrew translation
> by
> **Dr. M. Letteris.**

Unlike Yaakov Ẓevi, Letteris uses the different languages and alphabets to convey slightly different messages. To the Hebrew readers, he exploits the metaphorically allusive "Gold Dust" to describe his "Precious Poems from the Great Poets of the World." Those who know German, however, are literally informed that the book contains Hebrew translations of poems by Schiller and Byron. The double message is continued in the introduction, where the generally acceptable Hebrew message (like Yaakov Ẓevi's, also in Rashi script) is punctuated by classical allusions in Roman type, to imply—for those capable of deciphering it—a more subversive agenda. For the Hebrew-reading audience, Letteris associates his translations with Jewish culture, exclaiming: "How good and how pleasant [*ma tov umah na'im*] to bring them delights and fruits of excellences, songs about the land of our fathers, to restore the soul—according to the longed-for reward to give them like the satisfaction of good meat and wine."[12] His purpose, as he concludes his introduction, is to make available a variety of poems:

> And thus I heard, like the voice of a master to an apprentice, to bring this to light, dedicated in one collection, and with the blessing of God, some words I will add to these songs here and there. Grant them time and space! In addition, consider convention and wisdom a sign of their souls, and take teaching [*torah*] from it with all of your heart; go in the delight of our language to give you stubborn/rebellious support,

because in poetry, the angels above and the stars of the heights take joy; and the word of our God is in the mouth of a poet/prophet in an important song for the dwellers of this world. And to you peace.

Two things stand out in this paragraph. First, his principle of translation seems rather loose—he "will add to these songs here and there." Also, the content can be read as a Judaization of the epigraph from Horace, that good literature both delights and teaches, which is printed in Roman letters at the beginning of the introduction:

> Aut prodesse volunt aut delectare poetae,
> aut simul et iucunda et idonea dicere vitae.
> Horat.

In addition to the epigraph, Letteris uses the Roman alphabet in the first paragraph to compare himself to Cicero. By using only non-Hebrew letters for these classical allusions, he seems to be addressing himself exclusively to *maskilim,* that is, to those who will understand what the Hebrew readers cannot: that like a Cynic, he will teach unexpected lessons through some delightful poetry. The Byron translations in particular—"Ancient Melodies, from the Profundity of the Songs of the English Poet Lord Byron" (on pages 24 through 31 of the collection)—are selected and organized in such a way that they comprise what can be read as a five-act play in which religion is subtly indicted for perpetuating Jewish exile. Specifically, he includes "Oh! Weep for Those," "The Wild Gazelle," "Song of Saul Before His Last Battle," and "On Jordan's Banks" from the *Hebrew Melodies,* and finally, the non-Jewish *Darkness.*[13]

For his exposition about Jewish exile, Letteris bypasses completely the more idealistic "She Walks in Beauty," "The Harp the Monarch Minstrel Swept," and "If That High World," and temporarily skips over "The Wild Gazelle," to open with an ironic version of "Oh! Weep for Those," Byron's expression of mourning:

> Oh! weep for those that wept by Babel's stream,
> Whose shrines are desolate, whose land a dream;
> Weep for the harp of Judah's broken shell;
> Mourn—where their God hath dwelt the godless dwell!
>   *(ll. 1–4)*

CHAPTER 2

In his untitled translation, Letteris exploits the Jewish liturgy to question the concept of prayer itself:

> Bitter praise [*helilu*] for a people who forsook their land
> On the rivers of Babel with a pain in the heart they settled
> Next to a holy harp that was shattered on a rock
> Together with their glory because it was hurled against a rock.

The first word (in the Hebrew text, the adjective "bitter" comes second), *helilu,* derives from the root *halel,* "to praise," most commonly encountered as Hallel, the name of a prayer of joy and thanksgiving for redemption.[14] In addition, however, the root could also mean "to be foolish." By combining *helilu* with the second word of his translation, *mar,* "bitter," Letteris undercuts the concept of a joyful prayer, this being "bitter praise," with the implication that to rely on prayer alone is "to be foolish." In contrast to the Hallel, a prayer that anticipates redemption, Letteris concludes with Byron's ending: "and Judah—the grave!"

Next, the dramatic complication is provided by the also-untitled translation of "The Wild Gazelle," in which Letteris transforms Byron's depiction of how non-Jewish life has flourished "on Judah's hills," into an emblem of Jewish exile. As an artistic genre, the emblem consists of a symbolic picture, a short poem, and a motto. Similarly, Letteris begins with an image:

> The ram in the field nimble is seen
> On the mountains of Israel her feet flit by,
> On the stream of water, to know the explanation
> There you will be pleased there you will be astounded even more about her appearance
> Her feet were not weak were not even tired
> Her eyes like doves grace grace they appeared.
>
> (ll. 1–6)

In the third line, Letteris indicates that, unlike Byron, he will allegorize the picture of the mammal roaming around; and beginning in the next stanza, he provides his analysis. As he says: "Effortlessly from this the daughters of Zion I envisioned" (l. 7).

Both poems end with the skeptical motto: "And Mockery sits on Salem's throne." In Byron's version, the Jewish God has been replaced by a personified "Mockery," who has appropriated "Salem," the anglicization of the Hebrew *shalem*, meaning "complete, peace," a word posited as a possible etymology of the name Jerusalem. In his translation, Letteris emphasizes his symbolic approach to the poem, replacing Byron's appropriation with a linguistically embedded Jerusalem to be sought by the reader. In Hebrew, Letteris's last line reads: al kes *shalem* yoshev la'ag *rish*enu. Translated literally as "on the chair of peace/completion sits mocking our poverty/chief/inheritance," the third and sixth words contain possible Hebrew roots of the word Jerusalem: *rishenu*, "our inheritance," from the root *yerush*, and *shalem*. However, *rishenu* could also mean poverty, indicating that the inheritance of Jerusalem has been dissipated.

The loss of the inheritance was caused by poor leadership, as suggested by yet another meaning of the root *rish*, "head, chief, leader." This meaning connects with Letteris's choice of a Hebrew word for gazelle. In his translation, he deliberately bypassed *zvi*, a word that literally means "gazelle," for *ayelet*, whose root *ayil* signifies the more general "hart, stag, deer," but also means "head, chief, leader." Thus, Letteris's choice introduces an associational cluster revolving around the concept of leadership, that which caused the Jewish heritage, Jerusalem, to be buried. This also could indicate why Letteris omitted a title: there is nothing at the head of the poem to guide the reader.

For his third poem, Letteris includes a title—"Of Saul Before His Death," in place of Byron's "Song of Saul Before His Last Battle"—to suggest that the translation will indict passive religiosity for causing poor leadership. In the original, Byron seems to be parodying the jingoism of officers leading their troops to battle, having Saul exhort his followers to place the cause ahead of the leader:

> Warriors and chiefs! should the shaft or the sword
> Pierce me in leading the host of the Lord,
> Heed not the corse, though a king's, in your path:
> Bury your steel in the bosoms of Gath!
>
> (*ll. 1–4*)

At the end, Saul reveals his stiff upper lip, bravely accepting the possibility of death:

> Bright is the diadem, boundless the sway,
> Or kingly the death, which awaits us to-day!"
>
> (*ll. 11–12*)

CHAPTER 2

In the Hebrew, Letteris Judaizes the militarism that Byron parodies. Instead of exhorting the troops to "Bury your steel in the bosoms of Gath!" Letteris's Saul reminds his that they are fighting a holy war: "Truly, the sword to God you shall lift up and raise high!" (l. 4). Similarly, at the end, instead of bravely facing death, he articulates a belief that it is all part of God's plan: "The crown is very bright, the government is very strong; / Even death has an important function, [it is] the king of rest" (ll. 11–12). The result of Letteris's translation is a parody of a parody: either way, Saul will die; and despite assertions that "the government is very strong," Jerusalem will ultimately be lost.

The tragedy reaches its climax in the fourth poem, in which Letteris retitles Byron's "On Jordan's Banks" as "The Land of the Gazelle." By using the word *zvi* in the title, Letteris creates a linguistic progression from "The Wild Gazelle," his symbolic representation of poor leadership, through his "Of Saul Before his Death," its actualization, to a poem that blames tyranny for causing the loss of the Temple. Byron's final couplet focuses on the empty temple:

> How long by tyrants shall thy land be trod?
> How long thy temple worshipless, Oh God?
> *(ll. 11–12)*

In the translation, Letteris Judaizes the image:

> Your land for how long will the tyrant be bowed down to?
> For how long still will he defile the house of your glory!

Letteris seems to be indicting a religion that values the building more than the people themselves.

The denouement of Letteris's five-act tragedy is "A Vision of Darkness," a translation of Byron's poem that, according to Marchand, "pictures with immitigable cynicism and despair the unheroic end of the last men on a dying planet."[15] Letteris interprets *Darkness*, as he explains in a footnote, as an explanation of Isaiah 13:10: "For the stars of the heavens and their constellations will not give their light; the sun will be dark at its rising and the moon will not shed its light." In the Bible, the passage is part of Isaiah's oracles against foreign nations, in this case against Babylon. By including in his collection a later poem, itself not part of the *Hebrew Melodies,* Letteris seems to be criticizing the postexilic state of the Jews, who seem to prefer universal darkness to Enlightenment. In the original version, Byron concludes with the triumph of a personified Darkness:

> The moon, their mistress, had expired before;
> The winds were wither'd in the stagnant air,
> And the clouds perish'd; Darkness had no need
> Of aid from them—She was the universe.
> *(ll. 79–82)*

In the translation, Letteris shifts the focus onto the Jews:

> Also the coarse clouds passed by, they went,
> They wandered; [even] without them darkness was considerable
> World-wide. Beneath earth was dark, beneath
> Filled with confusion [*tevel*] ruin darkness [*minudaḥ*] thrust forward *selah*.

Here, the clouds evoke the wandering Jews—they "passed by, they went, / They wandered," but without attempting to illuminate, leaving everything in a state of confusion.

When the poems are viewed as a group, the linguistic choices suggest that Letteris used his Byronic translations to produce a kind of anti-psalm, implying, possibly, a criticism of Jewish messianism, the belief that a scion of David will restore the Jews to their homeland. The first translation, "Oh! Weep for Those," begins with the root *halel,* an echo of the opening of Psalm 113, which begins the Hallel prayer. Then, in the third line of the lyric, for Byron's "the harp of Judah's broken shell," is the phrase *kinur kodesh,* the "holy lyre," usually a reference to David's instrument. In the sixth line, however, for Byron's "And when shall Zion's songs again seem sweet?" is: "Who will play music on *asur* your lovely songs?" The choice of an alternate, rarely used term for *kinur* suggests that David is unavailable. This implication is underscored by the choice of "Song of Saul Before His Last Battle" for the third of the translations. The introduction of David's predecessor seems to be implying that prayers for a familial descendant are fatuous. The last word of the Byronic translations, which concludes the skeptical *Darkness,* is *selah,* a musical notation used to indicate a pause, frequently to mark the end of a psalm. By the end of Letteris's Hallel, he seems to be implying that the Jews need to take action in the real world rather than passively wait for divine assistance.

CHAPTER 2

Matisyahu Simḥah Rabener and Eliezer Eliyahu Igel—Mature Compromise

Appearing a little over a decade later, the 1864 Hebrew edition of the *Hebrew Melodies*, which embodies all of the problems associated with introducing secular literature into central-eastern European Jewish culture in the mid-nineteenth century, seems to have been designed to transform Letteris's skepticism into an optimistic view of the future. Containing preliminary materials and dedicatory poems not accounted for on the title page, whose epigraph may be a later addition, the book appears to have been altered after its initial composition, suggesting that the publisher and translator were responding either to actual or to anticipated pressure, and felt the need to justify their publication of Byron.

The title page and table of contents suggest that the edition was originally intended primarily as a straightforward Hebrew translation of Byron's song cycle. In translation, the title page reads:

> Hebrew Melodies
> Various Songs Based on Holy Illumination
> Which I Translated
> From the Songs of the Magnificent English Poet
> In the Estimation and Praise of the Name
> Lord Byron
>
> I Am the Hero
> Matisyahu Simḥah Rabener,
> First Teacher of the Hebrew Language in the School of Chernowitz

At the bottom of the title page is the imprint:

> Czernowitz.
> Published by the Preacher . . . Eliyahu Igel
> The Year [1864]

The table of contents at the end contains only one oddity. Entitled "Contents of the Songs of Lord Byron," the page lists, in two columns, twenty-four titles: the first twenty-three correspond to the twenty-three songs conventionally included in the *Hebrew Melodies*; the last, however, "A Dark Vision (a poem in six stages)," is likely a response to Letteris's translation of Byron's *Darkness*.

Besides the inclusion of *Darkness,* textual anomalies suggest that at some point in its production, the book evolved from a straightforward translation of Byron into an indirect defense of the Haskalah. First, inserted on the title page between the identification of the text and the imprint, is a passage from Isaiah: "Neither let the son of the stranger, that hath joined himself to the Lord, speak, saying, The Lord hath utterly separated me from his people: . . . I will give them an everlasting name, that shall not be cut off" (46:3, 5).[16] In addition, there are two sets of page numbers: an initial sixteen pages of preliminary materials, and then, starting the numbering over again at page 1, the lyrics themselves, which continue on consecutively to page 32, the table of contents, which does not contain any reference to the first part of the book. The preliminaries begin with a three-page preface signed by "the younger, Eliezer Eliyahu Igel, ha-Levi"; this is followed by a six-page introduction by the translator, Matisyahu Simḥah Rabener; a four-page poem dedicated to Moses Montefiore; and a dedicatory verse to Byron.[17] Taken together, these extra materials constitute what might be interpreted as a protracted argument in favor of the secular use of Hebrew, a major subject of dispute, at least in the Czernowitz of 1864, if not among Jews worldwide.

Czernowitz, the capital city of Bukovina, was uniquely situated in the mid-nineteenth century.[18] Beginning in 1775, the area was under the control of the Austrian Empire, and though it suffered discrimination, there was still a significant amount of emigration into the city, especially among Ḥasidim and *maskilim*, leading to a period of internal as well as external struggle in the Jewish community. After 1848, when the degree of governmental discrimination decreased, there was an influx of *maskilim*, especially from the Galician city of Lvov,[19] the nearby center of Enlightenment activity. The increased presence of *maskilim* threatened both the Orthodox and the Ḥasidim, leaving the Jewish community at midcentury embroiled in a three-way struggle for control.

By 1851, the conflict erupted over the controversy of choosing a new rabbi. While the Orthodox supported hiring a traditional rabbi, the *maskilim* rebelled and in 1853 hired Eliezer Eliyahu Igel (1825–92), on the basis of his reputation for great Talmudic knowledge and high moral character.[20] Igel came from a well-known family of antique book dealers in Lvov. His father, while a firm believer in Orthodoxy and learned in Talmud, was also a specialist in Polish bibliography, his clientele including leaders of the Polish and eastern scholarly communities. Igel had both a religious and a secular education. After completing his studies at the gymnasium of

Lemberg at the age of eighteen, he went to Padua, where he studied at the Rabbinical College under Samuel David Luzzato (1800–65), Hillel ben Shelomo Tore (1805–71), and Mordecai Samuel Ghirondi (1799–1852); and he received a doctorate of theology. He then returned to Lvov in the hope of obtaining an official post. When that failed, he accepted the offer from Czernowitz.

Upon his arrival, Igel found himself embroiled in an ongoing battle between the Orthodox and the *maskilim*. The specific area of conflict had to do with questions about whether the ritual slaughterer was adhering strictly enough to the rules for keeping kosher. After investigation, Dr. Igel found that the trouble had been instigated by a group of fanatics in Lvov, and he settled the upheaval by contacting the governmental authorities. After things calmed down, the community again voted, and on May 10, 1854, Dr. Igel received 147 votes, with only 34 against him. This was the first significant victory of the *maskilim* in Czernowitz. Dr. Igel accomplished many things during his tenure, most notably the construction of a Reform temple in the 1870s. Before that, in 1853, he established a Jewish school dedicated to teaching the values of the Haskalah.

Because Czernowitz had not yet produced its own *maskilim*, Dr. Igel brought from Lvov his nephew, Matisyahu Simḥah Rabener (b. January 23, 1826), to serve as the first Hebrew teacher.[21] Also the recipient of both a religious and a secular education, Rabener had worked with Rabbi Jacob Meshullam Ornstein (1775–1839), and was reputed to be a prodigy. At fifteen, he studied foreign languages and Hebrew grammar, and he wrote Hebrew stories. At the university at Lvov, Rabener learned philosophy, Oriental languages, and music, after which he traveled to Rawa-Ruska, where he became friends with leading *maskilim*. He started work as a merchant, but after losing everything, he sought employment as a secretary. In 1860, Dr. Igel hired him as a Hebrew teacher in Czernowitz, where Rabener became a leader in the circle of *maskilim*.

Intellectually active, Rabener published a Hebrew grammar and a collection of poetry that included translations of Schiller as well as the translation of the *Hebrew Melodies*. In 1867, Rabener was named headmaster and preacher at Falticeni, Rumania, and in 1869, at Jassy, Rumania, where he stayed until 1886. While there, he began publishing a quarterly, *Zimrat ha'arez*, though only two numbers appeared. Rabener is most known for his translations from German literature, though his original composition, *Shulamit* (1880), is the only play written about the Song of Songs.

Despite the fact that in his history of the Jews of Bukovina, N. M. Gelber barely mentions Rabener's translation of the *Hebrew Melodies*, the book itself can be viewed as a significant building block in the *maskilic* construction of a new Jewish identity, the text fulfilling the specific intentions associated with Haskalah publications. After the publisher justifies his publication, the translator then recontextualizes Jewish scholarship away from the older religious authorities and toward more modern activists, demonstrates the flexibility of the Hebrew language, and, finally, rationalizes the secularization of Jewish culture.

In the publisher's preface, Igel counters the negative, those arguments that had been proffered by the religious authorities against introducing non-Jewish secular literature into the Jewish canon. Using the epigraph from Isaiah as his justification, Igel presents Byron, in the words of Isaiah, as a "stranger [i.e., non-Jew], that hath joined himself to the Lord," defending publication of the book on the basis of the poet's life, the themes of the poems, and, finally, the quality of the translation.

There are no records indicating whether Igel was ignorant of Byron's history or just being disingenuous, but regardless, his preface transforms the licentious lord of British culture into the equivalent of a Jew from Czernowitz, Igel specifically using the words *ḥasid* and *ẓadik*—both indicating righteousness—to portray Byron in the terms of one who, like his imputed compatriots, suffered discrimination from those who failed to appreciate his true value. As Igel speculates: "Perhaps it was the hatred of the enemies who pursued him, and embittered all the days of his life, that made him like a witness to the innocence of the people sung about in these songs" (1:4).

Not surprisingly, given this view of Byron, Igel sees the songs speaking directly to the Jewish experience:

> The present translation, which is a sign of thanks to the poet Byron, is a joyous meditation for the hearts of all Jews who are scattered on the face of the earth, filled with feelings of love and honor toward the author whom no road in the footprints of other authors would convey half of the happiness of an upright heart or spark smiles about the faith of Israel, because the righteousness and truth of poetry are there, along with the strengthening love of a man for his friend. (1:4)

Most important is the emphasis on Zionism:

> And now the translator . . . confirms the spirit of the language which is miraculously found there, Zion spiritualized in the midst of the

> Hebrews by the English author. . . . And thus while others might rejoice in our destruction, all the lovers of our faith and our language will rejoice first, that the name of the author will be exalted for that which he honored and valued, and second, that the reader can expect to take pleasure from the dazzling language which not only exudes holiness but also restores the sublime idea of Zion, the return to which is the faith of Israel. (1:4)

The implication is that Byron, like no other poet, understood the pain of exile, and therefore was able to project faith in an ultimate restoration.

Next, Igel praises the work of the translator:

> But his name has already has gone forth in praise and beauty as the translator of the poetry of Schiller, . . . and the grammar book . . . as well as other books on which his hands waved with the same spirit that he dresses the songs of Byron with Hebrew rhetoric, so that there will be an increase of the heritage of the congregation of Jacob and thousands of Israelites. And the *Hebrew Melodies,* which hitherto resounded sweetly only in the ears that knew English or other languages into which they were translated, now shall go forth bound in holy dress, arranged in beautifully rhymed lines, made by the hands of a skilled translator, consistent with the rhyme of the author. (1:4–5)

Not simply an encomium for his nephew, this passage confronts head-on the rabbinic objection to bringing non-Jewish secular literature into the community. First, there is the already-existing context, which includes Schiller, among others. Then, there is the knowledge of the translator, who has already published books on Hebrew grammar. Finally, there is fidelity to his text, songs written, as already argued, by one with special sympathy for the Jews. Therefore, as Igel implies, there is no reason *not* to read the *Hebrew Melodies.* Continuing Igel's train of thought, Rabener uses his introduction to explain the reasons why Byron's lyrics should be introduced into the Jewish canon.

Rabener begins by defending himself against two opposing forces that would have condemned his translating the *Hebrew Melodies* into Hebrew. As discussed more fully in the introduction, from the conservative side were those who believed that Hebrew should be reserved strictly for religious purposes, and that dabbling in secular literature would endanger the soul. The extremists among the *maskilim,* in contrast, opposed the use of Hebrew entirely. In advocating a secular education, they favored the vernacular, believing that the Jews needed to assimilate with the dominant culture if they wished to receive equal rights. However, after 1848, when Jews in the Austrian Empire doubted that they would ever be liberated, many decided that they should develop their own culture in their own language. This is the position Rabener advocates in his introduction, where he rejects the criticism of both extremes in favor of the modern Jew who, though active in the secular world, still retains his own identity. The epitome of this characterization, the dedicatee of the book, is Sir Moses Montefiore.

Before getting to Montefiore, however, Rabener first counters the objections posed by his opponents on the right and the left with his opening statement: "I am Jewish and I love the language of God" (1:6). With this assertion as his theme, Rabener then, after acknowledging the concern that has been voiced by the religious over his soul, asserts his moral confidence with a catalogue of poets and philosophers, Jewish and non-Jewish, who, he believes, have strengthened him. The list, which includes Lamartine, Milton, Petrarch, Dante, Humboldt, Spinoza, Kant, and Mendelssohn, places Rabener in the context of the western Haskalah, his education comprising the classical European poets but culminating in the modern thinkers whose theories have had the most impact on the *maskilim*.

In the second paragraph, Rabener turns to the radical *maskilim* in particular, defending his choice of Hebrew by using the metaphor of a young man who, ashamed of his mother, seeks a bride from a different tribe. In contrast, Rabener claims that he loves his mother tongue: "Thus I gave my heart completely to this, from where I tried to my fullest ability as a translator into the Hebrew language, and this was my goal at all times, to draw out—stumbling until I improved—to ignite the love of our holy tongue in the hearts of the sons of Israel, and to elevate the rays of honor and the name of beauty, in the eyes of other nations, how good and wonderful it is" (1:7). Next, Rabener turns to Byron's poems, implying that they are enhanced by the Hebrew: "And now here I have brought it before you, read with pleasure! The gift is more like a whisper of a taste of the language of God, sweet fruits from the songs of Britain in a holy basket, it is the murmur of the songs of the author, Lord Byron, who called them by the name *Hebrew Melodies,* made more magnificent, glorified with much praise" (1:7). This is followed by a long description of the poems' contents. Written from an obviously Jewish perspective, the literary analysis is not, as the British view the subject, of "Old Testament" themes, that is, topics that prefigure Christ and the New Testament; rather, Rabener presents

CHAPTER 2

Byron's lyrics in terms of Jewish history: "Once revealing the people of Israel in the beauty of beauty in the realm of heroics, its value is grace—complete in itself the heaven is purified, and thousands of stars multiply in the moon's garland. They will be remembered and will be beautiful to the eye, appearing in time like the shadow and life of the soul mixed together—if, with his hand, faith in the knowledge of heritage, the Torah of a living God and its strength" (1:8). The reference to the Torah, the original five books of the first Moses, provides the transition to the new Moses, Moses Montefiore. Historically, the phrase "from Moses to Moses" was used to emphasize the importance of Moses Maimonides (1135–1204) to Jewish history.[22] Author, as mentioned in the discussion of Isaac Nathan, of both the *Mishnah Torah,* a strict-constructionist analysis of the Torah, written in Hebrew, and the *Guide to the Perplexed,* an Aristotelian analysis of faith, written in Arabic, Maimonides stirred controversy with his early advocacy of a secular education in the vernacular. Later, in the modern era, the Haskalah adapted the phrase "from Moses to Moses" to identify Moses Mendelssohn as Maimonides' successor, implying a direct descent from the prophet to the medieval rationalist to the contemporary philosopher. Here, in his translation of the *Hebrew Melodies,* Rabener extends the line to the newest Moses.

The most prominent English Jew of the time, Moses Montefiore (1784–1885) was not only a contemporary of Byron, he was both an observant Jew and a social activist.[23] Born while his Anglo-Jewish parents were on a visit to Lvov, he was prominent in both the British and Jewish worlds. As an Englishman, he was a successful merchant who eventually became sheriff of London (1837–38), was knighted by Queen Victoria, and received a baronetcy in 1846. Active in the Jewish community, Montefiore first visited the Middle East in 1827, at which time he became religiously observant. As a merchant, he was one of the twelve "Jew brokers" in London, and served as president of the Board of Deputies of British Jews from 1835 to 1874. Internationally, Montefiore was known for personal diplomacy, interceding in situations where Jews were being discriminated against: Syria in 1840; Russia in 1846 and again in 1872; Morocco in 1863; and Rumania in 1867. Even though not all of his missions were successful, Montefiore still earned his reputation as an advocate for the Jews.

Byron, Rabener implies, provides the connection that joins all of these threads of history: "Indeed, there will be found here by this hand, the name and what is left in the Holy Land—it is Jewish literature by the English poet Byron, which will reveal to the eyes of the sun astonishment at the songs of a Jewish heart; his songs are a thing of beauty about his love of the holy nation and its faith. Also to the savior and respected one, a man of God, the righteous one, Moses Montefiore" (1:10). The Hebrew translation of the *Hebrew Melodies,* consequently, provides the means by which the new Jew can adapt his Jewish identity to accommodate the exigencies of the modern world. Finally, balancing out the catalogue of intellectuals who provided the foundation for his interpretation of Haskalah is, in the last paragraph, a list of social activists—men who, in the middle of the nineteenth century, publicly strove to ameliorate the condition of the Jews. These include the Rothschild family, Joseph Montefiore, Abraham Albert Cahn of Paris, Nathan Adler of London, and Ludwig August Frankl of Vienna.

Following Rabener's introduction are two original compositions. The first, a three-page encomium in honor of Moses Montefiore, written in quatrains with the rhyme scheme *abab*, is distinct in that *every* word in the poem begins with the letter *mem,* the Hebrew *M,* for *Moses Montefiore.* The second poem is a nine-line acrostic in which the first letter of each line, read down, spells out "Lord Byron" in Hebrew:

> To the Composer of the Melodies
> A Poem to Lord Byron:
> Acrostic

> [L] To the composer of the holy melodies, in council with the heavenly company,
> [O] Indeed, a memorial tribute in the excellence of the Hebrew language.
> [R] You did much, glorious one, to give special insight,
> [D] How sweet are the words of your songs, like pressed from a fertile vine.
> [B] Rejoiced together, the scepter of God in the language of Zion and Jerusalem,
> [Y] Your name will be remembered for beauty, orator of great deeds!
> [R] You pleased the Jewess, the Muslim woman bowed down seven times.
> [O] You loved truth and faith, and you hated vacillation and deceit.
> [N] Your soul grew like an onion in complaining fields, preserved in the hostility of life. (1:16)

While the content of both poems is commonplace, containing the kind of praise expected in this sort of publication, they are remarkable for two reasons. The first is that through them, Rabener is demonstrating the flexibility of Hebrew, indicating not only that it is suitable for secular purposes, but that it is capable of extensive poetic gymnastics. The second reason why these two poems are notable is that their subjects are not religious figures. Historically, these sorts of poems would have been reserved for biblical figures or for rabbinic authorities. Here, however, one is a modern secular, though observant, Jew, and the other is a Christian poet.

Finally, after sixteen pages of preliminary materials, Rabener provides Hebrew translations of twenty-three *Hebrew Melodies,* kept in the conventional order. Given the limitations of contemporary Hebrew, the translations are relatively mechanical, and the vocabulary and syntax overwhelmingly biblical. On the practical level, this means that while Byron had attempted to infuse an overlay of biblical atmosphere onto his nineteenth-century English, when translated into Hebrew, the English connotations are perforce removed, and consequently, the Christian—or, at the very least, the non-Jewish—implications of the poems disappear. In their place, as both Igel and Rabener emphasize in their respective introductions, the poems reveal what might be interpreted as their inherent Jewish sensibilities: "holy melodies," as Rabener says in the first line of his acrostic, "holy melodies" that must have been composed "in council with the heavenly company."

The first two poems provide examples of the kinds of changes effected through the translation. In the first, specifically Jewish connotations force even the most basic, word-for-word translation into a religious context probably never imagined by Byron. To begin with the first lines, written even before Byron's active collaboration with Nathan:

> She walks in beauty, like the night
> Of cloudless climes and starry skies.

Compare with Rabener's version:

> In the beauty of beauty she walks, like the night silent
> Appropriate for the stars that seem dark in contrast to the essence of [*shamayim*].

From the beginning, the Hebrew translation creates an association with the Bible. Apparently lacking a more felicitous way to articulate "Of cloudless climes and starry skies," Rabener approximates the sense of Byron's poem by replacing "starry skies" with "stars that seem dark in contrast to the essence of *shamayim*," the Hebrew word meaning either "sky" or "heaven," though anyone with only a rudimentary knowledge of the Hebrew Bible would recognize the word from the first verse of Genesis, where "In the beginning, God created the heaven," *shamayim*. Beyond the biblical context, Rabener's diction also places the poem in a Jewish, quasi-mystical mode. The phrase "In the beauty of beauty," uses two different words for beauty, the second, *tiferet*, meaning also "splendor, glory," kabbalistically signifying the fifth of the ten divine attributes, the Sefirot.[24] Thus, the translation takes the poem yet another step beyond Anne Beatrix, wife of Byron's second cousin Robert John Wilmot, the literal subject.

Also notable is the title of the poem. Despite the fact that his first line, an almost word-for-word translation of Byron's, could be used, Rabener deliberately introduces a new title: "Bas yehudah." Literally, the phrase means "the daughter of Judah," suggesting in English the word "Jewess." The Hebrew, however, connotes the archetypal Jewish woman: culturally, the *eshet ḥayil*, the Jewish "woman of valor"; figuratively, the Shekhinah, the female spirit of immanence. Thus, in contrast to the English reader, who would interpret the poem as the description of an idealized, possibly platonic form of beauty, the Jewish audience, from the title alone, would place the lyric within a religious context. This new title, when combined with the word *tiferet*, yields a poem that should be impervious to the attacks of the opponents of Haskalah.[25]

Similarly, Rabener retitles the second poem, "The Harp the Monarch Minstrel Swept," to "*Kinur* David," "The Harp of David," thus emphasizing the identity of the monarch, and thereby placing the poem within the larger context of Jewish Zionism and messianism, David himself having built the Temple, and his descendant being prophesied to lead the Jews back to Jerusalem. The shifted focus is subtly underscored throughout the text, the most obvious example being the translation of lines 6–7:

> It softened men of iron mould,
> It gave them virtues not their own.

Rabener's version:

> It melted like wax a heart hardened like stone
> It uncovered hidden righteousness, not known in their lives.

The difference is striking. While Byron praises the ennobling qualities of the harp, that it brings "virtues not their own," Rabener inverts the meaning, saying that the innate nobility of humans is sometimes hidden, and that music melts away the external coverings so that their true goodness can be revealed.

While it is not possible to analyze each poem individually, it is instructive to note the changed titles:

Byron	**Rabener**
"She Walks in Beauty"	"The Daughter of Judah"
"The Harp the Monarch Minstrel Swept"	"The Harp of David"
"If That High World"	"The Binding of Life"
"The Wild Gazelle"	"The Land of Birth"
"Oh! Weep for Those"	"Jewish Grave"
"On Jordan's Banks"	"Sinai in Holiness"
"Jephtha's Daughter"	"Jephtha's Daughter"
"Oh! Snatch'd Away in Beauty's Bloom"	"By the Grave"
"My Soul Is Dark"	"Meditation on the Harp"
"I Saw Thee Weep"	"The Fine Dust of Her Lips"
"Thy Days Are Done"	"To the Hero"
"Saul"	"Song of Saul"
"Song of Saul Before His Last Battle"	"Saul and Samuel"
"'All Is Vanity, Saith the Preacher'"	"All Is Vanity, Saith the Preacher"
"When Coldness Wraps This Suffering Clay"	"Eternity of the Soul"
"Vision of Belshazzar"	"Vision of Belshazzar"
"Sun of the Sleepless!"	"God of the Moon"
"Were My Bosom as False as Thou Deem'st It to Be"	"Guardian of Faiths"
"Herod's Lament for Mariamne"	"Herod's Lament"
"On the Day of the Destruction of Jerusalem by Titus"	"Difficult Vision"
"By the Rivers of Babylon We Sat Down and Wept"	"The Poet of the Prisoner"
"The Destruction of Sennacherib"	"The Destruction of Sennacherib"
"From Job"	"A Vision of Job"

Of the twenty-three lyrics, the only ones for which Rabener retains the original titles are those with biblical associations: "Jephtha's Daughter," "Saul," "'All Is Vanity, Saith the Preacher,'" "Vision of Belshazzar," "Herod's Lament," and "The Destruction of Sennacherib." The others are all modified to emphasize, if not actually create, an aura that will resonate with the Jewish experience.

Finally, the book ends with Rabener's addendum to the *Hebrew Melodies,* a rereading of Byron's poem *Darkness.* As he explains in a footnote to his translation: "Because this song was not placed by the poet among the *Hebrew Melodies,* perhaps it will be comparable to a solid vision, like that of the strong prophets (Isaiah 13:10). Therefore, I sought to dress her also in holy clothes so she will be thought of as one of the Hebrew daughters" (2:27).

Rabener never mentions Letteris directly, though both external and internal evidence suggests that his version was a response to the way the earlier translator used *Darkness* to imply a pessimistic attitude about the future of the Jews. Historically, both translators traveled in the same intellectual circles, and both translated Schiller as well as Byron; also, it seems that Letteris is the only reader other than Rabener to have associated *Darkness* specifically with Isaiah 13:10.[26] Intertextually, there are enough similarities between their Hebrew versions to suggest that in the act of translating Byron, Rabener was at the same time revising Letteris's depiction of despair.

Rabener's title suggests that he was influenced by but also subverting Letteris's translation. Both translators juxtapose two nouns against each other, making it impossible to determine which is to be the substantive and which the modifier: Letteris, *ḥizayon ḥoshekh*; and Rabener, *ḥezyon maḥshakh*. The first word, *ḥezyon*, means "vision," and the second root, *ḥoshekh*, means "darkness."[27] In the later version, by adding the prefix *m,* Rabener could be retaining the same signification as Letteris, the word *maḥshakh*, as he vocalizes it, meaning "darkness." However, the prefix *m* also signifies the preposition "from," thus suggesting an alternate interpretation, "a dream from the darkness," as opposed to "a dream of darkness." The ambiguity is underscored by Rabener's subtitle, "a poem in six stages," through which he evokes a kabbalistic context, specifically *shemittah,* the belief that history consists of a series of seven-thousand-year cycles, during which creation plays itself out for six thousand years, and then, in preparation for the next cycle, reverts back to the primordial chaos.[28] Thus, instead of Letteris's linear tragedy that ends with *Darkness,* this cyclic *shemittah*, especially when associated with Isaiah's prophesy about the fall of Babylon,

CHAPTER 2

transforms what had originated as Byron's "immitigable cynicism and despair" into the preparation for a new cycle of Enlightenment. Being placed at the end of a volume in which a justification for reading secular literature and a dedication to the most influential secular Jew of the day precede the Hebrew translation of a collection of poems written by a non-Jew, "A Dark Vision," like a commencement address, simultaneously concludes the metaphorical Babylonian exile and initiates the new world of Enlightenment, rather the Haskalah.

In the poem itself, Rabener uses the language and imagery of Genesis to recontextualize Byron's *Darkness* from a Christian apocalyptic vision into a failed cycle of creation. Byron's original reads:

> I had a dream, which was not all a dream.
> The bright sun was extinguish'd, and the stars
> Did wander darkling in the eternal space,
> Rayless, and pathless, and the icy earth
> Swung blind and blackening in the moonless air;
> Morn came, and went—and came, and brought no day,
> And men forgot their passions in the dread
> Of this their desolation;
>   *(ll. 1–8)*

In Rabener's translation, this is comparable to the first stage in the cycle of creation:

> I envisioned a night vision, a dream like a discovery of eyes:
> The sun dressed in darkness, lightening-beauty was extinguished,
> Stars of pride were connected, together they collected their brightness,
> They celebrated in the breadth of the firmament, all of their paths entangled together.
> In the darkness, excommunicated, they wandered, in the chaos there was no path,
> The land fluctuated in darkness, like the cold of the condensation of its turning,
> The moon did not shelter, light trembled in the excess
> Come morning, it changed, and time and its days were no more.[29]

In his version, Rabener essentially undoes the work of the first day's creation. Considering the fact that the sun was not created until the fourth day, Rabener chooses to translate Byron's "bright sun" with the word *ḥarsa,* rather than the more common term, *shemesh*. In contrast, he uses *rakiya* (Genesis 1:6) for "firmament" (l. 4), and *tohu* (Genesis 1:2) for "chaos" (l. 5). Finally, the line "The land fluctuated in darkness" evokes, though with different vocabulary, the biblical "darkness was upon the face of the deep" (Genesis 1:2).

As a negative interpretation of the second day, the second stage (ll. 9–25) parodies the creation of the heavens, transforming the metaphor for the heights to which man might aspire into a negative portrayal of the depths to which man might sink:

> Man forgot his longing, from desire drawn forth from his heart
> From darkness distressed and constrained, from great flickering desolation
> Sons of innocence all of them, in heart broken and crushed
> To God for deliverance they prayed: Please, let there be light!
> *(ll. 9–12)*

In translating Byron's "and all hearts / Were chill'd into a selfish prayer for light" (ll. 8–9), Rabener incorporates the language of Genesis 1:3 to parody the biblical account. But his is not Byron's "selfish prayer"; instead, Rabener seems to be criticizing those who passively wait for deliverance, rather than actively seeking the light of Enlightenment, Haskalah. Instead, as he ends this section, "And there was eternal night, darkness, eternal darkness" (l. 25); or, as Byron said: "all was black" (l. 21).

Reversing the next day's creation, in his third stage (ll. 26–34), Rabener describes how men destroy vegetation:

> They lay waste trees with the shoulder to increase quickly the pile of fuel,
> Their eyes are astonished, the heart astonished at the dusty wilderness,
> Death stretched like curtains upon the carcass of the land.
> *(ll. 32–34)*

The result is an inversion of God's work on the fourth day, the creation of the lights in the heavens. Instead, in lines 35–48, Rabener depicts the darkening of humanity:

> Then they separated from the dead, they looked they feared the ruin,
> They groaned they ground teeth, they cursed and they blessed God.
> All dwellers in the [*ruaḥ*], in the bottom of the earth they trembled,
> They ascended to [*hevel*], they were weakened from flying higher,
> All their lives splintered for tender heart was reversed,

CHAPTER 2

> Snake and serpent crept in oppression at the heels of men,
> They hissed in a loud voice only the people perished,
> The man scraped them in the head, and they would be food for them.—
>
> *(ll. 35–42)*

In this passage, Rabener's use of biblical terminology and imagery undermines the metaphorical implications of the heavenly lights. Although the word *ruaḥ* literally signifies "breath" or "wind," making it the appropriate term to describe those who "tremble" "in the bottom of the earth," it is also the word for the "spirit" of God, in Genesis 1:2, as well as the kabbalistic term for the rational soul, two meanings that seem unavailable to these people. Similarly, while the word *hevel* literally means "air," it is also the term for "vanity," which dominates the opening of Ecclesiastes. That these people are so low that they would have to ascend to reach the level of *hevel,* vanity, is telling. Finally, Rabener transforms Byron's depiction of stingless vipers into a parody of original sin. In Byron

> vipers crawl'd
> And twined themselves among the multitude,
> Hissing, but stingless—they were slain for food.
>
> *(ll. 35–37)*

Using different vocabulary, Rabener transforms the biblical punishment—"he [man] shall bruise your head, and you [serpent] shall bruise his heel" (Genesis 3:15)—into an image of man's degeneration: "The man scraped them in the head, and they would be food for them."

On the fifth day, God created the animals; the fifth stage of Rabener's cycle (ll. 49–68), which opens with the word "Death," depicts the physical death of humanity, until "There remained only two from the multitude of people in the city, / They lived in the perfection of hatred, the hostility of the world between them" (ll. 62–63). In the final irony, the last stage (ll. 69–91) parodies the creation of man, describing the final destruction of the world:

> Eternal storms and tempests will oppress the multitudes,
> Cloud and mist wandered, vapors will walk on them,
> Beyond them sufficient darkness, abundant ruin and darkness,
> But darkness is the master, it is the [*tevel*] rejected.
>
> *(ll. 88–91)*

However, unlike Byron's linear account, in which "Darkness had no need / Of aid from them—She was the universe" (ll. 81–82), Rabener depicts this as part of a larger cycle.

To signal the transformation of Byron's linear account into the Jewish *shemittah,* Rabener opens the sixth stage with the word "Compassion": "Compassion was captured in it, here a spark was sparked. / Fire growls its breath" (ll. 69–70). The word *raḥamim,* "compassion," an alternate term used for the fifth of the divine emanations (as seen above, the other, *tiferet,* is used in the translation of "She Walks in Beauty"), is defined as the unifying center of all creation. The "spark," literally from the fire, kabbalistically signifies the divine spark of humanity. Finally, the poem ends with the word *tevel,* generally defined as "confusion, violation of the natural order, abomination," as seen in Letteris's version of the last line: "Filled with confusion [*tevel*] ruin darkness [*minudah*] thrust forward *selah*." Kabbalistically, however, the word refers to the lowest of the seven earths, which "is the whole and perfect symbol of all the *Sefiroth* of construction and man, dwelling on it, is the image of the Sefirothic decade; this is why *Tebel* is said to include, in complete harmony, all the possibilities of the other six earths."[30] Combined, the kabbalistic terminology places *Darkness* into the cycle of creation, indicating that even the destruction of the world can be viewed positively, as part of a larger cosmic plan.

Whether intentional or not, Rabener's translation of the *Hebrew Melodies* at the very least responds to the skepticism inherent in Letteris's. By prefacing Byron with a defense of the secular culture of the Jews, and then reenvisioning Byron's vision of *Darkness* to signal the beginning of a new age, the 1864 edition seems to embody the optimism that Czernowitz, under the religious guidance of Igel and the intellectual leadership of Rabener, will emerge as a new center of Enlightenment. That optimism, unfortunately, was unavailable to the final Byronic *maskil,* Judah Leib Gordon.

Judah Leib Gordon—Ultimate Disillusionment

In contrast to Letteris, who was afraid to voice his own skepticism, or Igel and Rabener, who couched their radical program in the socially acceptable garb of prominent secular Jews, Judah Leib Gordon (1831–92) had no trouble articulating or defending his own attitudes, though he would be forced to pay for antagonizing many of the Jewish leaders he came in contact with. While still young, possibly as early as 1860, he turned to Byron's *Hebrew Melodies* for help developing his attitudes; and later, as published in his *Collected Poems* of 1884, he translated seven poems to create his own song cycle, illustrative of his belief that any return to Zion must be preceded by the educational principles of the Haskalah.[31]

Unlike most of the other Jewish Byronists, Judah Leib Gordon, the first Hebrew national poet and the major polemicist in the eastern Haskalah, was a leading intellectual in the Jewish community.[32] Born in the Lithuanian city of Vilna to an enlightened father, Gordon received both a Jewish and a European education, the former being taught by a disciple of the Gaon of Vilna (Elijah ben Solomon Zalman, 1720–97), and the latter (including Russian, German, Polish, French, and English) under the guidance of his brother-in-law, Mikhel Gordon (1823–90), a minor poet in his own right. After graduating from the government's teachers' seminary in Vilna, he began teaching in various government Jewish schools in the Kovno province (Lithuania): Ponevezh (1853–60); Shavli (1860–65); and Telz (1865–72), where he established a girls' school.

Growing up around Mikhel Gordon, Judah Leib was, from a young age, surrounded by poets, though he was not confirmed in his own vocation until when, near the age of twenty, he transcribed and edited the work of a seriously ill friend, Micah Joseph Lebensohn, whose father, Abraham Dov, recognized Gordon's abilities and influenced his early works. In addition to poetry, Gordon began writing essays for the Hebrew periodical *Ha-Maggid,* as well as other Jewish publications, formulating his attitudes toward the Haskalah.

In 1872, Gordon moved to St. Petersburg, where he became secretary to the Jewish community and director of the Society for the Promotion of Culture among the Jews of Russia.[33] Established in 1863 by wealthy members of the community, the society was intended to counter the persistent excuse that the religious, social, and cultural separatism of the Jews was the main reason for their being denied civic equality. As finally organized, the society had three stated aims: of acculturating the Jews of Russia through education in the vernacular; of supporting Jewish culture through the publication of original books, translations, and periodicals in Russian and Hebrew; and of supporting the education of youth through financial grants.

Gordon's work for the society pitted him against the rabbinic establishment, which rightly feared a diminution of power and authority. Antagonisms came to a head in 1879 when, having been falsely denounced by an opponent in a dispute over the appointment of a new rabbi, Gordon was arrested and imprisoned for anti-czarist activities. Although he was finally exonerated in 1880, he never forgave the community leaders for failing to pursue his release actively, and for failing to reappoint him to his former position. Therefore, he accepted the position as editor of *Ha-Meliz*, the leading Hebrew periodical in St. Petersburg. Gordon maintained a stormy relationship with the publisher, Alexander Zederbaum, and finally resigned in 1888. In 1892, Gordon died of cancer.

Broadly speaking, Gordon's work progresses from the early Romanticism of long epics on biblical themes through the realism of polemical essays and social satire to the nationalism of his later life, especially after his arrest in 1879 and the pogroms of 1881. Despite these evolutions, he maintained a core set of beliefs throughout his life. First, as an adherent of the Haskalah, Gordon was a vocal advocate of secular education in the vernacular. Still, he was a staunch Hebraist who felt that the essential character of the Jews lay in their language. Yet he advocated the kind of religious reform then being enacted in Germany. Finally, though believing in the messianic prophecy that the Jews would return to their homeland, he also felt that prior to such a return, they had to be educated in western ways before they would be competent to establish their own European-style nation in the Middle East.

These beliefs pitted Gordon against most factions of the Jewish community. His advocacy of a secular education in the vernacular, along with religious reform, ran into strenuous opposition by the rabbis, whom Gordon accused of malfeasance in the performance of their duties. In response, they strove to eliminate Gordon as a threat to them. But if the more conservative elements resisted Gordon, so, too, did the liberal factions. Gordon's insistence on Hebrew as the Jewish national language threatened the assimilationists, who feared provoking anti-Semitic accusations of Jewish separatism, if not of outright anti-Russian activism. In addition, in this pre-Herzl period, his adherence to a form of *Golus*-Nationalism raised the ire of Ḥovevei Ẓion, the "Lovers of Zion," who wanted to purchase land for colonizing the Middle East.[34] And finally, the Jews then living in Palestine also felt threatened by Gordon, his advocacy of a Europeanized government in the new Jerusalem jeopardizing their position as the primary beneficiaries of Jewish philanthropy, in favor of those who believed money should go toward constructing a new Jewish identity, rather than reinforcing the old. Though, in his own mind, Gordon was steering a middle—and rational—course between extremists, he succeeded during his career in alienating almost everyone, and by the time of his death, history had passed him and his core beliefs by.

Apparently, Gordon first turned to Byron and other Romantic poets relatively early in his career. According to Stanislawski, in the mid-1850s, after suffering the repercussions of going too far in an argument against leading western *maskilim* and after abandoning work on an epic cycle about King David, Gordon "set to work on shorter poems on incidental themes that either emerged from his own experiences or from works by Schiller, Byron, and other masters." Several years later, in 1861, Gordon published "short pieces, including reworkings of poems by Byron, Leopold Scheffer, and various French authors."[35] Finally, his *Collected Poems* of 1884 contains translations of seven of the *Hebrew Melodies*: "If That High World," "The Wild Gazelle," "Oh! Weep for Those," "On Jordan's Banks," "Jephtha's Daughter," "Herod's Lament for Mariamne," and "On the Day of the Destruction of Jerusalem by Titus."[36] Viewed as a unit, these particular lyrics, especially in the order preserved by Gordon, transform Byron's *Hebrew Melodies* into a literary representation of Gordon's own particular brand of Jewish messianism. Specifically, he uses Byron first to establish the abstract ideal and then to sketch out the historical condition of the Jews, though Gordon stops short of a projected return to Jerusalem, presumably because the Jews had not yet, in his lifetime, been appropriately acculturated.

Gordon opens with a brief one-paragraph introduction in which he describes Byron in terms of Jewish messianism:

> Wherever he saw oppression and distorted justice he quietly helped however he could. And where there was an enemy, like the enemies that then crushed the Greeks beneath the hand of the Turks, he hurried to assist them with his strength. This is the inheritance of those who crush Joseph, for he assists the children of Israel with a pen. This Byron was the first to breathe in these songs to reveal the love of Zion and affection for Jerusalem in the heart of the sons of the people of our land, and this love protects us in the heart of this people better than all the people of the earth. Therefore, we should honor the name of this poet and speak of the memory of his nearness to us. (161)

In contrast to the Christian Messiah, who is said to bring about the end of time, the Jewish Messiah, as descendent of David, the poet-king, is to lead the Jewish people back to their homeland in Jerusalem. Similarly, Byron, the British poet, as friend of the downcast, provides both material and artistic help wherever he can. Therefore, as Gordon says, the Jews should honor his name.

After the introduction, Gordon begins with what is actually the third poem of Byron's collection, using "If That High World" to introduce the messianic theme of exile and return. On the literal level, Byron's poem, containing two stanzas, posits belief in the immortality of the soul as consolation for the separation caused by death. In the first two lines, the speaker postulates the hypothetical—"If that high world, which lies beyond / Our own, surviving Love endears"—the implications of which he traces in the next six lines:

> If there the cherish'd heart be fond,
>   The eye the same, except in tears—
> How welcome those untrodden spheres!
>   How sweet this very hour to die!
> To soar from earth and find all fears
>   Lost in thy light—Eternity!

The inference to be drawn is that though the loss will be mourned in this life, the lovers will, if the theory is correct, be reunited in the next, the only difference being "except in tears." In the second stanza, the speaker takes the leap of faith: "It must be so" (l. 9). There must be something larger than the individual—"'tis not for self / That we so tremble on the brink" (ll. 9–10), in which case, the souls must be immortal and the two will be reunited: "And soul in soul grow deathless theirs!" (l. 16).

In Gordon's translation, the use of diction shifts the focus from the literal love between two human beings to the figurative love between God and his people:

> If it is a true thing that in heaven
> Yet Love dwells [*shokhenet*] among spirits,
> Because there is not there disaster, no tears in the eyes
> No heart grieving, soul wailing—
> Then peace to them, eternal without searching
> And blessing comes to you, at the moment of death
> A time of eternal light from the beauty of the morning
> Will pull away the troublesome night, will evaporate all pain.
>
> That thing is true! and how good [*mah tov*] is our portion!
> This hope will separate woe from our hearts
> Our feet standing on the remote parts of a corrupt pit

And our changes will appear shorn of vanity.
Everything descends to the pit! They remembered this and were strengthened:
There, in the place that the spirits are united,
There is no more enmity, the hearts are joined together,
They were buried before God and they were sanctified.

Consistent with Byron's, Gordon's two stanzas sketch out the hypothetical proposition of a reunification of lovers, the first postulating "Yet Love dwells among spirits," and the second "That thing is true!" However, the Hebrew words echo morning prayers associated with Jewish messianic belief. In the second line, the verb *shokhenet* is based on the root *shokhen*, used in *shoken ad*, from Nishmat Kol Ḥai, the morning prayer for eternal peace and blessing.[37] In the second stanza, immediately after affirming the messianic theory of the first, Gordon echoes the language of Balaam's blessing in Numbers: "How goodly are thy tents, O Jacob, and thy tabernacles, O Israel!" (24:5), the Hebrew for "how goodly" being *mah tovu*, and Gordon's line *mah tov*. In alluding to Balaam, Gordon shifts the focus from the lovers to the "tabernacles" of Israel, the Hebrew for tabernacle being based on the root *shakhan*, the place where "love dwells" in the second line. While Gordon does not literally alter Byron's lyrics, his Hebrew diction creates its own figurative level, as the love being discussed implies, in addition to the Byronic connotations, the connection between God and his people.

Having used Byron's poem to establish the theory of God's love, in the next six poems Gordon traces out the historical cycle upon which Jewish messianic belief is predicated. In the second poem of the group, "The Wild Gazelle," Gordon delineates the historical context for Jewish messianism, deliberately placing Byron's poem within a Zionist context, and even substituting the word "Zion" for "Judah," Byron's choice. Both versions emphasize the separation between God and his people, described in terms of the exile from Zion. In Gordon's, though, Byron's first two lines—"The wild gazelle on Judah's hills / Exulting yet may bound"—become "Gazelles leap and pass over the field / On the mountains of Zion and Jerusalem." Similarly, in the second stanza, Byron's "A step as fleet, an eye more bright, / Hath Judah witness'd there" is transformed into "Like these gazelles the daughter of Zion was." Not only does Gordon make the comparison direct, he expands the Zionist context to the Jewish people, "daughter of Zion." Finally, in the last stanza, Gordon substitutes for Byron's irony the Jewish messianic prayer. As Byron concludes his poem:

> But we must wander witheringly,
>   In other lands to die;
> And where our fathers' ashes be,
>   Our own may never lie:
> Our temple hath not left a stone,
> And Mockery sits on Salem's throne.
>
>   (*ll. 19–24*)

Here, Byron subverts any messianic hope, the temple being destroyed and the God of Israel being replaced by "Mockery," use of the English Salem being an ironic allusion to a poetic name for Jerusalem (see Psalm 76:2: "His abode has been established in Salem, his dwelling place in Zion"; also see discussion of Letteris above). Now, Gordon's version:

> And we will wander from our land
> On strange land the spirit goes forth
> Cut off from all land our essence is dispersed
> And in the graves of the fathers it will not find rest;
> Let God hallow our desolate city that is arid
> And where the wings of idols sit on the seat of God.

Gordon replaces Byron's despair with a prayer of restoration, that God will again hallow his city and enable his people to resanctify his Temple. Thus, if Gordon's version of "If That High World" articulates the theological basis of Jewish messianism, his "The Wild Gazelle" places that belief in its historical context.

The next two poems in Byron's sequence explore the postexilic condition of the Jews. The first, "Oh! Weep for Those," laments the loss of the homeland, both Byron and Gordon ending with despair: Byron "Mankind their Country—Israel but the grave!" and Gordon "The badger has a crag, and the Jew—only a grave!!" In the next one, "On Jordan's Banks," Gordon seems to soften the tone. Byron seems accusatory:

> On Jordan's banks the Arab's camels stray,
> On Sion's hill the False One's votaries pray,
> The Baal-adorer bows on Sinai's steep—
> Yet there—even there—Oh God! thy thunders sleep.
>
>   (*ll. 1–4*)

The verb "sleep" seems to suggest that God is neglecting his obligation. In his translation, Gordon modulates the effect, replacing Byron's "sleep" with silence:

> On the Jordan's banks Arabs stretch out
> On the heights of Zion your name they blaspheme
> On Sinai to Baal they bow down the knee
> And the uproar of your thunder still is silent, my God! —

In his version, the adverb "still" implies that the silence will, at some point, end.

Both versions end with the rhetorical question "How long?" Byron:

> How long by tyrants shall thy land be trod?
> How long thy temple worshipless, Oh God?
> (*ll. 11–12*)

Gordon:

> Until when will the feet of the enemy trample your land
> Until when will enemies plunder your temple?!

In Judaizing Byron, Gordon substitutes the generic "enemy" (*zar*) for Byron's more politically charged "tyrants." Then, in the last line, replacing Byron's "worshipless" temple, Gordon, like Letteris, alludes to its desecration, a far greater tragedy to Jewish sensibilities.

Gordon's answer to the question "how long" is as long as it takes for the Jews to modernize their religion and become Europeanized. Symbolizing the need to leave the older cult are the final three poems, "Jephtha's Daughter," "Herod's Lament for Mariamne," and "On the Day of the Destruction of Jerusalem by Titus," all three literally tied to ancient beliefs that, Gordon felt, were not only archaic but inhibited Jewish progress in the modern world. The first, as symbol of both the older religion and the historical adaptability of the Jewish religion, is "Jephtha's Daughter," Byron's poem about the nameless woman who willingly permits herself to be sacrificed in fulfillment of a promise her father made to God (Judges 11). As discussed in the previous chapter, Byron emphasizes the dignity of the daughter, as she willingly accedes to self-sacrifice for the sake of her father's honor:

Byron and the *Maskilim*

> Since our Country, our God—Oh, my Sire!
> Demand that thy Daughter expire;
> Since thy triumph was bought by thy vow—
> Strike the bosom that's bared for thee now!
>
> (*ll. 1–4*)

Although she does accept what is presented as her familial obligation, in so doing, the daughter also emphasizes the reality that she has no alternative, her references to country, God, and father indicating that she has no recourse—all of the social institutions are stacked up against her. As a nameless female, her only option is to accept her death with dignity.

Without changing the poem substantively, Gordon brings out the problems inherent in the biblical source. Given the emphasis on the daughter's virginity, not to mention Jephtha's own illegitimacy, the story is associated with a kind of fertility ritual considered archaic by the biblical period. Therefore, its mere inclusion in Judges stands as testimony that ritual and belief had evolved to the point that a blind promise entailing sacrifice was no longer sanctioned by the Jews. The biblical context underscores Judaism's history of religious reform, not unlike that being advocated by *maskilim* in the West.

Gordon's version remains fairly close to Byron's, except, most notably, for the last two lines of the second stanza, where he changes Byron's

> If the hand that I love lay me low,
> There cannot be pain in the blow!
>
> (*ll. 7–8*)

to

> If the hand of my father brings death to me
> His fear about me is unnecessary. The pain is numb.

Instead of Byron's romanticized notion of martyrdom, implying that the act of self-sacrifice committed out of love is painless, Gordon emphasizes biblical law, stressing the legal obligation of child to parent, implying that according to the Law, the child must obey the father. Therefore, even though the daughter accepts her social and filial obligation to die, the result is not the physical absence of pain but the emotional deadening of sensation.

CHAPTER 2

The next poem, "Herod's Lament for Mariamne," can be read as both Byron's and Gordon's indictment of corrupt authorities in their respective societies. Based on Josephus's account of the execution of Mariamne (*Antiquities of the Jews,* book 15, chapter 7), the poem lodges two complaints against an absolutist law: first, the real possibility that an innocent person might be executed; and second, the emotional likelihood that those implicated in the law's implementation might be adversely affected. According to Josephus, Herod, distrusting his wife, has her tried and executed, only to realize her innocence later and mourn her loss. As a lamentation, Byron's poem plumbs the depths of remorse, the first stanza articulating Herod's intellectual acceptance of guilt, the second his abandonment of any false hope that she might still live, and the third the emotional recognition that his guilt can never be assuaged:

> And mine's the guilt, and mine the hell,
>   This bosom's desolation dooming;
> And I have earn'd those tortures well,
>   Which unconsumed are still consuming!
>   (ll. 21–24)

Except for the exigencies of idiom, Gordon's version is essentially the same as Byron's, an implicit indictment of a law whose execution renders its adherents powerless:

> In me is the indictment, to me also is the fixed cup
> My portion I will drink I will find in myself a murderer
> And in the walls of my heart will be extended the humiliation
> And will crush its foundation into eternal desolation.

Despite the cover of the law, Byron's and Gordon's Herods both indict themselves for murder and articulate the dimensions of their guilt.

In the last poem of this sequence, "On the Day of the Destruction of Jerusalem by Titus," Byron and Gordon both sever the ties between the historical need for the physical Jerusalem and the contemporary condition of the Jews. Written as a flashback in which the speaker recalls his experience on the day of the Temple's destruction, the poem juxtaposes the sentimentality of loss with the modern realization that God can be prayed to anywhere; moreover, the fact that the Temple was destroyed implies that he wanted it that way anyway—otherwise, Titus wouldn't have succeeded. As Byron concludes:

> But the Gods of the Pagan shall never profane
> The shrine where Jehovah disdain'd not to reign;
> And scattered and scorn'd as thy people may be,
> Our worship, oh Father! is only for thee.
> *(ll. 17–20)*

Gordon even more explicitly differentiates between the physical Temple in Jerusalem, which can be defiled, and the metaphorical temple in the heart, which cannot:

> But whether also in the innermost part of your temple God will stand unfit
> In the innermost part of the heart of your people folly will not come:
> Also there in the place of exile, also between flouted anguish,
> Only to you, the one father, only to you we will pray.

According to the conventional narrative of Jewish history, the pogroms of 1880–81 effectively ended the Haskalah, graphically demonstrating that the Jews would not be permitted to assimilate into the Russian Empire. From that perspective, these Hebrew versions of Byron, given their limited circulation, might be considered part of the larger failure of the movement. However, by the last decades of the nineteenth century, neither the secular use of Hebrew nor the inclusion of gentile materials in the Jewish canon was controversial, both practices having been accepted by the vast majority of Jews. Moreover, the work of *maskilim* like Yaakov Zevi, Meir Halevi Letteris, Matisyahu Simḥah Rabener, Eliezer Eliyahu Igel, and Judah Leib Gordon together created a space in which the Jewish identity could evolve into its post-Enlightenment forms. As will be seen in the following chapters, two major factions competed to fill that space: the Yiddishists, who wanted to create a Jewish nation in the Diaspora; and the Zionists, who have established a Jewish state in Israel.

CHAPTER 3

Byron and the Yiddishists

As Benjamin Harshav explains, the Yiddishist movement was part of a larger Jewish revolution, "not directed against a political power structure but rather against a governing semiotics, a set of beliefs, values, and behavior, and toward internalized ideals of a new world culture."[1] In their attempt to bring the Jews into the twentieth century, Yiddishists used their language as the vehicle through which to restructure the Jewish mode of thought, by eliminating the religious component and by translating—or, to be more precise, Judaizing—non-Jewish literature. In their quest for acculturation, they turned first to Russian literature, Russian being the vernacular of many of the intellectuals. Russian literature, for its part, was heavily influenced by German Romantic philosophy and by English Romantic poetry; and Byron was the avatar of the English Romantic poet.[2] Thus, both directly through the English and indirectly through the Russian, Byron became a significant figure to at least nine Yiddishists.

Comparable to the Byronic materials produced by the *maskilim*, the Yiddish texts punctuate the evolution of the movement as a whole. In its early periods, *Golus*-Nationalism was dominated by the anti-Zionist, anti-religious ideology of Chaim Zhitlowsky, who hoped to use Yiddishism as a vehicle for converting the Jewish masses to Marxism. By the early 1920s, the conditions that had produced *Golus*-Nationalism had been obviated. The Balfour Declaration of 1917 legitimated the Zionist cause. Similarly, the Reform and Conservative religious movements of Judaism, as well as newly gained rights of citizenship, especially in the West, effectively loosened the controls previously exerted by rabbinic authorities. Moreover, given the anti-Semitic purges within the Communist Party, few of the Jews who had emigrated wanted to return to Russia. Consequently, western Jews in general, and Yiddishists in particular, began to reexamine their attitudes toward *Golus*-Nationalism, trying to find the means by which to incorporate the new realities of Zionism and religious reform, especially as related to social activism in their new world. By the early 1930s, the attempt to create a Yiddishist identity had begun to collapse. The Zionist dream of a Jewish homeland in which Hebrew was spoken was becoming realized; and purges in the Soviet Union were being publicized. Consequently, it was neither possible nor necessarily desirable to posit Yiddish as *the* Jewish language or *Golus*-Nationalism as the governing ideology of the people. In addition, religion had been restored to its central position, the vast majority of Jews identifying Judaism as the major component of their identity. Therefore, from the perspective of Yiddishism, the Holocaust precipitated an ending already anticipated in the Jewish community.

In each of these phases, Yiddishists used Byron to help work out their attitudes toward *Golus*-Nationalism. In the earliest period, three in particular were influenced by Zhitlowsky's ideology: The first, Ezekiel Bleicher, translated *Childe Harold,* canto 1, and *Heaven and Earth,* and also wrote a brief biographical sketch of Byron; the second, Elkana Zilberman, translated into Yiddish what had originated as a Russian book-length biography of Byron; and finally, Max (Mordechai) Hershman published his Yiddish version of *The Prisoner of Chillon* in an anarchist periodical.

During the middle period, when the western Diasporas began replacing central and eastern Europe as the center of Yiddish culture, a second group of three Yiddishists turned to Byron for help in establishing their new Anglo- and American-Jewish identities: Nathan Horowitz, Abraham Asen, and Chaim Gutman. In London, Horowitz translated the *Hebrew Melodies, Manfred,* and *Cain* into Yiddish, and then the *Hebrew Melodies* into Hebrew, in deciding to return to a religious Jewish identity; and in America, Asen translated *The Prisoner of Chillon,* the *Hebrew Melodies,* and *Cain,* with a Yiddish introduction by Gutman, to advocate Labor Zionism.

Finally, the last three Yiddishists represent three responses to the rise of Nazi Germany. Shelomo Simon, not a translator but a reviewer, criticized Asen's *Cain* for possibly fueling anti-Semitism. Similarly, Shea Tenenbaum reinterpreted Byron's *Cain* to privilege the obedient Abel over the rebellious Cain. Finally, Moisei Khashtshevatski, the last in the series of nine Yiddish Byronists, was a Polish Communist who translated *The Prisoner of Chillon* before fighting in the Red Army against the Nazis.

CHAPTER 3

Golus-*Nationalism*

Ezekiel Bleicher—Yiddishist Ideology

Included in Zhitlowsky's first issue of *Dos neie leben* was the earliest Yiddish version of Byron, a translation of *Childe Harold*, canto 1, by Ezekiel Bleicher (b. 1884). An adherent of the leftist ideology articulated by Zhitlowsky, Bleicher seems to have advocated the Bund's antireligious and anti-Zionist policies, using his Byronic materials to criticize the contemporary Jewish religious establishment.[3]

There are very few details extant about Bleicher's life, though what is available leads to the inference that he considered Byron a kindred spirit.[4] Born in Russia, Bleicher apparently left some time around the pogroms of 1904–6, though not before graduating from a surveying school there; he later studied mathematics in Rome. Around 1906, he came to the United States where, under Zhitlowsky's guidance, Bleicher became interested in literature. In 1909, he translated the first canto of *Childe Harold*, the only Yiddish version of the poem. The next year Bleicher moved to Warsaw, where he lived from 1910 to 1911. While there, he translated Goethe's *Faust* for Abraham Reisen's *Eyropaeishe literatur* (European Literature), which also reprinted his Yiddish *Childe Harold*. From then until around 1919, Bleicher lived the peripatetic life of his Byronic hero, traveling through France and Italy and staying periodically in England and America. Like Byron's, his travels provided a source of inspiration, Bleicher writing original lyrics, travel literature, a series of stories entitled *Parisian Times*, articles about art and theater, correspondence, and *Veh un unruh* (Woe and Restlessness, 1915), a book containing both his own verse and another reprint of his *Childe Harold* translation. Continuing the Byronic parallel, Bleicher, too, participated in what he believed to be a war of liberation, returning, after the March Revolution, to the Soviet Union, where he served as an officer in the War Commissariat starting in 1919. Also in that year, Bleicher published a translation of Byron's *Heaven and Earth*, as well as a collection of his own ballads, *Der shtumer monakh* (The Dumb Monk), both from Kiev (a major Yiddish publishing center). After that, Bleicher seems to have retired from his Yiddish literary career. Nothing more is known of him.

If, from the British perspective, Bleicher's biography resembles Byron's, from Bleicher's perspective, Byron's biography suggests a Bundist manqué, that is, a would-be revolutionary impeded by decadent aristocratic genes and the interference of a conservative religious establishment. Needless to say, in his brief four-page sketch, "Lard Beiran: Biagrafishe natizen" (Lord Byron: Biographical Notice), printed in Reisen's *Eyropaeische literatur,* Bleicher had to leave out a great deal of information about Byron's life, though what he includes suggests that he intended his biography to serve as a kind of negative example of a life whose great promise was impeded by moral and social obstacles.

Bleicher's thesis for the biography is that Byron was caught in a struggle between the aristocratic establishment on the one hand and his poetic inspiration on the other. In the first three sentences, he introduces Byron's paternal heritage—there is no mention of the maternal line or even of Byron's mother at all. Characterizing Captain Byron as "a reckless squanderer," Bleicher explains that Byron's father "died young, leaving his family in very constrained circumstances." As luck would have it, though, "ten-year-old George Byron all of a sudden became a rich heir and a representative of the highest English aristocracy." However, Byron was not simply the scion of the degenerate aristocracy: "The poetry counts as much as the aristocracy for his identity. With the exception of King David, one knows of no other princes, counts, other lords, who were as noble or as important as Byron. Byron himself was as proud to belong to those Byrons who came over from Normandy with William the Conqueror, as to be the creator of *Childe Harold* and *Manfred*" (23). The rest of the text works out the conflict between these two components of Byron's identity. In school, he gained a reputation for wildness, though trips to the mountains enabled him to develop his poetic sensibilities. He was both sexually and creatively precocious, and in 1810–11 (a century before Bleicher's own travels), Byron and Hobhouse traveled to the Levant. Upon his return to England, Byron assumed his seat in Parliament, though because his maiden speech was unsuccessful, he abandoned any political aspirations he might have had. Still, Bleicher speculates, one can only imagine what might have happened if Byron's speech had been as well received as the first two cantos of *Childe Harold.*

In any case, as Bleicher continues, the religious establishment began to intrude into Byron's life. After his return to England, Byron published a series of works, culminating with the *Hebrew Melodies,* "elegies," as Bleicher explains, "fit to the old Jewish events. With them, Byron acquired for himself a name with the religious faction." Bleicher completely ignores the anti-Semitic response to the *Hebrew Melodies,* simply asserting that

that was Byron's high point, after which he "fell very far backwards." The problem was that "English conservative public opinion mixed itself into the poet's family life." In 1816, when Byron and his wife separated, "society cast the entire fault on the poet and forbade him to stay in his homeland any more, so he decided to leave permanently" (25).

As Bleicher continues, in his self-exile, Byron struggled with the two parts of his identity, still writing prolifically, though from the time of his stay in Venice on, "In his palace he had a harem; day or night passed in crazy tumult, the highest and the lowest were found done in that place. The poet himself changed so much that his friends barely recognized him" (25). Even worse, according to Bleicher, Byron used opium as an appetite suppressant, only to become addicted. Luckily, through the good influence of Countess Teresa Guiccioli, he regained his self-control and was able to complete some of his most famous work. Finally, Byron joined the revolution: "Inspired by the idea to help liberate this land of art and poetry, he went to Greece. His intention was realized, and he decided to install his own brigade. In Missolonghi he was inspired by the Greek imperative to be their redeemer. He willingly took on himself the high command . . . when a strong fever forced him to bed, from which he did not get out again. Byron died on the 24th of January 1824" (26).

This brief biographical sketch is significant for the way Bleicher recontextualizes the British Romantic poet into an archetypal figure of the Jewish intelligentsia, with bundist sympathies. Comparable to the leftist interpretation of the traditional Jew from a rabbinic family, Byron's true nature is impaired by his aristocratic heritage; and like the Socialist, Byron first tries to placate the religious authorities with his publication of the *Hebrew Melodies,* though the establishment still turns against him in the end. Finally, Byron redeems himself by joining the revolution and fighting for the people.

Equally significant are the parallels to Bleicher's own life. Born roughly a century apart (1788 and 1884), Bleicher and Byron both lived through the evolution of what began as a revolution against tyrannical monarchies, both were self-exiles, both were poets, and finally, both actively supported their causes, assuming formal titles. Although clearly Bleicher never achieved the level of a Byron, still these parallels suggest reasons why he was so attracted to the British poet that he would choose to translate *Childe Harold*, canto 1, as his first contribution to the Yiddish intelligentsia, and *Heaven and Earth,* upon his return to the Soviet Union, as his last.

For Bleicher and his Jewish audience, the first canto of *Childe Harold* would have resonated on several different levels. Most obviously, Harold specifically identifies himself as "The fabled Hebrew wanderer" ("To Inez," 5.2). Historically, the setting is tied to one of the seminal events of Jewish history, the expulsion of the Jews from Spain in 1492, dislocating what had been a long-established community from its home, and thereby affecting Jewish history from the sixteenth century on.[5] Previously, Spain had been the center of their culture, so the expulsion wrenched from the Jews any sense of security they might have achieved. The edict itself, which called either for the conversion of the Jews or for their exile, was enforced by the Inquisition, the most virulent engine of anti-Semitism before the Holocaust. Because the Catholic Church was so committed to extirpating Jews from Iberia, some did convert to Christianity, though as "New Christians," they still remained suspect to their neighbors who, it must be admitted, did have cause, considering the fact that others became crypto-Jews, conforming to Christian mores in public while retaining whatever vestiges of Jewish rites they could manage in private. Those Jews who could, however, left Spain, relocating variously to the Levant, Spanish colonies in the New World, or Amsterdam, whose tradition of tolerance enabled them to make new homes for themselves. Thus, Childe Harold's wanderings through Portugal and Spain would echo in the cultural consciousness of the Yiddish audience.

More immediate, however, were the parallels between the Spain of Byron's time and the Russia of Bleicher's, it being quite likely that Bleicher himself left Russia because of a political situation evocative of that in Spain during the time of Byron's visit. Historically, the period between 1808 and 1813, known as the Peninsular War, was characterized by the Spanish people's opposition to French domination, the Peninsular War being key to Spanish nationalism. Under Napoleon, the French took advantage of the turmoil surrounding the conflict between Fernando, heir to the throne, and Godoy, the prime minister and reportedly the lover of the queen. In March 1808, Godoy fell, King Carlos IV abdicated, and Fernando ascended to the throne. Seeing his opportunity to supplant the Bourbons, Napoleon compelled Fernando VII to abdicate in favor of his father, who, in turn, abdicated in favor of Joseph Bonaparte. Technically, French control was accomplished in accordance with the legal formalities; however, the people refused to accept the new monarch, considering him illegitimate and the product of treason. Although not precisely the same situation, Czar Nicholas II's subversion of the Duma, after it had been granted expanded powers at the insistence of the people, reflects the same tyrannical impulse; and Byron's meditations on the state of the peninsula during 1809–10 can be assumed to reflect Bleicher's on the state of Russia a century later.

In his translation, Bleicher decontextualizes Byron's romance, limiting himself strictly to canto 1, the Iberian Peninsula.[6] Specifically, he entitles his translation merely *Childe Harold,* despite the fact that Byron intended his eponymous hero to be on a pilgrimage, and the work to be a romance. He excludes the epigraph from *Le cosmopolite,* in which Fougeret de Monbron (1753) derives a sense of patriotic nationalism from the observation that all countries are equally bad. Also omitted is the preface, in which Byron specifically identifies Childe Harold as a fictional character, explains his choice of a Spenserian stanza—it "admits of every variety"—and insists that Childe Harold "never was intended as an example, further than to show that early perversion of mind and morals leads to satiety of past pleasures and disappointment in new ones, and that even the beauties of nature, and the stimulus of travel (except ambition, the most powerful of all excitements) are lost on a soul so constituted, or rather misdirected."[7]

Finally, Bleicher leaves out the dedication, "To Ianthe." The effect is a pared-down narrative that conforms to a leftist ideology. Even though he does nothing to distort the text itself, just by removing the outer contexts, Bleicher renders *Childe Harold* more amenable to the Bund's educational program. Also, it should be noted, Bleicher's language is the Yiddish of the hard-liners who attempted to extirpate Hebrew from their orthography and vocabulary, thereby making their language more consistent with its old Germanic origins than with modern Yiddish. Without Byron's context and minus the religious component of the language, the Yiddish *Childe Harold* can be read as a projection of Bleicher himself, a member of the Jewish intelligentsia attempting to bring his culture into the twentieth century.

As a pilgrimage, canto 1 both telescopes and parodies the archetypal structure of the first book of Spenser's *Faerie Queene,* the book of holiness. Initially traveling with the true Una and the instinctive dwarf, Red Crosse, the Christian knight, embarks on the first adventure of his until-then innocent life. In the course of his travels, he encounters the dragon of error, whose deceptively easy defeat he erroneously interprets as the measure of his own prowess; and he subsequently falls prey to the sins of the House of Pride, and therefore must be schooled in his faith at the House of Holiness, so that he can then defeat the dragon in a three-day battle proleptic of the apocalyptic agon in which Jesus will defeat Satan. As a parody of *The Faerie Queene,* canto 1 of *Childe Harold* can be read as an indictment of the church/state relationship lauded by Spenser. The hero of this ironic pilgrimage is the opposite of an untested knight: he is a world-weary dilettante who, traveling alone except for servants, visits areas in Iberia that subvert the theme underlying the allegory of *The Faerie Queene,* that is, the advantages of a constitutionally established church. Specifically, the visit to Portugal suggests the deceptively easy victory at the Cave of Error; Cava resembles the House of Pride; the Maid of Saragossa is a transformation of Dame Caelia; and finally, the three-part bullfight in Cadiz parodies the defeat of the dragon who has imprisoned Adam and Eve. As an adaptation of the Spenserian prototype, Byron's poem is overtly Christian; yet, when placed in a Jewish context, the hero's quest can be read as the construction of a *golus* Yiddish identity, especially in the light of the pogroms of 1904–6. To Bleicher's audience, Harold's visit to Portugal becomes an indictment of state-sponsored religion, the primary error of history; Cava, of tyranny; Seville, the rise of the proletariat as the means of counteracting tyranny; and Cadiz, the dangers of bourgeois hypocrisy.

The first section of the canto, roughly stanzas 1 through 14, introduces Harold in terms that associate him with a combination of the myth of the Wandering Jew and the Jewish self-identity, with the originating sin transformed from the rejection of Christ into sexual licentiousness. Although the specific sin is not really part of the Jewish sense of self, it can be interpreted metaphorically as *alterity,* the real sin for which both Byron and the Jews are condemned. The result is a feeling of pride and isolation, a psychological state characteristic of both Harold and the Jews:

> And now Childe Harold was sore sick at heart,
> And from his fellow bacchanals would flee;
> 'Tis said, at times the sullen tear would start,
> But Pride congeal'd the drop within his ee.
>
> *(6.1–4)*

Therefore, Harold leaves his home, knowing, as did the Jews who left Russia, that he would not be missed by the natives: "My greatest grief is that I leave / No thing that claims a tear" (Harold's farewell, 8.7–8).

In his description of Portugal (stanzas 15–27), Byron transforms Spenser's Cave of Error, Red Crosse's deceptively easy initial victory, into an indictment of both religion and nationalism. Upon seeing the land, the narrator, like Red Crosse, confuses a pleasing appearance with a deadly reality. First, he places Portugal into an Edenic context—"Oh, Christ! it is a goody sight to see / What heaven hath done for this delicious land!"

(15.1–2)—to be sullied by man's "impious hand" (15.5), the punishment being the ravages of the Napoleonic wars: "Gaul's locust host, and earth from fellest foemen purge" (15.9). As he goes further, however, he realizes the difference between appearance and reality:

> But whoso entereth within this town,
> That, sheening far, celestial seems to be,
> Disconsolate will wander up and down.
>   (17.1–3)

Asking "Why, Nature, waste thy wonders on such men?" (18.2), he locates the fault with the Inquisition, the religious institution in which, "In hope to merit Heaven," authorities responded "by making earth a Hell" (20.9), the result being "here and there, as up the crags you spring, / Mark many rude-carv'd crosses near the path" (21.1–2). Noting that people have not learned from their mistakes, he brings the history to his time, alluding to the 1808 Convention of Cintra—"Behold the hall where chiefs were late conven'd! / Oh! dome displeasing unto British eye!" (24.1–2)—when the victorious British permitted the weakened French army to return home intact. Harold summarizes the lessons of Portugal during a meditation on the way out of the country:

> Though here awhile he learn'd to moralize,
> For Meditation fix'd at times on him;
> And conscious Reason whisper'd to despise
> His early youth, misspent in maddest whim;
> But as he gaz'd on truth his aching eyes grew dim.
>   (27.5–9)

The lesson here, for both Harold and Bleicher's Jewish audience, is the disastrous effect of abdicating personal responsibility to established authority. Using the city of Mafra as an object lesson, Harold summarizes the particular dangers of an integrally connected religious and civil administration:

> Yet Mafra shall one moment claim delay,
> Where dwelt of yore the Lusian's luckless queen;
> And church and court did mingle their array,
> And mass and revel were alternate seen;
> Lordling and freres—ill sorted fry I ween!

> But here the Babylonian whore hath built
> A dome where flaunts she in such glorious sheen,
> That men forget the blood which she hath spilt,
> And bow the knee to Pomp that loves to varnish guilt.
>
> *(29.1–9)*

The criticism of the Roman Catholic Church would resonate with the Protestant British and the Jews, both having been victims of papal excesses. But even more important, the criticism can be generalized to apply to all religious establishments that hypocritically use the power of the state to create their own hegemony, and to all civil authorities who cynically garb themselves in the robes of religion to sustain their own power.

In the central portion of canto 1, the tour through Spain, Byron breaks this theme down into its major components, as illustrated through the cities of Cava, Seville, and Cadiz. As the first stop in Spain, the tour of Cava (stanzas 33–44) transforms Spenser's House of Pride into an indictment of religion as the root of Spain's problems. Starting with the early history of the country, Byron alludes to the Crusades, finding little difference between the Christians and Muslims:

> Whilome upon his banks did legions throng
> Of Moor and knight, in mailed splendour drest:
> Here ceas'd the swift their race, here sunk the strong;
> The Paynim turban and the Christian crest
> Mix'd on the bleeding stream, by floating hosts oppress'd.
>
> *(34.5–9)*

He then recounts the entry of the Muslims into Spain, granted permission by Count Julian in 711, bringing the history of war to the present—"The Grave shall bear the chiefest prize away, / And Havoc scarce for joy can number their array" (40.8–9): "There shall they rot—Ambition's honour'd fools!" (42.1).

In Spenser, the House of Pride is counterbalanced by the House of Holiness; in Byron, the pride of the religious-civil authorities is counterbalanced by the voice of the people, the Maid of Saragossa (stanzas 45–64). When the adulterous queen undermined the stability of the throne, giving the French the opportunity to seize control of Spain, it took the representative of the people to defeat Napoleon:

CHAPTER 3

> Who can appease like her a lover's ghost?
> Who can avenge so well a leader's fall?
> What maid retrieve when man's flush'd hope is lost?
> Who hang so fiercely on the flying Gaul,
> Foil'd by a woman's hand, before a batter'd wall?
>
> (56.5–9)

At this point in *The Faerie Queene,* the Red Crosse Knight, having been schooled in holiness, is fit to confront the dragon that has kidnaped Adam and Eve; and in his three-day battle, he liberates our first parents from original sin. In his parody, Byron transforms the emblem of the apocalypse into a bullfight in Cadiz (stanzas 65–79), a city that "Calls forth a sweeter, though ignoble praise" (65.4)—a city of religious hypocrisy that Byron compares ironically to London: "London! right well thou know'st the day of prayer" (69.2). Elaborating upon the bullfight, Byron includes three attacks, comparable to Red Crosse's three-day battle against the dragon, though this is a "light-limb'd Matadore" (74.2), and the bull, "Without a groan, without a struggle dies" (79.5), hardly an apocalyptic agon.

After his battle, the Red Crosse Knight is betrothed to Una, though their marriage is postponed until after he fulfills his obligations to the Faerie Queene. In Byron's poem, there is no such denouement. Rather, Childe Harold returns to status quo ante, as "life-abhorring gloom / Wrote on his faded brow curst Cain's unresting doom" (83.8–9). Not betrothed, he instead sings a song "To Inez," in which he explicitly identifies himself as the Wandering Jew:

> It is that settled, ceaseless gloom
>   The fabled Hebrew wanderer bore;
> That will not look beyond the tomb,
>   But cannot hope for rest before.
>
> (5.1–4)

Considering the Christian myth but a dream—"Oh! may they still of transport dream, / And ne'er, at least like me, awake" (7.3–4), Harold completes his song and nihilistically sails on: "Here all were noble, save Nobility; / None hugg'd a Conqueror's chain, save fallen Chivalry!" (85.8–9).

This is the state of Bleicher and Russian Jewry in 1910. The expansion of the Duma had been subverted by the monarchy, and the Jews had been scapegoated by everyone for everything the different factions felt had gone wrong. There had been a mass Jewish exodus from Russia, though many of the self-exiles were keeping a close watch on the events, hoping, as would Bleicher a decade later, to return to their homeland in the Diaspora, where they could assist what they hoped could become the Communist equivalent of the Maid of Saragossa in the liberation of their country from the religious and monarchical establishments that had thwarted the will of the people.

When Bleicher returned to the Soviet Union after the May Revolution, he likely became part of the Bund's antireligion campaign, the purpose being to wean the Jews away from the traditional religious establishment so that they could become part of the larger Communist movement being consolidated at the time. It seems logical to infer, therefore, that Bleicher's decision to translate *Heaven and Earth* was made in conjunction with his ideology, Byron's play easily being read as an allegory of the debilitating effect religion has had on the proletariat.

According to Daniel P. Watkins, *Heaven and Earth* can be interpreted as an attack against the exploitation of religion for political purposes.[8] Set in the period immediately preceding the flood, Byron's play questions the efficacy of a law that, applying only to a limited segment of the population, is used as a weapon for social control, preventing both free choice and independent thought. The dicta of the law are pronounced by Noah, a strict authoritarian whose primary goal, it would appear, is to maintain his power. To that end, he emphasizes two points: that there should be no intermarriage, whether between humans and spirits or between sons of Seth and daughters of Cain; and that his family must not stray beyond the strict boundaries he imposes on them. In order to justify his edict, he claims election, that his are the laws of God, though when that fails, he uses the ultimate weapon of a religious establishment, the accusation of blasphemy, to halt any inquiry that might threaten to undermine his hegemony.

When *Heaven and Earth* is read as an allegory of Yiddishist ideology, Noah can be seen to embody the position of the rabbinate, those who used religion as an instrument for social control, ignoring and/or denigrating alternative readings of the Bible in an attempt to prevent assimilation with the dominant community. The daughters of Cain, who are also children of Adam, represent the Bund, the socialist union that advocated secular education as the means of diminishing religious hegemony. That Japhet, after exploring both sides, would choose his father over Anah, reflects what Bundists considered their primary challenge, the emotional tie exerted by the religious over the young. In contrast, Bleicher, who left Russia to become an active member of the intelligentsia, and who returned to become (fatally, apparently) an official of Soviet Russia, makes the kind of authentic choice advocated by Aholibamah, self-sacrifice for principle, regardless of the personal cost.

As with Bleicher, the other two translators dedicated to constructing a Yiddishist identity, Elkana Zilberman and Max Hershman, both seem to have used Byron in conjunction with the Bund's effort to acculturate Jews after the Russian Revolution. As a general policy, leftists advocated translation as a method for transforming the older Jewish Zionist into the modern secular internationalist who would work for proletarian rights in the Diaspora. In this context, Byron could be presented as a symbol of the individual who transcends background and personal shortcomings to engage in a war of both national and intellectual liberation.

Elkana Zilberman—Yiddishist Biography

Not much is known about the next Yiddish Byronist.[9] Elkana Zilberman (b. 1893) was born in Poland, eventually moving to Warsaw, where he studied in Jewish schools and attended a Russian gymnasium. Zilberman worked as a businessman, and in 1922, he began contributing to the Yiddish-Polish press. In 1928, he moved to Brazil to work in commerce, though he returned to Warsaw in 1931. In the summer of 1939, he went to France, and was last seen in Paris on September 1, 1939. Zilberman's literary career consists of some early Polish translations of Yiddish literature, but mostly Yiddish essays, humourous pieces, literary criticism (especially about Reiner Maria Rilke), and translations from Russian, Polish and German literature. Zilberman was the proprietor of the periodical *Orient,* which published Yiddish translations of classical literature. In book form, he published Yiddish translations of Dostoyevsky's *Memories of a Death House* (1927), and Polish writer Kazimierz Tetmajer. On Byron, he published *Lord Byron: His Life and Work,* identified on the title page as a free translation of N. Aleksandrav's biography.[10]

Produced in the early 1920s (possibly to coincide with the centenary of Byron's death), Zilberman's biography has a subtle leftward tilt, suggesting Bundist sympathies, though without the overt propaganda of an ideologue. Still, there are several anomalies in the text to suggest the presence of some sort of redaction before publication. For the most part, the biography is consistent with the standard chronology, though chapter titles and concluding essays present the British Romantic in terms of the Yiddishist

Jewish identity: a religious skeptic, a *Golus*-Nationalist, and a committed revolutionary. The 157-page text consists of nine chapters:

1. The Heritage and Childhood
2. In School
3. In University—The Earliest Works
4. Travels—*Childe Harold*
5. The Oriental Poems—Marriage
6. A Voluntary Exile
7. In Greece—Death
8. Byron as a Man
9. Byron's Place in Literature

Although Zilberman remains objective throughout his text, citing what are presumably Aleksandrav's chief sources,[11] the emphasis seems to be on Byron's personal liberation from the bonds created by ancestry, parentage, and repressive religious and social institutions, a liberation accomplished through early travels and eventual self-exile from his homeland, all to prepare him for heroic death in the struggle for Greek independence.

Zilberman reserves his own analyses for the last two chapters, summarizing Byron's personal and professional lives, respectively. In chapter 8, "Byron as a Man," Zilberman concludes that Byron's selfless advocacy for Greek independence redeemed him from the excessive individualism and pride of his youth. Citing the passage quoted above in the introduction, in which Macaulay describes Byron as "a strange union of opposite extremes," Zilberman blames Byron's mother's own inconsistent personality, alternately doting and raging, as caused by her religious excesses, for Byron's problems. As he concludes the chapter:

> As a result of contemplating the world, Byron became a skeptic. In his work, the poet posed great questions, though he could never provide answers for them. He had laid out the responses contemplated at that time, but his own had not become definite or firm enough. His understanding grew more and more analytic, yet never reaching the point of synthesis. When home, Byron felt as though he was in the tumultuous domain of pure criticism. Only through complete skepticism was he able, finally, to counter his mother's foolishness: he had believed in prophecy and premonitions, and was anxious, really, that he might be overtaken by fright.

CHAPTER 3

> The author of *Childe Harold* had a loving nature, but he would be overcome by uncontrolled and grandiose wildness. He loved the sea and the mountains, and he really adored endless deserts when he saw them.
>
> This should not seem strange—Byron's esthetic accomplishments are restricted enough. He had no taste for architecture, painting or sculpture; as for music, he was only interested in folk song, which had the least to do with art. (144–45)

Despite the fact that Byron's character was flawed, his work—as Zilberman argues in his ninth chapter, "Byron's Place in Literature"—is still significant because of its subjectivity and its universalism. Through the articulation of his own sorrow, Byron was able to express the pain of his contemporaries as well, conveying the spiritual disharmony of the time, while simultaneously exposing the "madness of the social order." Byron's gift lay in

> giving voice to new aspirations. He sang about freedom for oppressed people; he sang about their independence. The greatness of his poetry increased not only because he sang about them, but also because he struggled for those of whom he sang. Byron died physically in the struggle for Greek liberation; his personal success was destroyed in his struggle with English society. He had no specific political or religious outlook, and limited himself merely to denials. That is where his strength really lay, using the essential importance of his poetry for the spiritual and political development of his contemporaries. (152)

Basically, Byron had "the heart of a poet and the head of a scholar" (153). Because of his cosmopolitanism, Byron's influence spread throughout Europe, though contemporary Englishmen considered him an epicurean; still, he would gain popularity in the century after his death.

The most significant aspect of this Yiddish biography is the complete absence of any reference to the *Hebrew Melodies*. Probably related to this is the anomaly of numbering: chapter 5, "The Oriental Poems—Marriage," ends on page 86, and chapter 6, "A Voluntary Exile," begins on page 91.[12] Given the fact that there is no break of narrative, only missing pages, it would seem that the text was altered after Zilberman sent the manuscript to the printer and after the sixth chapter was set. There is nothing to indicate why the four pages are missing, or whether it was Zilberman or an editor/censor who decided to tamper with the text. Still, it seems hardly coincidental that the only work excluded from the biography is the one whose themes are religious and frequently associated with proto-Zionism.

Zilberman's only reference to the Jews comes in the form of a complaint at the end about the absence of Byronic texts in the Jewish canon: "In Jewish/Yiddish literature, deplorably, Byron's name is almost unknown. Besides *Cain,* it seems, there is nothing more. It is therefore a great injustice that work like *Childe Harold, Manfred,* and *Don Juan* have not yet entered our literature" (155). The only Jewish *Cain*s that predate Zilberman are the Hebrew translations by Yaakov Zevi (1851–52) and David Frishman (1900). Also, it is possible that Zilberman is using the word *yidisher* to signify the Yiddish language, but as far as I know, there were no Yiddish *Cain*s before the early 1920s, when this biography was published. Nathan Horowitz probably completed his *Cain* around 1925, and Abraham Asen first published his in 1928. Also, it seems odd that Zilberman would omit Bleicher's translations. Although the Yiddish *Childe Harold* was originally published more than a decade before Zilberman's biography, it was reprinted twice; and Bleicher's *Heaven and Earth* was issued in Kiev, a major Yiddish publishing center, only a few years before Zilberman's biography. Interesting, also, is the inclusion in the list of *Don Juan,* which was never to be translated, and the omission of *The Prisoner of Chillon,* which would be translated into Yiddish at least three times in the next decade. Not surprising is the omission of any reference to Jewish *Hebrew Melodies.*

Max (Mordechai) Hershman—Yiddishist Anarchism

The third Byronist to contribute to the Yiddishist identity is Max (Mordechai) Hershman.[13] Born in Berditchev, Ukraine, in 1891, to a poor working family, he attended *ḥeder* (religious school) until he was thirteen, when he began to study secular subjects as well. In 1910, he moved to Warsaw, where he worked as a private teacher while, as a nonresidential student, he was able to complete gymnasium. From Warsaw, Hershman went to London, in 1911, where he began to write, first in Russian, but later back to Yiddish and then in English. He contributed to *Di tseit, Di post,* and *Di frei yidishe tribune un lashon un leben* as well as to *Drum Africa* in Johannesburg. In Yiddish, Hershman published two collections of poems: *Erd-veh* (Cry of the Earth, 1924) and *Bereshis* (*In the Beginning,* 1954). In English, he published a collection of essays and aphorisms, *Bound and Shackled* (1944). In addition to Byron's *The Prisoner of Chillon,* Hershman also translated a French poem by Francois Coppeé, both published in 1922 in *Der arbayter fraynd* (The

Worker's Friend), a monthly and weekly that was published, with interruptions, from July 15, 1885, to January 1932.[14] As the first avowedly Socialist Yiddish periodical in the world, it ran as a Socialist and anarchist journal until 1892, after which *Der arbayter fraynd* was strictly anarchist. Therefore, it seems logical to infer that its Yiddish readers would respond to Hershman's *The Prisoner of Chillon* as if it were a quasi-allegorical statement of anarchism.

Conventionally, *The Prisoner of Chillon* is read from a psychological perspective, as detailing the mental deterioration that occurs when someone is isolated from other human beings and from nature.[15] The theme was historically inspired, Byron having conceived of the poem after he and Shelley visited Chillon Castle on June 25, 1816.[16] François Bonivard was imprisoned in Chillon Castle between 1530 and 1536, though Byron's account strays from historical fact: Bonivard was one of three, not six, brothers; and his father was likely not a martyr to faith. Still, Shelley, in his *History of a Six Weeks' Tour,* said that the castle was "a monument of man's tyrannical inhumanity to man."[17]

If the physical scene was influenced by Chillon Castle, the psychological exploration might have been influenced by Hamlet's bantering with Rosencrantz and Guildenstern in the second scene of act 2, where Shakespeare's prince laments "that this goodly frame, the earth, seems to me a sterile promontory," or, in Bonivard's words:

> And mine has been the fate of those
> To whom the goodly earth and air
> Are bann'd, and barr'd—forbidden fare.
>   *(ll. 8–10)*

Hamlet's interchange begins with his expostulation that "Denmark's a prison," a notion he further explains: "for there is nothing either good or bad, but thinking makes it so: to me it is a prison. . . . O God, I could be bounded in a nut-shell and count myself a king of infinite space, were it not that I have bad dreams." The conversation culminates with Hamlet's description of man, as introduced by the phrase Byron adapts for his poem:

> [T]his goodly frame, the earth, seems to me a sterile promontory; this most excellent canopy, the air, look you, this brave o'erhanging firmament, this majestical roof fretted with golden fire, why, it appears no other thing to me than a foul and pestilent congregation of vapors. What a piece of work is a man! how noble in reason! how infinite in faculty! in form and moving how

express and admirable! in action how like an angel! in apprehension how like a god! the beauty of the world! the paragon of animals! And yet, to me, what is this quintessence of dust? man delights not me.[18]

In *Paradise Lost,* Satan echoes Hamlet—"myself am Hell" (4:75)—Milton associating the state of psychological despair with the loss of faith. Byron, in turn, ironizes Milton's morality, attributing the despair to the physical effects of religious persecution: "But this was for my father's faith / I suffered chains and courted death" (ll. 11–12). Bonivard could have remained free had he renounced his faith; but because he retains it, he is imprisoned.

Psychologically, although Bonivard himself is the only source of information the reader has, and although he has clearly been affected by years of isolation, still, even filtering the account through his impaired mind, one can trace his attitude toward his altered mental capacity as he effectively actualizes Hamlet's assertion that he could find himself "king of infinite space," though Bonivard chooses ultimately to remain self-confined in his prison. In this respect, *The Prisoner of Chillon* seems to echo Wordsworth's sonnet "Nuns Fret Not at Their Convent's Narrow Room." Although the emphasis on the number seven—"We were seven—who now are one" (l. 17)—literally echoes Wordsworth's "We Are Seven," with the ominous shift into the past tense, Byron's poem figuratively suggests the sonnet whose speaker notes that "In truth the prison, unto which we doom / Ourselves, no prison is" (ll. 8–9). Thus, despite the fact that a psychological interpretation might yield the conclusion that Bonivard is mad, a more figurative reading suggests that the poem can be interpreted allegorically, with Bonivard as a kind of everyman, and his narrative symbolizing the inward journey to an elevated state of consciousness, one in which, as in "Nuns Fret Not," the mind, "hav[ing] felt the weight of too much liberty, / Should find brief solace" (ll. 13–14) in self-imposed confinement. Thus, the sense-deprivation in part 9 of *The Prisoner of Chillon* might project a kind of death/rebirth, in which Bonivard transcends the empirical mode of thought to an intuitive plane of consciousness:

> What next befell me then and there
> I know not well—I never knew—
> First came the loss of light, and air,
> And then of darkness too:
> I had no thought, no feeling—none—
> *(ll. 231–35)*

CHAPTER 3

His ultimate, apparently insane, choice to remain in prison, even after having been freed from his physical bonds, might imply a spiritual regeneration:

> We were all inmates of one place,
> And I, the monarch of each race,
> Had power to kill—yet, strange to tell!
> In quiet we had learn'd to dwell
> . . .
> My very chains and I grew friends,
> So much a long communion tends
> To make us what we are:—even I
> Regain'd my freedom with a sigh.
> (*ll. 385–88, 391–94*)

The appearance of *The Prisoner of Chillon* in an ideologically anarchist periodical suggests the formation of an entirely different interpretive community, one less concerned about Bonivard's relationship with nature or his state of mind than with the social institutions that compromised his existence in the first place. Basically, anarchism is the rejection of any authoritarian government in favor of voluntary associations as the means of satisfying natural social tendencies.[19] Although the term *anarchism* was not used until the mid-nineteenth century, the concept itself was first delineated by Gerrard Winstanley (1609–60?), whose pamphlet *The New Law of Righteousness* (1649) advocated a rational form of Christianity to replace the corrupting nature of authority. Winstanley was followed at the end of the next century by William Godwin (1756–1836). In the first edition of his *Enquiry concerning Political Justice* (1793), Godwin argued against revolution. Attributing criminal behavior to the laws that favored property owners, Godwin posited the theory that formal institutions would eventually manifest their own corrupt nature and disintegrate, to be replaced by voluntary social associations. It should also be noted that Shelley, Byron's traveling companion during the visit to Chillon Castle, was an admirer of Godwin's theories, so it would not be far-fetched to suspect that Bonivard's history provoked a discussion of anarchism that found its way into the poem. Regardless of Byron's actual intention, *The Prisoner of Chillon*, when viewed from the perspective of anarchism, can be read as an allegorical representation of Godwin's theory, parts 1–9 demonstrating the deleterious effects of government, and parts 10–14 the regenerative powers of voluntary associations.

The first part establishes the central conflict of the poem and of anarchism itself: the fear by those in authority that spiritual beliefs will undermine the power of laws designed to protect material property. Having been imprisoned for maintaining his "father's faith," Bonivard is the emblem of the idealist whose very existence is a beacon for those who reject government, his having been summarily thrown into a dungeon indicating the lengths authorities will go to in order to retain their hegemony. The description of the prison can be interpreted as the law that protects property rights at the expense of the human spirit, with its "seven pillars of gothic mold" (l. 27), the "seven columns, massy and grey" (l. 29),

> And in each pillar there is a ring,
> And in each ring there is a chain;
> That iron is a cankering thing,
> For in these limbs its teeth remain,
> With marks that will not wear away,
> Till I have done with this new day.
>   (ll. 36–41)

Byron inverts Plato's allegory of the cave to suggest the intellectual effects of imprisonment. At the end of part 2, Bonivard explains that he has "not seen the sun so rise / For years" (ll. 43–44), and at the beginning of part 3, he echoes Plato's description of people who are chained down in such a way that they cannot turn around to see the fire behind them:

> They chain'd us each to a column stone,
> And we were three—yet, each alone,
> We could not move a single pace,
> We could not see each other's face,
> But with that pale and livid light
> That made us strangers in our sight.
>   (ll. 48–53)

The result is that "Our voices took a dreary tone, / An echo of the dungeon-stone, / . . . They never sounded like our own" (ll. 63–64, 68). The implication is that Bonivard's government has used Plato as a negative instructor. If the philosopher's purpose was to demonstrate how to liberate oneself from mental bonds, Bonivard's captors use the allegory as a guide for imposing those bonds on freethinkers. The result is that prisoners lose touch with who they really are.

Bonivard's brothers symbolize the qualities of the freethinker—youthful idealism and mature strength—their deaths suggesting the aging process, on the one hand, and the human values that are sacrificed to property laws, on the other. The result is a living death: "A double dungeon wall and wave / Have made—and like a living grave" (ll. 113–14). Absent human contact, Bonivard dies spiritually:

> First came the loss of light, and air,
> And then of darkness too:
> I had no thought, no feeling—none—
> Among the stones I stood a stone.
>   *(ll. 233–36)*

Almost in fulfillment of Godwin's theory, Bonivard's spiritual death yields the death of the law as well, the last half of the poem reflecting the rebirth of both. As Bonivard's spirit regenerates—"But then by dull degrees came back / My senses to their wonted track" (ll. 259–60)—his jailors no longer feel bound by the law: "A kind of change came in my fate, / My keepers grew compassionate" (ll. 300–1), not repairing the chain that had broken. He then successively is able to walk around his cell, climb up to the barred window, and look out at nature. Still imprisoned, however, Bonivard must return,

> And when I did descend again,
> The darkness of my dim abode
> Fell on me as a heavy load;
>   *(ll. 359–61)*

until, finally, "At last men came to set me free" (l. 370).

No longer constrained by the law, Bonivard can freely choose how to live, and he opts to remain in his cell: "These heavy walls to me had grown / A hermitage—and all my own!" (ll. 377–78). At this point, the physical circumstances of his existence are less important than the fact of his freedom. Now, he is free to establish the kind of voluntary relationship advocated by the anarchists:

> In quiet we had learn'd to dwell,
> Nor slew I of my subjects one,
> What Sovereign hath so little done?
>   *(ll. 388–90)*

Still, there are aftereffects to the experience:

> My very chains and I grew friends,
> So much a long communion tends
> To make us what we are:—even I
> Regain'd my freedom with a sigh.
> *(ll. 391–94)*

Westernized Yiddishism

To the Yiddishists, Bonivard's sigh would resonate with the *Golus* movement as a whole, history undermining the need for, and practicality of, a nation within a nation, with Yiddish as its official language. Starting with the pogroms of 1880–81 and spurred on by later pogroms as well as the Russian Revolution, Jews migrated to the West, where more advanced laws and customs afforded them the means to gain legal citizenship and social integration, not to mention educational opportunities to provide material security. As a result, there was no need for *Golus*-Nationalism in the western Diasporas, so in the middle phase, Yiddishists explored alternative modes by which to retain their Yiddish identity, some again turning to Byron for help in articulating the problem.

Nathan Horowitz—Religious Apologetic

In addition to being the first Yiddish translator of the *Hebrew Melodies*, Nathan Horowitz is also noteworthy for being the only one to translate Byron into both Yiddish and Hebrew. As with so many of the other translators, not much specific information is available about Horowitz, but the little that is known suggests the possibility that his turn to Byron was part of an attempt to deal with a personal conflict that, originating in the contradiction between his religious upbringing and the appeal of secularism, seems to have resolved itself in a turn to the occult.[20] Born in Vilna in 1888, Horowitz, who spelled his name variously Hurvitsh and Horovits, attended the Slobodka Yeshiva. Founded in 1882 in conjunction with the Musar movement, the Slobodka Yeshiva was devoted to instilling a strict ethical education in conjunction with *halakhah,* Jewish law, a curriculum designed to counteract the secularizing forces—not least those of the Yiddishists—that drew

CHAPTER 3

Jews away from the religious authorities.[21] Horowitz left the *yeshiva* at the age of seventeen and moved to London where, from 1907 on, he published poetry, essays, and translations into English under his own name as well as under pseudonyms such as N. Rahlin and Y. Funk. He eventually became a reporter and proofreader for the London *Yiddish Express*. Between 1911 and 1929, Horowitz published several books in England: *Ferzen—Funm bavusten perzishen dikhter Omar Khayyam* (Verses by the Famous Persian Poet Omar Khayyam, 1911); *Treumen un gedanken* (Dreams and Thoughts, 1924), with an introduction by the author's editor from the *Yiddish Express*, Harry Sperling; *Tefilah un shirah* (Prayers and Songs: Poems, 1926); *Himnen un fantazien* (Hymns and Fantasies: Melodies Founded on Hebrew Liturgy, 1927); *Idishe tefilos un pitutim* (English title: *The Hebrew Liturgy* [A Study], 1929). In English, Horowitz published *Sabbath and Other Tales* (1926) and *Souls in Exile: A Play in Four Acts* (1928). He also wrote *King Saul: Biblical Play in Seven Acts* (1933). Horowitz died in Vilna in 1934, largely forgotten by the Anglo-Jewish community.

Most of Horowitz's Byronic work was in Yiddish, including translations of the *Hebrew Melodies* (1925), *Manfred* (1925?), and *Cain* (1925?);[22] but in 1930, he published his only Hebrew work, a new translation of the *Hebrew Melodies*. This return to Byron seems to have been part of an attempt to resolve personal conflicts. The pre-Byron material conveys a sense of ambivalence; his early translation of *Omar Khayyam*, completed in 1911, several years after his arrival in London, might be indicative of an imaginative, if not actual, excursion into Epicureanism, the Persian poem being the antithesis of the Musar movement. Following *Omar Khayyam*, Horowitz's adoption of pseudonyms and variant spellings of his name suggests an identity crisis, perhaps a reluctance to repudiate Musar entirely. Within this context, the specific references to Byron seem fairly unremarkable. First, the preface to the Yiddish *Hebrew Melodies*, in 1925:

> The good response which my first original book of poetry *Treumen un gedanken* received in literary circles encouraged me to issue a similar series of translated poems, namely *The Hebrew Melodies*, of Lord Byron.
>
> The translation, which was mentioned in *Jewish Chronicle* on the hundred-year anniversary of Byron, I now issue revised and improved.
>
> Byron, as is known, wrote the series of songs for his contemporary, the Jewish composer Mr. Nathan, who at that time had composed music for a famous vocalist. The music of Nathan can be found somewhere in the British Museum; it has not succeeded in the musical

world, but the series itself remained some of the most sublime lyrical poetry in world literature.

I took strict pains to retain the spirit of the poems, and therefore I hope I have been very ethical in respecting their esthetic value. (2)

Second, the author's note to the English translation of his *Sabbath and Other Tales* in 1926: "The good reception given in Anglo-Jewish literary circles to my Yiddish book of poems entitled 'Dreams and Thoughts' and my Yiddish rendering of Byron's 'Cain,' 'Manfred' and the 'Hebrew Melodies,' has prompted my friends to ask me also for some stories" (2). Finally, the introduction to the Hebrew *Hebrew Melodies,* in 1930:

The purpose of my work is to provide a translation of [songs of Israel] *Hebrew Melodies* of Lord Byron, that is, to show the love of Hebrew poetry and Hebrew songs by the English authority, rendered in clean and pure Hebrew.

I strove to make them in an appropriate style, beautiful and befitting. And my heart is happy in the thought that in my translation I met the need of the literature to be accessible. (2)

The only thing that stands out is the different purposes for the two versions of the *Hebrew Melodies*. Regarding the earlier Yiddish translation, Horowitz seems most interested in making Byron available for a Yiddish-reading public, hoping "to retain the spirit of the poems." Conversely, in the Hebrew translation, he seems less interested in the author's intention than in his own, using the English originals as the basis for a new Hebrew song cycle, written "in an appropriate style, beautiful and befitting."

The shifted emphasis seems to have resulted from a developing interest in Kabbalism. The most direct evidence available is from his publications: in 1924, *Treumen un gedanken,* with the subtitle "otherworldly songs"; and in 1927, *Himnen un fantazien.* Tellingly, the introduction to *Treumen un gedanken* was written by Harry Sperling, best known as the translator of the *Zohar* ([The Book of] Splendor)*,* the most mystical of kabbalistic texts.[23] The evolution of Horowitz's intellectual interests can be traced through the two Byron translations. The earlier version uses Hebrew to Judaize Byron, emphasizing the specifically biblical or religious connotations of the poems. In contrast, the Hebrew version, published five years later, contains an overlay of kabbalistic terminology that, to the adept, effectively transforms Byron's secular Christian originals into a collection of Jewish mystical poems. A comparative analysis of three poems—"She Walks in Beauty," "The Harp the Monarch Minstrel Swept," and "On Jordan's Banks"—can suggest the differences between the two translations.[24]

The most notable characteristic of the Yiddish translation is the juxtaposition of selected Hebrew terminology against a Germanic-appearing linguistic base.[25] Though Horowitz was publishing after the *Golus*-Nationalist movement had waned, his Yiddish appears to be that of the hard-liners, with a Germanic vocabulary and spelling. Emphasizing its Germanic base, Horowitz frequently introduces the letter *he* in places where it is not usually found, either in normative or phonetic spelling of Yiddish, apparently to evoke, at least visually, a Germanic context. To take an obvious example, in the word for "beauty," in "She Walks in Beauty," he approximates the German umlaut by using an *ayin-he* combination instead of the more usual Yiddish spelling *yod-yod*. The Yiddish word is usually *sheinheit*, the German is Schönheit, and Horowitz's is *shehnheit*. Similarly, in his version of the line "The smiles that win" (l. 15), Horowitz rejects the normative Yiddish *nemt*, from the root *nemen*, "attract, excite," in favor of the German *nehmt*. (It should be noted that Horowitz changes Byron's plural to the singular "smile.")

Within this Germanic context, the few Hebrew words stand out. In "She Walks in Beauty," there is only one, *ḥen*, "grace," in Byron's "nameless grace" (l. 8). Significantly, in choosing the Hebrew term, Horowitz rejects the more common German cognate *gnad*, "grace, favor." As the only Hebrew term in the poem, the word *ḥen* seems deliberately to associate the poem with the religious concept of grace, suggesting, as had Rabener before him, an association between Byron's abstraction and the Shekhinah, a connection Horowitz would exploit more fully in his Hebrew version.

Even more evocative, the four Hebrew words in "The Harp the Monarch Minstrel Swept" associate Byron's poem about musical inspiration with Jewish messianism. According to Jewish tradition, the Messiah, a descendant of King David, will have the mission of restoring the Jews to their homeland in Jerusalem. While Byron refrains from naming David until the end of the first stanza, Horowitz identifies the "monarch minstrel" in his title and first line, using the Hebrew *melekh* rather than the Germanic *konig*. Similarly, Horowitz changes Byron's "tone"—"That felt not, fired not to the tone" (l. 9)—to "song," not the Germanic *lider*, however, but the Hebrew *shirah*, which not only rhymes with *lireh*, "lyre," but, more significantly, connotes a religious song. Still, Horowitz differentiates Byron's *shirah* from the psalms of David, which are specifically identified through the Hebrew root *zmr*. The third Hebrew word is *boreh*, "creator." In the first two lines of the second stanza, Byron praises the theme of the harp's song: "It told the triumphs of our King, / It wafted glory to our God" (ll. 11–12). Emphasizing the Jewish differentiation between God and his Messiah, Horowitz replaces Byron's metaphor God/King with a literal reference to God; but in selecting the word *boreh*, he ties the poem in with Genesis, whose first line—"In the beginning God created the heaven and earth"—contains the same root, *bara*, "he created." The last word, *neugen*, is based on the Yiddish *nigun*, "melody, tune," itself derived from the Hebrew root *nagan*, "to play a musical instrument." Most usually, the word refers to the traditional tunes used for chanting the Bible in religious services. In translating Byron's "The cedars bow, the mountains nod; / Its sound aspired to heaven and there abode!" (ll. 14–15), Horowitz has "The cedars and mountains bow and play [a musical instrument] / It is a heavenly attainment." Through the root *nagan*, Horowitz brings all of these meanings to bear—the harp as an instrument whose music, like the chanting of the Bible, can help bring the Messiah.

In the last example, Horowitz uses four Hebrew words in his Yiddish "On Jordan's Banks" to ironize Byron's theme of a lost Zion. In translating Byron's second line—"On Sion's hill the False One's votaries pray,"—Horowitz uses the Hebrew word for "pray," *mispalel*. While it is true that virtually all of the Yiddish words for "pray" derive from Hebrew, that is, from Jewish religious contexts, it is also true that Horowitz frequently Yiddishizes German terminology. The Jewish prayer to the idols who have usurped "Sion's hill" suggests a violation of the covenant, though it could be either the Jews who have turned away from their God, or God who has abandoned his people. The ambivalence is underscored by the next Hebrew term, *luaḥ*, "tablet," the word used in Exodus (24:12) for the stone on which, in Byron's words, "thy finger scorch'd the tablet stone!" (l. 5). Next, for living creatures in "none living see and not expire" (l. 8), Horowitz again uses the root *bara*, in this case the plural *baru'im*. Finally, for "Oh! in the lightning let thy glance appear" (l. 9), Horowitz adds thunder to the lightning, choosing the root *kol*, thus alluding as well to the voice of God: "In thunders and in lightnings again, again make manifest yourself!" Together, these four words combine to suggest the spiritual dilemma of one who blames God for not making himself manifest but, at the same time, prays that he would.

If in the Yiddish version, the Hebrew words Judaize Byron's lyrics, in the Hebrew version, kabbalistic terminology transforms them into esoteric poems. Believing that in addition to the surface meanings, mystical texts contain levels of meaning inaccessible to the ordinary reader, Kabbalists, among other techniques, derive hidden significations of particular words through which they interweave entirely different readings for a given text. So, too, with Horowitz's Hebrew translation of the *Hebrew Melodies*. While to the general reader, they can be seen to represent Byron's lyrics, to the adept, the profusion of kabbalistic terminology implies mystical significations.[26]

In the first poem, whose title is rendered as "She Is Modest Walking in Beauty," Horowitz develops the earlier intuition that the subject of Byron's poem is the Shekhinah. In addition to her exoteric identification as the female spirit of the Godhead, esoterically the Shekhinah is described as the female counterpart of the Godhead, whose presence constitutes his true unity. At the initial fault, she is said to have gone into exile and will be redeemed only at the final restoration of the cosmos. The Shekhinah, also identified as the mystical community of Israel, is the tenth Sefirah, divine emanation; and her passive manifestation is the *avir*, the divine ether.

Horowitz's Hebrew translation of "She Walks in Beauty" contains at least a half dozen specifically kabbalistic terms that underscore the association of the poem's subject with the Shekhinah. In the second line, Horowitz renders Byron's "Of cloudless climes and starry skies" as "In the air are no clouds or stars in the firmament." He specifically transforms Byron's "climes" into the kabbalistic ether, *avir*; and for Byron's "skies," he uses the word from Genesis 1:6, "firmament," *rakiya*, the term that is used kabbalistically to denote the second heaven, location of the cosmic foundation, which is resplendent with divine radiation. Next, Horowitz transforms Byron's third line, "And all that's best of dark and light," into "And the best of darkness and splendor from exile." The word for "splendor," *zohar*, is the title of the most mystical kabbalistic text; and *goleh*, "exile," refers to the exile of the Shekhinah. Later, in line 10, he uses the word *hod*, name of the eighth divine emanation, generally translated as the "divine glory"; and in line 13, he describes the "brightness" of her brow with the word *bahir*, title of another kabbalistic text.[27]

Along the same lines, Horowitz's Hebrew translation of Byron's "The Harp the Monarch Minstrel Swept" mystifies the concept of messianism. Omitting any reference to the historical King David, this version, entitled "The Poetic King," evokes the Jewish concept of the Messiah, the Hebrew word *mashiaḥ*, "messiah," appearing at the beginning of each stanza: in the second line—"In front of his faithful servants, in the Messiah of the righteous God," in contrast to Byron's "The King of men, the loved of Heaven"; and in the eleventh—"All of his songs told about the brilliance of the Messiah," as opposed to the original "It told the triumphs of our King." Horowitz's version hinges on the word *tevel*, with which he concludes both stanzas of the poem. As seen in the discussion of Rabener's version of *Darkness*, *tevel*, often generalized to mean "world," is kabbalistically associated with the upper earth, and is the location of the earthly paradise where, according to some Kabbalists, souls that have been purified through the process of *gilgul*, transmigration, wait until the final restoration. By having each stanza end at the upper paradise, Horowitz uses Byron's poem to create an image of *gilgul*.

The first stanza refers to the physical experience of hearing the harp's music, its effect being to "hallow the holy in weeping" (Byron: "Which Music hallow'd while she wept," l. 3), enabling fallen souls to rise: "And it provided good ascent for all who are contemptible and low" (Byron: "It gave them virtues not their own," l. 7). The result, as Byron says at the end of the stanza, is that "David's lyre grew mightier than his throne!" Horowitz translates "throne" as "his chair in *tevel*," thus introducing the mystical concept of *tevel*, as upper earth, as well as ending the line, and stanza, with the word *tevel*. In the next stanza, he emphasizes the mystical properties of the harp's music. On the first line, "All of his songs told about the brilliance of the Messiah" (Byron: "It told the triumphs of our King," l. 11), Horowitz uses the Hebrew *siprah*, for "told," the same root used for Sefirah, divine emanation. Then, in the next line, he includes the sixth Sefirah, *tiferet*, "divine beauty": "And compliments to God that are uplifting beautiful." In the next to the last line, for "sounds that seem as from above," Horowitz uses the phrase *bat kol*, "daughter of the voice," one source of mystical knowing. And in contrast to Byron, whose "In dreams that day's broad light can not remove" implies that the only way to apprehend the *bat kol* is through dreams, Horowitz ends with "the light is not of this world!" repeating the root *tevel* to imply that, contrary to Byron's belief, it is possible to achieve the level of earthly paradise. Thus, the Hebrew translation implies that the harp can be the vehicle through which consciousness can be elevated to higher levels of thought.

Finally, there is enough kabbalistic terminology in Horowitz's Hebrew translation of "On Jordan's Banks" to justify reading Byron's proto-Zionist allegorically, as a mystical vision of the exile of the Shekhinah. In translating "There—where thy shadow to thy people shone!" (l. 6), Horowitz uses the phrase *zel Shaddai*, *zel* literally meaning "shadow," though kabbalistically interpreted as the external projection of the inner identity; and Shaddai is a name of God. In the seventh line, he uses the root *tiferet,* the sixth Sefirah, "divine beauty," to render "Thy glory shrouded in its garb of fire." For the next, "Thyself—none living see and not expire!" (l. 8), Horowitz's "In honor, the strength which is not seen by the flesh of life!" contains the word *gevurah,* "power" or "strength," one identification of the fifth Sefirah.

In the last stanza, Byron's prayer that the exile end, Horowitz is much more explicit. First, his translation of "Sweep from his shiver'd hand the oppressor's spear!" (l. 10) contains a series of ambiguous words that could conceivably be seen as a rendition of Byron's line or, with a little mystical prodding, could represent what might be interpreted as the real kabbalistic truth behind the English. Taken in order, the first word, *ha'ever,* could mean "past tense," "the region beyond" (either physical or mystical), and is also a possible source of the word *Hebrew.* The second word, *ha-ḥerev,* could be "desolation" or "sword." Next, *mezukat,* is an adjectival form of either "distress" or "support." This is followed by *be-torat, be* a prefix meaning "in" or "of," and *torat,* genetive form of "instruction, teaching," or the Jewish term for the Pentateuch. Finally, *sheḥakim* could mean either "pulverized" or "heavenly." To a Kabbalist, any or all of the possible permutations and combinations could have mystical significance. Finally, though, Horowitz's last line is explicitly kabbalistic. Instead of Byron's "How long thy temple worshipless, Oh God?" (l. 12), he has: "Until when will your jubilee be desolated by the absence of your Shekhinah?" The word *yovel,* "jubilee," refers to the "Great Jubilee," the belief that the cosmos comprises a series of seven seven-thousand-year cycles of existence (*shemittot*), at the end of which everything will be reabsorbed into *binah,* the third of the divine emanations. Most significantly, Horowitz concludes his version with the word Shekhinah. Kabbalistically, Byron's "How long thy temple worshipless, Oh God?" (l. 12) would be interpreted as the exile of the Shekhinah; Horowitz simply makes the inference explicit.

Abraham Asen—American Yiddishism

Horowitz's American counterpart, Abraham Asen (1886–1958), was the most prolific of the Yiddish translators. Like his father before him, Asen combined his vocation—a dentist, in his case—with his intellectual pursuits, translator of the British and American classics into Yiddish.[28] Asen was born in Brest Litovsk into a prominent family, his maternal grandfather, Yehudah Leib Ruben, having been a founder of the northern Israeli colony Yesud ha-ma'alah in 1883.[29] Until the age of ten, Asen studied at *ḥeder* and under his father's tutelage, and then he attended the Jewish Lerer Institute of Vilna until the family moved to America in 1903. Starting in 1907, Asen began contributing translations to the New York press, a practice he continued even after becoming a dentist in 1912. In addition, Asen also wrote biographical sketches of major writers and composed poetry of his own. In 1921, he co-published the new journal *Der Humarist,* and starting in 1925, with Byron's *Prisoner of Chillon,* Asen published a number of Yiddish translations in book form, including *The Rubiyat of Omar Khayyam* (1926), Byron's *Hebrew Melodies* (1928), Tennyson's *Enoch Arden* (1930), Byron's *Cain* (1931), selected poems by Longfellow (1933), twenty-five poems by Walt Whitman (1934), twenty-five poems by Thomas Moore (1935), Shakespeare's *Sonnets* (1944), and *King Lear* (1947). He also translated into Yiddish Israel Herbert Levinthal's *Judaism: An Analysis and an Interpretation.*

An overview of his career as a translator suggests that Asen might be viewed as a paradigm of the American Yiddishist.[30] Most significant, he was not ideologically opposed to Zionism. When they left Europe, his family did choose to settle in New York rather than Palestine. Still, whether because of his grandfather's ties to Yesud ha-ma'alah, or possibly because of personal conviction, Asen seems to have avoided publishing in radical journals. He did contribute to the *Forvarts,* the dominant Yiddish newspaper, which originally espoused a staunch anti-Zionist ideology. However, by the time Asen began writing, the editorial policy had been modified to accommodate the more moderate attitudes of the New York Jewish community. Actually, he seems to have been drawn more to Labor Zionism, publishing in *Freiheit,* an organ of the Workers' Party of America; *Zekunft,* a publication of Yiddish-speaking branches of the Socialist Labor Party; and *Yidisher kemfer* (called *Yidisher Arbeter* between 1924 and 1931), a periodical dedicated to Labor Zionism. Rather than propaganda, Asen seems to have been more interested in literary quality, publishing in *Di feder,* a serious literary periodical, and in *Der oyfkum: Khoydesh zhurnal far literatur un kulturinyonim* (The Rise: Monthly Journal of Literature and Cultural Matters).

As with his attitude toward Zionism, Asen, who was active in the local Jewish community, seems also to have avoided the antireligious extremism of many of the original Yiddishists. The New York Jewish community was large and varied enough that local religious authorities never gained the kind of control that had been exerted in the pale of settlement. Therefore, Asen was able to combine his Yiddishist educational program with religion, actually publishing the biographical sketch, "Lord Byron: His Life and His Loves," in a newspaper with the explicitly religious section "From Shabbos to Shabbos."[31] Finally, his last book-length translation, published after the Holocaust and the establishment of the State of Israel, is a Yiddish translation "of a series of lectures delivered at the Friday night services of the Brooklyn Jewish Center during the seasons of 1932 and 1933," by Rabbi Israel H. Levinthal.[32]

In several ways, Asen's interest in Byron parallels that of Nathan Horowitz. Both turned to Byron in the mid-1920s, when the western Yiddishists were revising the focus of their educational program; both translated the Persian *Rubiyat of Omar Khayyam;* and both chose specifically to translate *Hebrew Melodies* and *Cain*. However, given their different backgrounds and interests, it seems likely that while Horowitz used Byron to facilitate his return to religion, Asen originally turned to Byron as a way to rationalize the apparent contradictions between his endorsement of Labor Zionism and the Yiddishist program of *Golus*-Nationalism.[33]

Asen's first move in this direction came in the introduction to his translation of *The Prisoner of Chillon*.[34] Removing the poem from the anarchist context into which Hershman had placed it, Asen transforms the Byronic hero into a combination of Labor Zionist/*Golus*-Nationalist, that is, one who finds it most expedient to wage the struggle for liberty in a self-imposed exile. In a brief, four-page biographical sketch, Asen presents Byron as the one honest man in a sea of hypocrisy, who, though achieving early success, found his acclaim less than satisfying: "But he was not satisfied, not with himself and not with the whole life." After his marriage ended, he fled his home because "[t]his Puritanical England had from this a new hot theme to shout about. And wicked tongues spoke a lot about things they knew little of" (6). Still, his self-imposed exile was salutary: "Separating from his wife and traveling from England in 1816 became a significant event in Byron's life and caused a deep change in his creativity. His despair and bitterness stimulated his imagination." Joining the Greek cause, Byron went to Italy in the summer of 1823, where "he encountered noise and chaos. But in the course of three months he was successful in bringing about great order." Unfortunately, by then "[h]is health, though, had grown worse and worse" (7), and he died. In the conclusion, Byron is presented as the personification of Asen's own version of a Yiddishist:

> Byron was famous more for the strength of his personality than his greatness as a poet. Byron became the spiritual mirror of the time. In his work he evoked the restless spirit of his generation. The struggle

against religion and tyranny was then new. Although he was a lord, Byron was a courageous revolutionary and freedom fighter. In his first speech to the English Parliament, he defended the English worker.

His poem *The Prisoner of Chillon* is important for the suffering which the hero of freedom was forced to undergo in his time.

Although Byron personally was not imprisoned in a jail, still he had himself undergone the same sorrow as the prisoner of Chillon. For Byron, as for the spirit of freedom, the whole world is a prison. Despite the fact that being a lord, Byron could obtain virtually whatever he wanted—still, he suffered more like a common citizen. He suffered from the world that misunderstood him. His fame extended beyond his time. But despite all misunderstandings, he had with his energetic personality exerted a great influence on the freedom movement of his own generation and also on later generations. (8)

On the one hand, Byron resembled the Labor Zionist, struggling against religious hypocrisy and political tyranny, using his power to defend the workingman. On the other, he was like the diasporean, recognizing that "the whole world is a prison" for those who lack liberty. Most of all, though, regardless of how it might have seemed at the time, his contribution to freedom, like all others, reverberated for later generations.

Chaim Gutman—Yiddish Zionism

Consolidating the presentation of Byron as a Labor Zionist, Asen ceded the introduction of his next translation, the book *Cain* (it had originally been published in serial form), to satirist and theater critic Chaim Gutman (1887–1961).[35] Descended from a wealthy and noble family, Gutman, born in Minsk, attended *ḥeder* until the age of thirteen, while also studying Russian and German with private teachers; later, he studied in Pinsk and Vilna. At the end of 1904, Gutman emigrated to America, where he stayed with relatives in New Jersey and attended Woodbine's Baron Hirsh Agriculture School. After a year, he left New Jersey for New York to work in a paper factory. At this time, he began publishing poetry, first in *Frei arbiter shtime,* and then in the daily *Forvarts* and weekly *Der arbeiter.* In 1909, he began contributing to *Der kibitzer,* a comic weekly, under his pen name Der Lebediker (the Lively One). From that time on, he was a continual presence in the Yiddish press, writing essays, satires, and drama reviews. Although a humorist, Gutman was known for the philosophical-moral themes of his work.

CHAPTER 3

To Gutman, the primary advantage of a Yiddish translation of Byron's *Cain* is that it enables the reader to explore a biblical theme without any "preaching": "The danger of writing in Yiddish a discourse on biblical themes is—the preaching. About the Bible and around the Bible one had by us so much sermonizing—as if at once one moves himself only to a theme that springs from a sermon" (3).

Gutman praises Byron for finding in Cain the first rebel, dreamer, and philosopher who, seeing "the great injustice which hovers over creation," asks: "And where is the explanation from God to man?" (4). Reinterpreting the Fall, Cain questions why one should be grateful to a God who would trap man.

Gutman sees Lucifer as a tragic figure "who wanted to be a god but couldn't," and who therefore became "the seducer and the seduced." After showing Cain the wonders of the world, Lucifer challenges him to liberate himself intellectually: "Doubt and believe and be not punished!" (6). Returning home with "strong love of life, hate towards death and rebellion," Cain, the brother who had such an aversion to spilling blood, ironically "brought the first death to the world" (6, 8).

Gutman concludes by reiterating his thesis, that the English play enables the reader to avoid the preaching endemic to a Jewish text: "Byron's *Cain* is not like an explanation on a bit of *Ḥumash*. Only an explanation from a poet, philosopher and rebel. A poet knew by nature not to suffer about sin. From a fratricide Byron made a judgment against God. And Cain the accused became an accuser" (8). According to Gutman, the two brothers are not merely individuals but character types. The Abelist is passively obedient, exhibiting "subservience and flattery to the creator of the world." In contrast, the Cainist "is the eternal rebel against a God who seeks sacrifices from men. And only blood sacrifices. The fruits of the earth don't smell good to his nostrils. He is the ancient God-tyrant, eternally bloodthirsty: a God who only wants altars and prayers and flattery and bribery." Gutman concludes: "Byron's *Cain* is a great work that probes the deepest secrets of our existence. It is a unique work, reflecting a man who himself knows the pain of seeking the secret of life but is unable to find it" (9). Thus the character Cain, like his literary creator, represents the image of the Jewish activist of 1931, the rebel who rejects the passive obedience inculcated by the religious sermons on the biblical story.

Two years after *Cain* was published in book form, the world changed radically, the Nazis seizing power in 1933. Consistent with the times, in 1934 Asen published "Lord Byron—His Life and His Loves," an expanded biographical sketch of Byron, this time transforming the British Romantic hero into an icon of Jewish pride and stoicism in the face of growing anti-Semitism.[36] In his introduction, Asen relates his subject to his audience, suggesting that the British lord is a symbol of the Jew in general, the victim of Nazi Germany in particular. Asen begins:

> It is already a hundred years since Lord Byron (George Noel Gordon Byron) died, but the personality of the immortal poet still affects everyone with his charm on human fantasy. Lord Byron had with his poetic vision put forth a new color of the spirit of the European world. He created a pattern out of whole cloth, from passionate longing and pessimism, which became the literary voice of a whole century, inspiring Goethe and a whole school of romantic poets in Germany, as well as in other European countries.

Comparable to the Jewish people, Byron's importance is long lived and wide ranging, extending even to "Goethe and a whole school of romantic poets in Germany." In this way reminding his audience that Germany has a rich cultural history, Asen implies that the current troubles will pass.

The political and social disabilities imposed on the Jews in early Nazi Germany, then, might be symbolized by Byron's physical disability: "By the age of ten, he already appeared stoic, because of his pride. From the time of his birth, one of his feet was a little lame. This used to cause him physical and emotional suffering, but he never let this show. And the way he was as a child, he stayed his whole life." But rather than be defeated by his deformity, Byron exerted great effort to overcome its effects: "In body and in spirit, Byron strove to prepare himself for the struggle of life. For long hours each day he used to practice boxing, jumping, swimming, shooting, fencing with a sword, in order to achieve the appearance of physical strength or hardness. In this way, he also used to exercise his spiritual powers. For example, he used to deliberately make enemies in order to have someone to battle with." Most important, though,

> Byron was the poet of revolution, the lyrical heir of Rousseau's lesson about freedom and liberty having been corrupted by society. He despised the conventional ways of his class; he attacked all of the social concepts of his period. And because he was a lord, his business establishments challenged many interesting and astonishing things. His life was a scandal of the highest grade. All of the other lords exerted themselves to conceal scandals which they committed. Byron, however, with

the combination of individual freedom and a compulsion to dramatize events in his life, actually strove to reveal the noisy and stormy business publicly.

Hating hypocrisy, Byron fought against a corrupt society that indicted him rather than confront its own flaws. Similarly, the implication seems to be, the Jews in the early 1930s must resist Nazism and "reveal the noisy and stormy business publicly."

As indicated by its title, the essay itself focuses on the loves of Byron. While sexual escapades are generally not a subject for the Yiddish press, it seems that figuratively, the liaisons, as the source of Byron's rejection by the dominant community, might symbolize alterity, the trait that differentiates a minority, like the Jews, from those who, in turn, discriminate against the *other*. Thus, just as Byron must choose between hypocritical conformity and self-exile, so, too, throughout history, have the Jews been forced to choose between conversion and the Diaspora.

Yiddishism and the Holocaust

Asen's essay initiates the turn to be taken in the last phase of *Golus*-Nationalism. As the realities of Nazi Germany and the Holocaust became known, Jews in the Diaspora sought ways of dealing with the threat, some indicting the antireligious ideology of the Yiddishist movement; in contrast, others, acknowledging the horrors of the Nazis, fought back, like Byron in the Greek War of Independence, demonstrating their moral integrity in the face of inevitable doom.

Shelomo Simon—Hebraic Yiddishism

Among Byronists, the return to a religious sense of identity was foreshadowed by Shelomo (Solomon) Simon (1895–1970).[37] A decade younger than Asen, Simon was born in a *shtetl* in the area of Minsk, where his father was a shoemaker and his mother a baker. He studied at traditional *yeshivas* until 1913, when he moved to New York. There, he worked variously as an operator and a presser at clothing factories, and in 1916, he became active in relief organizations for war victims. In 1918, he enlisted in the U.S. Army. Simon later became a Hebrew teacher, and from 1920 to 1924, he studied dentistry at New York University. Simon was also active in New York Jewish organizations, from 1926 working at the Sholem Aleichem Folk Institute, where from 1940 to 1955 he served variously as vice president and president; and from 1947 to 1950, Simon was vice president of the Jewish Ethical Society in New York. In addition, beginning in 1930, he served as the director of the Chavera Tanakh in Brooklyn.

As an educator, Simon focused primarily on children's literature and ethics in his writing. His career began in 1912 with an epigram in a Hebrew children's journal; and once in America, he published his first work, "A griner italianer," in *Tag* (1915); and from then through 1951, he was a regular contributor to various journals, especially *Kinder zhournal,* for which he served as assistant editor from 1948 to 1951. Simon was a prolific contributor to the international Yiddish press, publishing in Buenos Aires, Warsaw, Paris, and Mexico, as well as New York, writing essays on dentistry, children's stories, and the Bible, and editing and annotating a study Bible. Finally, he also published some polemical articles about Yiddish literature.

Simon's review article of Asen's translation of *Cain,* published in 1932, initiates the revised view that would effectively end the relationship between Byron and the Yiddishists.[38] Ignoring the earlier interpretation of Byron as the skeptical iconoclast who challenged the authority of organized religion, Simon argues that the problem with the Yiddish translation is that it removes Byron from the religious context, and for that reason, David Frishman's admittedly inferior (in Simon's opinion) Hebrew translation is preferable to Asen's superior Yiddish.[39] Basing his reasoning on the problem of heteroglossia, that is, the difficulty of retaining connotations when translating from one language to another, Simon begins by providing his own associations with the word for *table* in three languages—Yiddish, Hebrew, and English:

> Here is the example of a word—table. I express the word in three languages, Yiddish, Hebrew, and English.
> Yiddish—*tisch.*
> I see a long room, whitewashed brown. On one side of the wall lies a canopy, on the second an oaken commode. In the middle of the room a long table painted red. The middle is white—the paint is chipped from much washing. Soon like this word—table—spoken out loud I see the red table soon. First then I strain myself to see other tables.
> Hebrew—*shulkhan.*
> A desert. Sand and sky. A wandering community. A *cohen gadol,* a breast plate and *ephod*—a cap, silver bells—sound from pipes, a scent

> from sacrifices. A tent—a dwelling place, bedecked with all kinds of colorful skin—badger skins. A long golden table. On it this holy bread [*broit*]—the bread [*lekhem*] apparently. Around the table are four poles. English—table.
>
> A kitchen, the smell of cooking, a gas oven—a high hanging cupboard filled with glassware. Near the kitchen wall a small white porcelain table. (11)

Whether deliberately or even consciously, Simon ignores the obvious, that these impressions reflect his own experiences, that he associates Yiddish with life in the *shtetl*, Hebrew with the Bible and religious rituals, and English with contemporary New York. Not surprisingly, although the text is written in Yiddish, the vocabulary for the Hebrew scene is Hebraic. Thus, while the point about heteroglossia is well taken, its implications are circular, that Hebrew reminds him of the Bible.

In any case, this demonstration becomes the basis for Simon's denunciation of Asen's translation of *Cain*. He does recognize its merits:

> One can cite half-scores. One can say that Dr. Asen gave over the contents of *Cain* truly—one can feel in the translation Byron's great swaying and rhythm. One can hear in the Yiddish text the eternal sins of men against God, against nature. One hears in the lines the eternal protest of the inexcusable thinking animal, which the venerable Creator created in a capricious hour. We hear Byron's outcry in one of the lines against the strong Jehovah who made and destroyed worlds—to amuse himself. The weak man mismeasured himself against God and wasn't afraid, and therefore one sees the human immortality. (12)

Unfortunately, Simon claims, Yiddish is incapable of conveying the religiosity of Byron's original: "Dr. Asen's translation is more accurate than Frishman's, the rhythm is the same as in Byron. David Frishman ignored in the whole book Byron's rhythm. Yet Frishman's translation sounds better than Asen's, because Frishman translated *Cain* into Hebrew. Holy, holy—sounds biblical exactly like 'all hail'; let the heavens be lit—doesn't resonate. There is no canonical biblical issue in Yiddish and not a biblical style in Yiddish" (11). The problem, actually, is that the times have changed: "It is in truth a loss, that the book did not appear thirty years ago, when we all were in the epicurean mode and thought that there was someone to lash out against" (12).

Thus Simon implies his view of the Yiddishist movement: in the beginning of the twentieth century, left-wing radicals could use Byron as the symbol of their antireligious ideology; now, however, Jews have progressed far beyond their earlier Epicureanism; therefore, Yiddish should remain the province of the masses, while theological texts should be discussed in Hebrew, that is, among an intellectual elite. Through this argument, Simon places Byron within a strictly religious context. The allusion to events yet to unfold, unfortunately, is prescient.

Given the circumstances, it seems likely that Asen's biographical sketch, in which he applauds Byron's pride and stoicism, was a response to both Simon's review and events in Germany. Two years later, an unsigned essay, "Byron and Jews: On the 150th Birthday of Lord George Byron," appeared.[40] While brief, the essay is significant for portraying Byron as a conventionally religious person who had a special affection for the Jews. The author begins by implying a commonality between Byron's struggle in his times and the Jews' in theirs, opening with a reference to how the French Revolution, which had begun with the proclamation of freedom, equality, and brotherhood, had been subverted "in the period when freedom was tread on by the despotism of Napoleon and then through the 'Holy Alliance,' and the equality and brotherhood of people were swallowed up in the blood of the Napoleonic wars. It is therefore not news that Byron's love of freedom was mixed with a degree of pessimism." Just as in his time, Byron was forced to struggle against Napoleonism, now the Jews must oppose Nazism.

In discussing Byron's importance to the Jews, the author focuses on the *Hebrew Melodies*, noting that they were based on Byron's knowledge of the Bible: "Byron was an avid *ḥasid* and a distinguished savant of *Tanakh*." The diction here is significant, the word *ḥasid* meaning "pious man," and *Tanakh*, the Hebrew acronym for the three sections of the Jewish Bible: *Torah* (the Pentateuch), *Nevi'im* (prophets), and *Ketuvim* (other writings). On the basis of the unknown author's reading of the *Hebrew Melodies*, which were written in collaboration with the man identified as "his friend Isaac Nathan," Byron is transformed into a conventionally religious man. Furthermore, the author continues, as a collection, the *Hebrew Melodies* enabled Byron to redeem himself by focusing on "tragical moments from Jewish history, accentuating with a special sympathy the steadfastness of the Jews in their national misfortune, their faithfulness to *Yiddishkeit* and the people, their soul of patriotic betrayals." Most of all, "[t]he *Hebrew Melodies* defends not only the political equality of the Jewish people in itself and the real dogma of the self-sustaining Jewish culture, but is, in addition, written in a beautiful form." Surveying the different translations of the *Hebrew Melodies* in Hebrew and Yiddish, the author also mentions Bleicher's as well as Asen's.[41]

Shea Tenenbaum—Anti-Nazi Protectionism

The next essayist, Shea Tenenbaum (1910–89), placing *Cain* within the context of the Holocaust, inverts the earlier interpretations of the play, seeing Cain, the Byronic hero, as but a romanticized version of one man who kills another. Born in the village of Bobrinik in the area of Lublin, Poland, Tenenbaum went with his parents, at the time of World War I, to Kariv, and later Pilaf, where he studied in *ḥeder* and a Yiddish folk school.[42] Eventually traveling to Belgium, Tenenbaum, who was trained as a typesetter, worked in publishing and then at a textile factory. Contracting tuberculosis in 1934, he went to America for treatment at a Denver sanitarium and eventually settled in New York. A prolific writer, Tenenbaum debuted with a poem, "My Beloved," in the Antwerp *Di yidishe presse* (1926), and after that issued numerous poems, stories, brief essays, longer articles, and novels in a variety of publications.

In his essay "Lard beyrans tanus" (Lord Byron's Pretensions/Arguments; the Yiddish could mean either), Tenenbaum places *Cain* in the contemporary context to suggest that even though Cain's challenge to God might be emotionally satisfying, it has been undermined by historical reality. After quoting Lucifer's response to Adah's inquiry about where he lives—"Throughout all space" (1.1.546), Tenenbaum opens his essay with a description of the here and now:

> In the day of the greatest world sorrow—one wants to look around in the old books of the greatest poets, especially from the British poets, which had with deep thought and feeling enveloped the whole world. The British poets were very true about *Tanakh*, and given their universal problems, the *Tanakh* made a deep impression on their souls. Of those great poets who had studied the old book of books, Byron had in his youth also energetically read the Greek dramatists and the question of fate was at the center of his work and the drama of his life.[43]

He then rehearses the conventional reading of the characterization of God in the play: "In his dramatic mystery *Cain*—God appears like the culprit of all sorrows of humanity, the liar, swindler, and above all dishonorable. God took pleasure in introducing to men a temptation, and then punishing men for not being able to withstand the temptation." From this perspective, the rebellion of "Cain in his pride and oppression, in his revolutionary feeling, in superhuman courage" is thus justified in his attempt to subvert a tyrant.

Tenenbaum makes the conventional link between the character and his creator, between Cain and Byron:

> Cain is Byron himself. Byron's dramatic poems were undermined—because all heroes were Byron himself. Byron—with his volcanic suffering, revolutionary courage, proud solitude, intense pain, exhibitionistic nature, oppressed by rubbish and scandal, brutal egoist and greater dramatist—Byron is embodied in all of his heroes. His sad and bitter sardonic jest, his hopeful pessimism, and his dramatic form. . . . His spectacular personality, stronger individualism, regal bearing, Don Juan–like smile, and the appearance of a dark outlaw. What are morality and constraint when applied to the fantasies and the spirit of the European poet? And in this way, it seems to me, "Cain" is Byron himself.

He then rehearses Byron's adventures, culminating in the Greek rebellion against the Turks: "He felt like he must crown his work—with the same deed. And deed led to death. The hero must die for the sake of truth. England's kinglike son—must die traveling in the old Greek land, for which he had in his youth such strong love."

Arguing from the perspective of the Holocaust, however, Tenenbaum finds the Byronic hero naive: "And such read we now—again *Cain*. It is the old drama with the old arguments against God. Atheism is already now old. And a God, amusing himself and making and destroying worlds—is already also a naive conception. This assumption about the universe—through the coming of the future—this belongs to the inflated pretenses of former authors who don't have anything else." If Cain had criticized Abel's passivity, Tenenbaum faults Cain for his arrogance, and in so doing associates the Byronic superhero with the Nazi *Übermensch,* and by contrast, the naive Abel with the Jewish victims:

> We return again to the beginning, and when we read one moment the newspaper—about the slaughter of a million men . . . and in the second moment the pages of *Cain*—about the unrighteousness which rules the earth—it seems that one is reading a historical work but the guilt from the unhappiness of our time—doesn't seem to be from God—only from the man Cain himself. Cain who must murder the

tranquil, naive, joyful Abel, a servant to his God, loyal, peaceful, living his life with his comfortable naiveté.

Tenenbaum concludes by raising the same question that Cain had asked—Why do people die? "Man in our time—is crazy, because death is natural, given us by God—to him we have already gotten used to enough. Why do good people bring us sorrow and death—this we cannot understand." But far from being a literary posture, Tenenbaum's question is motivated by historical urgency.

Moisei Khashtshevatski—Yiddish Communism

The story of the Yiddish Byronists begins and ends with ideologues who, like Byron himself, attempt to actualize the Byronic hero: Ezekiel Bleicher returned to the Soviet Union after the revolution; and Moisei Khashtshevatski (1897–1943) fought with the Soviets against the Nazis. Born in the Ukraine, Khashtshevatski was the son of a teacher in the local Talmud-Torah.[44] After studying in *ḥeder* and Talmud-Torah, in 1916 Khashtshevatski attended commerce school. In the last year of World War I and in the first year of the Russian Revolution, he studied at the Universities of Petrograd and Yekaterinburg, publishing, in 1918, his first poem. In 1921, he went to Kiev and from that time established his reputation as a true artist and contributor to Soviet-Yiddish literature. In the periodical literature from Kiev, Krakow, Minsk, and Moscow, Khashtshevatski published lyrics and ballads as well as translating poetry from other languages. Khashtshevatski was also a member of "Khaliastre" (Yiddish, "the Gang"), a post–World War I group of Yiddish expressionist and futurist poets centered in Warsaw; and he contributed to their second literary anthology in 1922.[45] For three years starting in 1923, he was a regular contributor to *Der emes,* the Yiddish Communist Party newspaper, and he was an active participant in Soviet social-political life. Shortly after the outbreak of the Soviet-Nazi war in 1941, Khashtshevatski volunteered to mobilize in the Red Army. He fought in the worst battles of that period and died on the front. According to Yiddish writer Samuel Niger, "Moshe Khashtshevatski, it seems to me, was the most sincere of all Yiddish poets in the Ukraine. His lyric was born with an older, more wrinkled, quiet lyrical soul; he wasn't ashamed and said that it was old, broken, wrinkled and sorrowful in the quiet. He didn't make any excuse and assumed no heroic or demagogic poses. He did not storm the earth and didn't know any heroics about the empty blue heavens."[46]

Strongly influenced by Byron in his own poetry, in 1937 Khashtshevatski both wrote a seven-canto epic, *Lenin*, and translated *The Prisoner of Chillon*. After that, during the Second World War, Khashtshevatski returned to Jewish themes, viewing the conflict with Hitler in the kind of biblical terms that, had he lived, would have been punished by the Communists after the war. When viewed from this perspective, Khashtshevatski's *Prisoner of Chillon*, which was published at the height of the anti-Semitic purges, can be read as a secularized lament by one who had joined the movement dedicated to acculturating Jews for the Soviet Union only to see his fellow travelers purged by the Communist Party he had devoted his adult life toward building.[47] If Byron literally places his poem within a religious context—"But this was for my father's faith / I suffered chains and courted death" (ll. 11–12)—Khashtshevatski makes it socialistic: "I have for my father's liberation struggle / Paid with chains and death-demands."[48] Figuratively, the cause of the imprisonment is membership in the Bund, the organization that was established for the purpose of gaining for the Jews full citizenship in the Soviet Union. Ironically, it is membership in that very organization that led to the deaths of so many Jews. Still, like Byron in Greece, Khashtshevatski found himself in the impossible position of one who, though no longer believing in the efficacy of his cause, still feels compelled to see it through. Consequently, his translation of the liberation scene is faithful to Byron's:

> At last men came to set me free,
>   I ask'd not why, and reck'd not where,
> It was at length the same to me,
> Fettered or fetterless to be,
>   I learn'd to love despair.
>   *(ll. 370–74)*

Thus, it seems in character that a few years later, when the Germans invaded the Soviet Union, Khashtshevatski would enlist.

As a group, the Yiddishists seem to have shared a closer affinity to Byron than did the *maskilim*. Though this movement, too, would eventually fail, the attempt to establish a form of *Golus*-Nationalism paralleled Byron's own effort to create a home in a geographically undefined exile where he, too, could generate his own identity, independent of the controlling religious establishment. In addition to secularism, a significant component of their respective identities was freedom fighting, an actual attempt to liberate people from various forms of bondage; and just as Byron fought for Greek independence, so, too, did Yiddishists fight for their own. Finally, comparable to the meaninglessness of Byron's final illness, the Nazis eliminated Yiddishism as a movement, destroying most of its European cultural centers. Still, as will be seen in the next chapter, the Jewish Byronists would survive in the Zionist movement.

CHAPTER 4

Byron and the Zionists

In contrast to the Yiddishists, many of whom were *Golus*-Nationalists, the secular Hebraists tended to be Zionists. After the pogroms of 1880–81, when central and eastern European Jews acknowledged what appeared to be the reality that they never would be fully assimilated into their dominant communities, a number of them turned emotionally, if not physically, toward Jerusalem, where they placed their hopes for a homeland. At first, they were spiritual Zionists who wanted to implement their idealistic values in Palestine. Later, however, with the consolidation of political Zionism as a movement, then with the Balfour Declaration, and finally, with the Holocaust, many Jews sought an internationally recognized state in the area. Nationalistic aspirations introduced an entirely new Jewish sense of identity. Starting with the earliest immigrants, the newcomers for the most part regretted their diasporean roots, and resented the control that had been asserted by the religious, who emphasized Talmudic learning and advocated passive obedience to established authority. In contrast, *sabras,* technically, native-born Israelis, tended to be secularists, rejecting the values of the Diaspora while privileging physical prowess and active pragmatism, though in the process, it would eventually be argued, compromising the moral authority that had been used to justify establishing the state in the first place.

Generally speaking, the Yiddish Byronists reflected the Yiddishist ideology as it evolved from Zhitlowsky through the Holocaust. In contrast, the Hebraists tended to use Byron as a counterweight, translating the British poet in conjunction with a call for moderation against the hard-liners who dominated the Zionist movement from the 1897 Congress through statehood. The first three, who began writing in the pre-Balfour period, used Byron to express the need to retain traditional Jewish values. The earliest of these, Solomon Mandelkern, published a bilingual edition of the *Hebrew Melodies*. Best viewed as a transitional figure, Mandelkern was born too late to participate fully in the Haskalah, though too early to be active in Herzl's movement. The next Hebraist, David Frishman, translated *Cain, Manfred,* and *Heaven and Earth,* and wrote an extensive introductory essay on *Cain,* all in support of Aḥad Ha'Am's position that the Jews had to develop intellectually before even considering the possibility of statehood. Finally, Isaac Loeb Baruch, whose translations of *The Prisoner of Chillon* (published twice, the second time with revisions) and *Mazeppa* span the time period during which he decided to emigrate from eastern Europe to Palestine, uses Byron as a means of focusing on the relationship between the Diaspora and Zionism.

The last four Byronists all dealt with the complications attendant on statehood. During the Holocaust, Jacob Orland produced another bilingual edition of the *Hebrew Melodies*, this one published in 1944, to suggest that cooperation with the British might help pave the way to statehood. After him, the other three Byronists, all publishing after 1948, confronted the complications that resulted from statehood: Moshe Giyora's translation of Harold's farewell to England can be read as questioning the extreme antidiasporean views of the new Israeli identity; Shmuel Friedman's translation of the *Hebrew Melodies* seems to imply that Israelis lost touch with their moral compass after the invasion of Lebanon in 1982; and Michael Desheh's essay on Byron's life and the composition of the *Hebrew Melodies,* appended to Friedman's translation, posits the British poet as the figure of a revised Israeli identity, one that balanced out militarism with the traditional values of intellectualism and ethics.

Palestinian Period

Solomon Mandelkern—Enlightened Mysticism

As the last of the eastern *maskilim* and the first of the Zionists, Solomon Mandelkern (1846–1902) can best be viewed as a man out of his time.[1] Born in Mlynow and orphaned by his father's premature death, Mandelkern was raised by his maternal grandfather, a follower of Ḥasid Menahem Mendel of Kotzk. At sixteen, Mandelkern, who was already married, began writing poetry, a violation for which he was sent away to Dubnow, where he became part of the *maskilic* community. At nineteen, he divorced his Ḥasidic wife and began studying Judaica at the rabbinical seminaries of Vilna and Zhitomir, as well as Semitic languages at the University of St. Petersburg. Like many of the eastern *maskilim,* Mandelkern served as a government-appointed rabbi, specifically in Odessa from 1873 to 1880. A fairly prolific writer, he produced a three-volume Hebrew history of Russia (1875) for the Society for the Promotion of Culture among the Jews of Russia; original poetry, notably *Bat Sheva* (1866); an anthology of original poetry and translations, *Shirei sefat ever* (1882–1901); and translations of Hebrew poetry into German and Russian, as well as German poetry into Hebrew. His major opus was *Heikhal ha-kodesh* (1896), still the most comprehensive Bible concordance available. Mandelkern's Hebrew translation of the *Hebrew Melodies* was published in 1890.[2]

There are probably two major reasons why, despite his prolific literary accomplishments, Mandelkern is pretty much forgotten, except as the compiler of the Bible concordance. First, as Meyer Waxman notes, Mandelkern wrote most of his poetry in the post-Haskalah period, after the younger poets began to eclipse writers of the older generation.[3] In addition, he seems to have been a less than honorable man. Disliking Alexander Zederbaum, editor of the Hebrew periodical *Ha-Meliz,* Mandelkern submitted a false report of a blood libel in Bessarabia. When the truth was discovered, the journal, having printed the false report, was forced to cease publication, and Mandelkern had to leave Russia, living out his life unhappily as an exile from his home. Settling in Leipzig, he translated Abraham Mapu's Hebrew poetry into German, though without mentioning the original author's name. In contrast to many *maskilim,* Mandelkern was a Zionist, early on sympathizing with the Ḥovevei Zion, and later attending the first Zionist Congress in 1897. In 1899, he traveled to the United States to solicit buyers for his concordance. Mandelkern was attracted to the theory and practice of spiritualism, and in his later life, he suffered mental illness.

By the time Mandelkern published his translation of the *Hebrew Melodies,* the culture wars that had dominated Hebraists in the mid-nineteenth century had pretty much been resolved. The introduction of secular literature written by non-Jews was no longer a matter of controversy, nor was there any need to be overly concerned about the religious implications of a given text. Instead, as this, the first bilingual edition suggests, the emphasis now was on *aliyah* and the concomitant need for diasporan Jews to learn Hebrew.

CHAPTER 4

To start with the end of the book, Mandelkern says in his advertisement that he hopes his bilingual edition will be used as a text for university students:

> [Shirei sefat-ever]
> HEBREW POEMS
> (with vowel points)
> of
> Dr. S. Mandelkern . . .
>
> These poems have been most favorably reviewed by the press both for their contents and purity of biblical language. They are also to be recommended to Universities for exercises in reading Hebrew.

Given the fact that the notice is in English, it would appear that Mandelkern expected a predominantly Anglophone audience, that the projected students would be British or American Jews studying Hebrew. For this reason, it can be inferred, he dedicated the volume to Leon Lewisohn, Esq., an Anglo-Jewish philanthropist, whom Mandelkern identifies as "[t]he Ardent lover of the Hebrew language."

Next is a bilingual dedicatory poem, both in English—

> Ah, would some angel deign to shew me grace,
> And lend my pen his own seraphic fire,
> So that my verse be worthy deemed a place
> Beside the Bard's who struck the Hebrew lyre!

and in Hebrew—

> Let fly from his wings who gives and causes me joy
> One of the holy angels, possessor of six wings
> As often as will come to me in spirit and awaken me
> To write in a book songs of Zion and Jerusalem!

The verses are conventional invocations for inspiration—in both of them, Mandelkern prays to an angel. The content of the inspiration differs, however. In the English version, Mandelkern seems to be placing himself on the same level as Byron and the biblical David, praying that his translation merit "a place / Beside the Bard's who struck the Hebrew lyre!" In contrast, the Hebrew verse focuses on the content, "songs of Zion and Jerusalem." The fact that he would bring the focus onto himself—"my verse"—indicates some confidence that the Anglophone audience would be unfamiliar with his earlier disgrace; in contrast, the Hebrew version's emphasis on "Zion and Jerusalem" introduces the Zionist ideology in place of what might be a reminder to a more knowing audience of who he was.

As with his biography, the Hebrew translations evince the ambivalence of a *maskilic* project produced by a biblical scholar with a Ḥasidic background; that is, Mandelkern transforms Byron's secular lyrics into a text capable of supporting the kind of polysemous exegesis applied to the Bible. In the title of the collection, *Shirei yeshurun*, Mandelkern expands the signification of Byron's "Hebrew" beyond its biblical and linguistic associations. By using *yeshurun*, which literally means "the righteous people," Mandelkern figuratively includes all of the people of Israel, the Jews. For his substantive, he selects *shir-ei*, based on the root *shir*, meaning "poem, song," with the suffix *ei* indicating the genitive, "songs of." Thus, the collection could suggest the full range of connotations for poems or songs associated with the Jews, through any number of historical, allegorical, or mystical levels of interpretation.

The title of the first poem, "She Walks in Beauty," underscores Mandelkern's polysemous intentions.[4] By choosing "Shulamit" as the name for his version of a poem about Anne Beatrix, Mandelkern associates Byron's encomium to female beauty with the "beloved" in the Song of Songs (in Hebrew, *Shir ha-shirim*; 7:1[6:13]). As one of the most heavily interpreted figures in the Bible, Shulamit has been identified historically as Abishag, the woman brought to King David in his old age (1 Kings 1:1–4), interpreted allegorically as the people of Israel, and associated mystically with the Shekhinah. The text itself is punctuated by terms that elevate the reading beyond the literal level. The second word, *tifartah*, associates her physical beauty with the "divine glory," the root, as already mentioned in the discussions of Rabener and Horowitz, signifying variously physical beauty, symbolic splendor, or the sixth divine emanation, "divine beauty or glory." The ending *ah* is the genetive, indicating that she, the Shulamit, embodies the range of beauty from the profane to the sacred. The second word of the second line is *bahir*, an allusion to the *Sefer ha-Bahir*.

Along the same lines, Mandelkern implies that Byron's third and fourth lines—"And all that's best of dark and bright / Meet in her aspect and her eyes"—can mean that the woman signifies physical beauty or embodies the divine majesty. On the literal level, Mandelkern attributes to the woman the symmetrical values of conventional beauty: "Shadow of delight and brightness together in value / On the majesty of her face her eyes are suitably joined together." The word for shadow, *ẓel,* is part of a pun based on the biblical word "image," *ẓelem* (from Genesis 1:26: "Let us make man in our image, after our likeness"), and *ẓel,* "shadow," the ethereal body of the *ẓelem*. In this reading, the woman's beauty would be the external manifestation of her essential nature. The second word of the fourth line, *hod,* is the eighth emanation, signifying "majesty." Mandelkern chooses to render Byron's "Meet in her aspect" with the root *ta'am,* "couple together, conform," a word also used in Canticles. The last word of the line, *ḥubaru,* derives from a root meaning "to be united" or "spell, charm," among other possibilities. Mandelkern concludes the first stanza with "The pleasures of Eden compared to these would surely be lacking," the word *eden* signifying the Garden of Eden, as well as "pleasure, delight, time, period, hitherto." Considering the fact that Mandelkern is best known for his linguistic studies, especially the Bible concordance, it seems plausible to infer that the polysemy is fully intentional, and that his translation of Byron's lyrics, while amenable to a superficial reading, are also designed to lead one to higher levels of interpretation.

On the biographical level, Mandelkern's early Ḥasidic background and later affinity for spiritualism are consistent with the overlay of mysticism in his translation of Byron's lyrics. Historically, though, the publication of this first bilingual translation of the *Hebrew Melodies* initiates the transition from Haskalah to Zionism. Explicitly suggesting that his bilingual translation be used as a text for Hebrew-language courses, Mandelkern obviously did not fear opposition to his introducing secular literature into the culture. Yet the biblical orientation of the language locates the translation in the pre-Zionist period, before the political movement consolidated, and before linguists moved Hebrew beyond its biblical roots, transforming it into an instrument capable of modern discourse.

David Frishman—Independent Intellectualism

Both the most prolific of the spiritual Zionists and the most well known of the Jewish Byronists, David Frishman (1859–1922) is also the most overt in his use of the Byronic materials for the construction of a new Jewish identity. In addition to translating *Cain, Manfred,* and *Heaven and Earth,* he wrote a thirty-seven-page essay, appended to the 1900 publication of the Hebrew *Cain,* in which he explicitly transforms the Byronic hero—in both its biographical and literary manifestations—into building blocks of the new Jewish identity.[5]

Born in Poland in 1859 to a traditional family that nevertheless approved of the Haskalah, Frishman received a secular education that included European literature in addition to his conventional religious training.[6] Considered a prodigy, at the age of fifteen Frishman began publishing lyrics and short stories, and as an adult he became a major figure in the Jewish press, writing literary criticism and translating texts from other languages. Although he preferred Hebrew, he also wrote in Yiddish, and as both editor and publisher of various journals, Frishman was a major intellectual force in the period between the pogroms of the 1880s and World War I; since then, however, his influence has been diminished, in part because he advocated spiritual rather than political Zionism, refusing to incorporate Zionist ideology into his writing. Consequently, as political Zionism gained strength in the years after 1897, Frishman became increasingly marginalized, essentially because he agreed with Ahad Ha'Am that as a movement, political Zionism was spiritually deficient, and therefore incapable of creating a new Jewish identity. Since his death in 1922, Frishman's value to Jewish culture has been practically erased, and there are virtually no scholarly materials in English dealing with this once-central figure.[7]

Refusing to affiliate himself with any particular party or movement, Frishman was an isolated intellectual who argued, according to Waxman, that the essential identity of the Jew "consists in the special sense of righteousness of the Jews or better still, in their inability as a group to wrong their fellow-men, on a large scale."[8] Possessed of a "zeal for genuineness and individuality," Frishman wrote about the nobility of ordinary men and women who confront the conflict between the active individualism of personal desire and the passive conformity of social obligation, and in that moment of conflict, reveal the innate nobility of their character. In this way, Frishman effectively converted the characteristics of the Byronic hero—the superior individual whose depth of feeling isolated him from his community, and often his land—into the Jewish everyman, whose innate qualities of intellectual elitism and moral integrity isolated him from the other nations of the world.

Consistent with his own work, Frishman uses his critical essay on *Cain* to transform both the poet and his main character from the Byronic hero and his fictional representation into manifestations of the Jewish everyman. Specifically, he divides his thirty-seven-page essay into two major portions. In the frame, consisting of the first nine and the last three pages, Frishman discusses the intellectual and moral commonality between himself and Byron, portraying them both as skeptical intellectuals who oppose the mindless pressure to silence uncomfortable questions; then, in the central portion of the essay, he interprets the character Cain as Byron's—and his—literary incarnation.

In the introduction, Frishman conflates Byron's history with his own biography to prepare his audience for the transformation of Cain from a religious symbol of evil into the intellectual hero. He opens with an account of the play's original reception in 1821, bifurcating Byron's audience into British counterparts of the Jewish community of 1900, that is, into the know-nothing masses versus the isolated intellectuals capable of appreciating genius. As he says:

> [T]he priests who kept guard over the faith, the hypocrites and the imposters, all of them laid siege to all of the hiding places, and the people were astonished and afraid both of the holiness that the leaders wrapped themselves in, and of the leaders who wrapped themselves in these sheaves. Then, thousands of disputations and thousands of inquiries were written and published about this book; and interpreters interpreted and preachers preached thousands of sermons and bombast in the public houses and from the altar, that the spirit of atheism descended and consolidated and threatened the entire land. And the spirit spread from that land to all of the other European states to wherever word of the book was mentioned—and everyone who had a soul in his heart and a thought in his mind read and was fed and was feasted. (iii)

Having thus privileged the skeptical intellectual, Frishman then moves on to his own position within the Jewish community, relating his first encounter, as a child in *ḥeder*, with the biblical Cain. While the class studied, the young Frishman pondered over a number of questions that he felt were simply glossed over. In particular, he wondered why God would favor Abel over Cain, and he pitied, rather than condemned, the marked alienate:

> And my heart softened and contracted from great suffering in my bowels and the great awful curse that came to this unfortunate man: Here, he was cursed from the earth; here, he had to work by the sweat of his brow, and he could not receive any of the fruits or vegetables for food; here, he had to keep moving through the land, and where he slept one night, he could not lie the next; and here, for everyone who encountered him, it would be a kindness to send him forth; here, a sign would be placed on his brow: Could there be a greater misfortune than to be a marked man for all who encounter him?

> This was the picture of Cain which I saw in my imagination when I was a small boy. (v)

When he grew up, Frishman, in contrast to rabbinic tradition, began to view Cain as a symbol for the troubles that afflicted the Jewish people, blaming Cain not for having killed Abel, but for having passively accepted his punishment, without questioning its validity:

> And many times, I would say to myself: Ah! Cain! Do you know that you only did half of the job, and that you stood and did not comprehend it? Here is your brother whom you killed—but where did your spirit suddenly go, and why didn't your heart stay to comprehend and why didn't your heart stay to complete the job, to kill also your father and your mother, and after that also your soul, because then it would be complete, all species of man removed from the face of the earth, and there would be no more agitation and toil and trouble and pain and sorrowful events—and after that there would be quiet and peace and great silence for all eternity?! (vi)

Seeking solutions to the mystery of human suffering, Frishman studied the Bible and European literature, but remained dissatisfied until he read Byron's *Cain:* "[T]he best of them all—as I said—was Byron's *Cain*. In truth, there is no book in all of world literature which approaches this one on the subject of the suffering, nature, and distress of the heart, to reveal the great evil which has been called 'the eternal evil'" (vii). Reminding his Jewish readers of Byron's knowledge of the Bible, and listing thematically sympathetic works—the *Hebrew Melodies,* as well as *Heaven and Earth* (which he would later translate)—Frishman then portrays the biographical Byron in terms of a "Wandering Jew," unfairly exiled by a prejudiced mob:

> On April 25, 1816, Byron left England by boat, unfortunately never again to return, because England was suddenly for him detestable as a result of the lies, stupidity, and prejudices which the hypocrites and guardians of public morals attributed to him. There was no false accusation and no abomination, no transgression and no sin, no wickedness and no evil that they did not attribute falsely to him, until—because they had no recourse but to slander him, including the evil from all of the sins on the face of the earth—until they brought forward against him the accusation that he defiled his sister. (xi)

CHAPTER 4

Having thus prepared his audience, Frishman is able to devote the remainder of the essay to his analysis of the play.[9] Discussing the main characters, he begins with Cain, whom he considers "among the confirmed rebels, the skeptics; he loved truth and right, and hated lies and profanity with all of his restored strength." Frishman considers Adah, Cain's sister/wife, "a symbol of innocence and love, such that her love was ideal, more exalted than any there was, and she loved her man despite his bitterness and everything he would do, and never considered living away from him" (xvii). Finally, he interprets Lucifer (the morning star, etymologically), as

> a spirit—and this spirit was not like the Satan who came to test Job and to incite him and to drive him on, nor was he like the Satan whom Milton created for Adam, nor the Mephistopheles whom Goethe created for Faust. The excellent ancient accounts in many languages call Satan, the master of darkness, by the name Lucifer—for this reason: because he is the one who brings light. Perhaps Byron's Lucifer is actually a spirit that brings light. (xx)

As an illuminating spirit, Lucifer, according to Frishman, does not tempt Cain toward evil but only exposes the doubts that the character had had all along.

Turning to the first murder, Frishman says that Byron displaces sympathy away from Abel and toward Cain:

> And Abel, not fully understanding this outpouring of rage, added to the incitement . . . and Cain forgot his soul and did not know what he was doing, . . . and smote his brother to the ground. The murder was committed without Cain knowing that he had killed.
>
> There is nothing else like the fullness of this dramatic action that explains the ancient event. But this is a great thing full of wonderful irony that will never occur again: Cain, the man who feared death and who, upon hearing about it, trembled to the depths of his being, he, himself, with his own hands brought death to the midst of the earth for the first time! (xxxiii)

Frishman then completes the move started by Byron, associating Cain, the condemned alienate, with all of us:

> Cain is everyman in all of his virtues and all of his vices, in all of his assets and all of his deficiencies. That which happened to Cain will happen to anyone who thinks about and questions the last generation.

> Cain forms his reality without dogma. He is a man whose soul and eyes will be annihilated for whatever purpose, and who only within himself knows why, a man who repents for what he did, a man who excites pity and compassion, a man of anger and rage, who laughs and mocks and weeps and cries out from the intensity of his pain, and he passes in front of our eyes creating a standard of all emotion of the heart from the profane to the most profound. *Cain* is the wonderful tragedy and threat of the life of man. (xxxv)

His sin, therefore, resulted from his inability to "see the purpose for the creation of the world, . . . he could not find in the world the knowledge through which man would be able to understand all that was there, and he could not trust any of the promises made to him, and saw wrong in everything that occurred beneath the sun; and therefore he saw wrong also in the fate that was imposed on his father and on his own soul and on his brother, who did not perceive this" (xxxvi).

At the end of the essay, Frishman returns to the historical frame he had begun constructing in the beginning. As he concludes:

> This is Byron's strength: He combined all of our tears that were shed in the duration of a thousand generations, and placed them in the container we call eternity, and he revealed them to have originated from the depths of the fountain of the eyes of one of the first men of the first generation. I, who write these things, and you who read them, both of us, who are here descended from the first generation on the face of the earth, we need not in all of our moaning and groaning to add even a single cry or another tear which is not already found in Cain, this man who was one of the first ones. This is the mysterious strength of this drama that explodes from his mouth into our hearts, like no other: it is because suddenly, we see and perceive and understand what was told to us about the first man, that there was no escape or refuge from the eternal trouble he caused. (xxxvii–xxxviii)

Frishman's use of the first-person plural pronoun takes the essay full circle, from criticizing the English masses who condemned Byron to complimenting the Jewish intelligentsia, those readers who are capable of understanding why and how Byron's inversion of traditional biblical exegesis is important. Even more significant, the first-person plural pronoun unites Byron with the Jews, implying a commonality among the alienates, those who actively seek the deeper truths, despite institutional pressures to conform passively.

Cain served so readily as a vehicle for articulating Frishman's views in large part because Byron presented himself in ways consistent with Jewish beliefs. To begin with, he had purged his own Calvinism of those doctrines that would have been anathema to the Jews. He had excluded the beliefs, as explained by Truman Guy Steffan, that "[t]o dim-witted or corrupt man, the divine design was inexplicable, but a devout person was certain . . . that apparent evil would eventually turn out to be good"; also excised was the assumption that "salvation and immortality had been vicariously ensured by Christ's atonement, through his crucifixion for the sins of the whole world." In addition to their theological affinities, there were psychological similarities as well, the Byronic hero resembling the self-image of the Jewish intellectual. As Steffan describes the Byronic hero in *Cain*: "As a proud and restless seeker of knowledge, he was a nonconformist, at odds with his environment. He had no intellectual companion, no one who understood his problems or sympathized with his skepticism. . . . he paid the usual penalty for excessive and criminal individualism—rejection by nature and society." He was "a malcontent" who, "isolated from his fellow men, rebelled against authority and became an outcast."[10] Clearly, Frishman and Byron were both descendants of Spinoza, if not of Cain. Finally, that Frishman would translate *Manfred* and *Heaven and Earth* in 1922 suggests he felt an even broader identification with the Byronic hero after political Zionism had been institutionalized by the Balfour Declaration.

Isaac Loeb Baruch (Brocowitz)—Israeli Immigrationism

In both his biography and his Byron translations, Isaac Loeb Baruch (1874–1953) epitomizes the early Zionist who left eastern Europe for a new life in mandated Palestine.[11] Originally named Brocowitz, Baruch was born in Tourogen, Lithuania, where he studied in *ḥeder*. After attending the University of Berne, he became a Hebrew teacher, first in Kavna, and later, after moving to Tel Aviv in 1925, at Hertzlia High School from 1926 to 1936. Despite the scant biographical information available, there is evidence of Baruch's fairly extensive intellectual range. Beginning in Yiddish, he published in *Der yid* in 1900 "The Yiddish Type in World Literature"; and in the *Yiddishe familie* (1902), he published a translation of Heine's poem *R. Yehuda Ha-Levi*, together with a biography of Judah Ha-Levi. He also published Yiddish poems in *Hilf* (1903) and *Dos yidishe folk* (1906). Baruch's Hebrew work began with a lyric in *Aḥiasaf*, and ultimately included poems, stories, critical essays, and translations. His first Hebrew book, *Ozar safrut yisrael* (Treasury of Jewish Literature; 1913–25), a three-volume compilation of biblical and postbiblical literature, was followed by around a dozen other compilations of religious materials. Baruch was also a prolific translator, providing Hebrew versions of texts written originally in Yiddish, German, and English, including works by Sholem Asch, Hayim Nahman Bialik, Meir Goldschmidt, Solomon Ibn Gabirol, Johann Wolfgang von Goethe, Heinrich Heine, Axel Munthe, Ralph Waldo Emerson, John Galsworthy, Rudyard Kipling, and Jules Verne. As an educator, he translated Thomas Percy Nunn's *Ha-Hinukh* (Education: Its Data and First Principles; 1923); as a Zionist, Joseph Patai's biography *Hertsel* (1936); and as an Israeli under the British mandate, Gustaaf Johannes Renier's *Ha-kekhol ha-adam ha-anglim?* (English: Are They Human? 1940).

Baruch's two Byron publications—the early translation of *The Prisoner of Chillon* published in Ahad Ha'Am's journal *Ahiasaf* in 1900, and the combined *Prisoner of Chillon* and *Mazeppa* published in book form by Omanut in the mid-1920s—suggest that he was using Byron to help generate a new personal identity for himself, as well as a national identity for the Jewish people.[12] The earlier translation of *The Prisoner of Chillon* (the first of five different Jewish translations), published under his given name Y. L. Brocowitz, contains only the poem itself, without the three notes or the sonnet appended by Byron. Also, there is only a condensed summary of Byron's more extensive quotation from his source, Jean Sénebier's *Histoire littéraire de Genève* (1786); and the summary, along with an explanation of the meter, is typeset as a footnote to the title, though it is extensive enough to occupy most of the first page, there being room for only four lines of text. The book, in contrast, contains an eleven-page biographical introduction, followed by a somewhat revised version of *The Prisoner of Chillon*, with the Bonivard material printed as a preface, rather than footnote, and Byron's three notes included as endnotes. The second half of the book contains a translation of Byron's advertisement, which itself is a translation of Voltaire's *History of Charles XII* (1772), followed by the complete text of *Mazeppa*.

In the interim between the two publications, the world had changed radically. World War I and the Russian Revolution had been fought; the Jews had experienced the pogroms of 1904–6, and the Balfour Declaration had been signed. Personally, Baruch had moved from eastern Europe to the West (the first *Prisoner of Chillon* is signed Odessa, May 9, 1900; and the revised translation Hamburg, 1924); he had shortened his name from Brocowitz and was preparing to emigrate to Palestine. From the perspective of this context, it seems likely that Baruch coordinated the combination of his own life, the Byronic hero, and Byron himself all through the biblical figure Joseph.

Historically, the biblical story has been interpreted as the archetypal pattern of exile and return that is the basis of Zionism. Being favored by his father, Joseph incurs the jealousy of his brothers, who first throw him into a pit and then sell him into slavery in Egypt. Once there, he serves Potiphar faithfully, rebuffing the advances of his master's wife, who then falsely accuses him of sexual impropriety. Imprisoned, Joseph helps fellow inmates by interpreting their dreams. Some time later, when the Pharaoh has portentous dreams, Joseph interprets them, too, advising how the country can prepare for the impending hard times. Out of gratitude, he is rewarded and later, during the famine, he arranges to have his family brought to Egypt, where they and their descendants thrive for generations. In time, after their service to the Pharaoh has been forgotten, the Israelites are again enslaved and must, therefore, escape and return to Jerusalem. As a hero, Joseph embodies the characteristics of the new Jewish identity: he has intellectual superiority, being able to interpret dreams and plan for the future; and he has moral integrity, remaining loyal to his brothers and masters despite their treatment of him. From this perspective, Baruch's choice to translate *The Prisoner of Chillon* and *Mazeppa* suggests that the Byronic materials were part of an effort to consolidate the new Jewish identity.

The first publication, completed in Odessa in 1900, uses the Byronic material to project an image of the new secular Zionist. Key to this interpretation is the initial action of the Joseph material—the young boy being thrown into the pit—an image Baruch himself introduces through his summary of the Bonivard material and his translation of the first sixteen lines of the poem. In what is presented as a footnote to the title, whose subtitle, "A Fable," is deleted, Baruch transforms Bonivard from the Christian martyr into the new Jewish hero. In his summary, Baruch streamlines the narrative, omitting references to the specific religious conflict, patriotism, the betrayal by friends, and the catalogue of qualities possessed by his hero. What is left is the story of a man who, like Joseph, is imprisoned for principle, and who, upon his release, then seeks liberty for his people, striving to ensure their intellectual as well as their economic well-being.

Baruch uses his translation to support this new interpretation of Bonivard. In the original, Byron uses the first ten lines to depict the effects of imprisonment on his hero:

> My hair is grey, but not with years,
>   Nor grew it white
>   In a single night,
> As men's have grown from sudden fears:
> My limbs are bowed, though not with toil,
>   But rusted with a vile repose,
> For they have been a dungeon's spoil,
>   And mine has been the fate of those
> To whom the goodly earth and air
> Are bann'd, and barr'd—forbidden fare.
>   (ll. 1–10)

To contrast with Baruch's:

> My hair is [grown] white, but not from time
> Even not from a night of fear and trembling
> It became suddenly gray
> Like lots of hair turns like a demon in less than a day.
> Body crushed, but not from a yoke,
> It is bent from inactivity, the daughter of *sheol*.
> I was sentenced in perpetuity to dreadful imprisonment
> Bitter is my fate, it is the fate of a difficult day,
> That is without air and without a sliver of light
> To rot slowly in the pit.

In his version, Baruch changes the predicate of the sentence. Instead of the Shakespearean "goodly earth and air / Are bann'd and barr'd—forbidden fare," he uses a distinctly biblical style, characterized by a reduplicated syntax in which different forms of the same root are used within the same line—"Bitter is my fate, it is the fate of a difficult day." More significant is the complete change of the tenth line, from Byron's "Are bann'd, and barr'd—forbidden fare," in which Bonivard emphasizes what he is being deprived of, to "To rot slowly in the pit," which focuses on the current condition, culminating in the signifier *bor*, the word used in Genesis (37:22–29) for the "pit" into which Joseph's brothers threw him.

Although Baruch overtly associates his translation with the biblical Joseph, he deliberately complicates the religious implications of Byron's poem, as indicated in the next four lines:

CHAPTER 4

> But this was for my father's faith
> I suffered chains and courted death;
> That father perish'd at the stake
> For tenets he would not forsake.
>
> *(ll. 11–14)*

And Baruch:

> This for being a *nazar* of my father's faith
> I was oppressed imprisoned and greatly afflicted.
> My father on the tree of death suffered a bitter death,
> For the sake of his holy belief he didn't waver.

What stands out most in the Hebrew version is the equivocation over the cause of the imprisonment, the change from the explicit "this was for my father's faith," into the overdetermined and culturally charged Hebrew *nazar*, a choice that could conceivably redound back on the translator's own ambivalence about faith. As a verb, the root *nazar* can mean "to watch, guard," or "to observe, keep secret"; as a noun, it means "sprout, shoot," thus accurately rendering Byron's line into "This for being an observer of my father's faith," or "This for being a scion of my father's faith." However, the root *nazar* also means "to convert to Christianity." In this case, the line could indicate that Bonivard had abandoned, not observed his father's faith. The contradiction points to the dilemma of the early Zionists who were attempting to develop a secular Jewish identity. Historically, the Jews had survived because of their faith; yet, even nonbelievers had been oppressed for being Jewish. Having been published in Odessa in 1900, the translation suggests that communally, the Jews had to deal with the implications of their being "oppressed imprisoned and greatly afflicted," regardless of their attitude toward their "father's faith."

In the later publication, the juxtaposition of the revised *Prisoner of Chillon* with *Mazeppa* shifts the focus to the second point of contention in the new Jewish identity: geographical specificity. Baruch's move to Palestine entailed his leaving what had been his home in the Diaspora, where for generations Jews had insisted that despite their Zionist beliefs, they could still be loyal subjects to their country. In the new book, Baruch filters the Byronic materials through the Joseph archetype to shift the onus back away from the Jews and onto governments, like the Pharaoh's in later years, that failed to appreciate Jewish contributions to the commonweal.

Baruch implies the Joseph associations in the introductory biographical sketch, citing the false accusation of sexual impropriety—"His wife did not understand his spirit and nature, and his actions were unfamiliar to her"—for instigating an exile that would transform Byron into a kind of Joseph: a leader whose intellectual superiority provoked jealousy and slander, but whose moral integrity enabled him to retain his principles and led to his struggle for the liberation of others:

> Byron was one of the great poets of our world. It was a time when all European literature was subordinated to his slant ("Byronism"); however, because of their splendor and height, many of his works were smeared in the passage of days. Still, he had the stature of a giant, the spirit of one who creates like those of earlier generations, reaching the depths of the secret of creation, the depths of the order of the world, the depths of the concealed soul of man, not wavering even a small bit. He was the poet of the suffering of the world, the settler of the nihilism and shame of man, the herald of the liberty of the covenant, that he fought for to the last drop of his blood. The pessimism about and hatred of his works, that for his sake were his portion and defense in his time, none flowing except from the depth of deep love for all the crushed and insulted in the world. And from the depth of this perception of love, he spent a great portion of his wealth on deeds of charity and benevolence, participating in the war of Italian independence, and gave his soul for the liberation of the Greeks. (10)

Following the introduction is a slightly revised version of *The Prisoner of Chillon,* and a Hebrew *Mazeppa* that transforms Byron's eastern European hero into a figure of Joseph, himself being used as a figure of the political Zionist.

As an organic unit, the book depicts the means of generating the new Jewish identity. In the introduction, Baruch pays homage to the Jews' religious origins and then effusively praises Byron's *Hebrew Melodies* for their ability to speak to the Jewish soul, and *Cain* and *Heaven and Earth* for their biblical origins. Yet instead of translating any of those works, Baruch turns to *The Prisoner of Chillon* and *Mazeppa,* which together can be read as an allegory of the means by which to achieve the new Jewish identity: by leaving what has become imprisonment in the Diaspora for liberation in a new land.

The differences between the 1900 and 1920s versions of *The Prisoner of Chillon* suggest that more than simply changing his name, Baruch had strengthened his voice in the interim. To compare the first four lines of the two Hebrew versions to Byron's original:

> My hair is grey, but not with years,
>   Nor grew it white
>   In a single night,
>   As men's have grown from sudden fears.

Baruch's 1900 translation:

> My hair is [grown] white, but not from time
>   Even not from a night of fear and trembling
>   It became suddenly gray
>   Like lots of hair turns like a demon in less than a day.

The 1920s version:

> My hair [is that of an old man] gray—before its time
>   But not the son of a night because of trembling
>   It turned suddenly white like a night
>   Like many old ones from violence/havoc/devastation and anguish.

In the first version, Baruch provides as literal a translation as possible, given the differences between the two languages. The first line in the 1900 version reads: "Sa'ar-ei hilbin, akh lo me-et." Structurally, Hebrew is based primarily on three-letter roots that, through a series of internal changes and affixes, indicate syntax. In this example, *sa'ar* is the root for "hair," and *ei* is the suffix indicating first-person possessive, "my," meaning "my hairs." *Hilbin*, from the root *lbn*, "white," means literally "to turn white," and the last three words, "but not from time."

The second version, in contrast, reflects a much more secure speaker, not to mention more fully developed language. Now, Baruch seems confident enough to place Byron's poem within a more idiomatic Hebrew, characterized by an elliptical syntax that leaves grammatical choices open to the reader, there being only four words, and no active verb form: "Sa'ar-ei sav—be-terem et." Beginning with the same construct as that used in the earlier version, this one substitutes for the literal *hilbin*, "has turned white," *sav*, "gray, old, an old man," a word connected to the root *siv*, an internal change that indicates action, "to turn gray." In contrast to the English and the earlier Hebrew version, here Baruch is much more economical and direct, as underscored by the alliteration "sa'ar-ei sav." Similarly, as with biblical parallelism, the two words of the second member complement the first. *Be-terem* is also a construct, the root *terem* meaning "not yet, before," and *be* a prefix signifying "in, within, as in the condition of"; and *et* is the noun for "time, appointed time." As with the 1900 version, Baruch uses alliteration here, too, though with a shift from *s* to *t*. These changes are not substantive but stylistic, indicating that Baruch, while remaining faithful to his Byronic original, is integrating the poem more directly into his own Jewish culture.

An emendation at the end of the poem is consistent with the changes made at the beginning. In Byron's version:

> My very chains and I grew friends,
> So much a long communion tends
> To make us what we are:—even I
> Regain'd my freedom with a sigh.
>   (ll. 391–94)

Baruch's 1900:

> Mostly from custom to love and be friends
> The chains of the pit [*pir*] were made for me.
> Until because in my leaving, at the loss of the enemy
> From a close heart I sighed sadly.

Baruch's 1920s:

> Mostly from custom became dear to me
> The chains of my oppression:
> And in time I went forth from the house of the pit [*bor*]
> I sighed sadly at greeting liberty.

Significantly, in the 1900 version, Baruch uses the word *pir* for "chains of the pit." In the later version, he makes them the "chains of oppression," omitting the word *pir;* however, in the next line, when referring to Bonivard's regaining his freedom, Baruch has him leave the dungeon, using *bor*, the same root he had used in the beginning, the one that explicitly connects this Hebrew version of Byron's poem with the Joseph story. Thus, like Joseph, Bonivard/

Byron/Baruch is being released from captivity to begin a new, constructive life, like the one described in *Mazeppa*.

When read as a Jewish allegory, the Hebraized *Mazeppa* brings the Joseph allusion to mandated Palestine. Historically, the poem is based on *Histoire de Charles XII* (1772), in which Voltaire describes the adventures of Ivan Mazeppa (1632–1709), a page in the court of John Casimir V of Poland who has an affair with a married woman. When her husband finds out, he ties Mazeppa onto a horse that instinctively runs back to its home in the Ukraine. Once there, Mazeppa finds succor from a young girl who nurses him to health; and when well, Mazeppa serves the Cossacks, rising in the ranks until one day, he decides to leave it all. He crosses the Bosporus and ends up fighting for Charles II. Framing the tale is Mazeppa's interchange with Charles who, in the beginning, asks Mazeppa about his past, but, as we learn at the end, almost immediately falls asleep, completely uninterested in what his soldier has to say.

While presumably not part of Byron's vision, the plot sequence has enough parallels to the Bible that the Hebraized version almost inevitably evokes the story of Joseph. Mazeppa's account of his history is initiated by the affair with a married woman. Although the biblical prototype is innocent of the accusations made by Potiphar's wife, he is still punished. The two men then both demonstrate their value to their new countries—Mazeppa's service to the Cossacks, Joseph's to Pharaoh. Finally, each escapes by going across the water to yet another country—Mazeppa crossing the Bosporus to Sweden, the Israelites the Red Sea to Jerusalem.

Together, the Mazeppa and Joseph stories can be used to project the new Zionist identity. Of immediate interest to Baruch's contemporaries is the fact that Mazeppa was born in Podolia, a major center in the Jewish pale of settlement. Like the Byronic Mazeppa and the biblical Joseph, the Jews had striven to be useful citizens, though also like their prototypes, they were always considered aliens and were never fully integrated into society or emancipated. Therefore, like Baruch himself, they relocated to a new country hoping that their contributions might be better appreciated; however, like Charles II, the British protectors were thankful for any service the Jews might be able to provide, though otherwise uninterested. Most of all, as the prototype of the *sabra,* Mazeppa's physical prowess—both military and sexual—replaces the studiousness that had defined the diasporean Jewish identity.[13]

The conventional reading, according to McGann, is that in *Mazeppa,* "Byron imagined the possibility of an individual escaping from the large destructive fatalities of history."[14] From the Jewish perspective, however, it would seem that *Mazeppa* is less about the need to escape than to create one's own historical narrative, as Baruch himself did by moving to Tel Aviv and contributing to the cultural base of the new Jewish identity. As the inverse of Byron, who had to leave his homeland for a self-imposed exile, Baruch was returning from the Diaspora.

Israeli Statehood

Jacob Orland—Moderate Nationalism

For Jacob Orland (1914–2002), playwright and poet, Byron seems to have provided the means to articulate a call to the hard-liners for moderation in their attitude toward the British, especially in light of World War II. Orland was born in the Ukranian city of Tatiov, near Kiev. At the age of five, he witnessed the murder of eight members of his family as part of the slaughter of four hundred Jews in a pogrom that took place on Passover eve.[15] In 1921–22, his family emigrated to mandated Palestine in the third *aliyah*, initially to the area of Giladi, though in 1923 they moved to Jerusalem. Orland attended the Hebrew University in Jerusalem, and from youth, he was a member of the Haganah, the underground military organization formed in 1920. While still a student, Orland became part of the Israeli literati and began publishing poetry in the early 1930s. Also interested in the theater, in 1936 Orland went to England, where he studied at the Royal Academy of Dramatic Art in London. He published his first collection of poems in 1939 and in 1942 became literary editor of the periodical *Ashmoret*. During World War II, Orland served as a soldier in the British Army from 1942 to 1944 and was cofounder of the Hebrew Military Theatrical Group. After the war, he was a delegate to the Jewish National Fund in South Africa in 1952. A prolific writer, Orland published a number of collections of original poetry and plays, three of which were performed. In addition, he translated British and American literature into English, including works by Oscar Wilde, G. B. Shaw, and P. B. Shelley. His bilingual edition of the *Hebrew Melodies, Manginoth 'ivriyoth*, was published in Jerusalem in 1944.[16]

Orland's own attitudes toward Jewish nationalism seem to have been mixed. As part of the third *aliyah*, he emigrated among a group considered to be hard-left ideologues. Similarly, his service in the Haganah places him in the military underground that was as opposed to British control as it

CHAPTER 4

was to Arab insurgency. In the 1930s, when confronted by Arab terrorism, the Haganah rejected the moderation advocated by the Jewish Agency; yet, it should be noted, after the British issued their 1939 White Paper advocating more support for the Arabs than had previously been exhibited, the Jewish Agency reversed its earlier position and considered using the Haganah as an instrument against the British. By the 1940s, though, the Haganah, too, had reversed itself somewhat, helping to form Jewish units within the British Army.

If Orland's arrival with the third *aliyah* and membership in the Haganah might suggest leftward leanings, his decision, in the 1930s, to study drama in England rather than stay and defend the Jewish settlement, as well as his choice to serve in the British Army, suggest that his was not the Zionism of the hard left that would define Israeli identity through military, as opposed to intellectual, accomplishments. Rather, it would seem that his translation of the *Hebrew Melodies,* published at the height of the Holocaust, was an argument in favor of cooperation with the British, rather than opposition.

Both the translator's introduction and the use of Hebrew suggest that Orland's bilingual edition of the *Hebrew Melodies* was intended as a plea for partnership between the British and the Jews. After the reproduction of a portrait of Byron, the dedication to Duglas [*sic*] Kinnaird, and a bilingual table of contents, Orland prefaces the poems with a brief, four-page introduction containing, in addition to a conventional biographical sketch, what is apparently the first Hebrew discussion of Byron's collaboration with Nathan, the historical relationship being a trope for the contemporary partnership between the British and the Jews. After acknowledging the likelihood that the reader is already familiar with the songs, Orland suggests that a fresh reading can revivify the texts for the Jewish reader: "A little bit of their greatness descends to the valley of the soul of Israel and the threshold of it turns thus." In reading them, one "forgets for a few minutes, because he is enchanted by them, that the poet is a stranger [non-Jew], born in a distant and blessed land, one that is secure on her earth and that governs other nations" (12). The point, of course, is less to compliment Byron than to remind the Jews of 1944 that in the past, "strangers" had been known to sympathize with the plight of the Jews. Even more important, though, is Byron's nationality. Given the mandate and Britain's role in the war, Orland seems to be urging the Jews to work with the British, in the hope of persuading authorities to permit Jewish immigration to Palestine. As he says: "The extent that the fate of Jews worldwide is given in the hand of England can be seen in the small pamphlet of poems that came from the pen of one of the great poets, even though now, at this time, it is a full 120 years since his death; but no matter how much time has passed since then, his songs about our exile in the forge of fire are still appropriate" (12–13). Orland follows this with his Hebrew translation of the last stanza of "Oh! Weep for Those":[17]

> Tribes of the wandering foot and weary breast,
> How shall ye flee away and be at rest?
> The wild-dove hath her nest, the fox his cave,
> Mankind their Country—Israel but the grave!
> (ll. 9–12)

In Orland's translation:

> The tribes of the wanderers and the weariness of the strength,
> O where can you get far away and find rest!
> There is a nest for the wild-dove and for the fox his cave
> And land for man, and for Israel—the grave.

As he concludes the essay: "Perhaps they will try to read afresh even the songs of England, the rhymes of Byron by the light of these days. He is a great poet, according to the greatness of our faith, a poet of the ages, and his songs are new forever" (13). Although Orland might seem to be addressing the British, the fact that he writes in Hebrew suggests that his real audience is the Israelis, whom he urges to moderate their attitude toward those with the power, if they wish to realize the dream of a Jewish homeland.

In the translations, Orland subtly introduces the language of Zionism throughout. For example, in the last line of "Oh! Weep for Those," he exploits biblical terminology to emphasize the need for Zionism. When translating the word "country," instead of the word for political entity, *medinah*, "state," he chooses *eretz*, "land," the poetical name for Israel. As a result, the last line contains the Jewish name for mandated Palestine: "ve-*eretz* le-adam, u-le-*yisrael*—kivrehu."

Similarly, in "If That High World," Orland changes Byron's paean to platonic love into God's covenant with his people. Compare Byron's first two lines:

> If that high world, which lies beyond
> Our own, surviving Love endears

CHAPTER 4

to Orland's:

> If the world which extends
> From across from us, will guard the covenant.

In the Hebrew, Orland inserts the word *ever*, "from across," which is from the same root as the word for "Hebrew," the term adopted by Israelis to replace "Jew," their signifier for those in the Diaspora; and instead of using "endear," he uses *be-rit*, "covenant," thus literally substituting the Jewish covenant with God for Byron's love beyond the grave. Metaphorically, Orland's alterations introduce the relationship between the British and the Israelis, "the world which extends / From across from us" implying Britain, and "guard the covenant," suggesting an appeal that the mandate be honored.

Orland uses his bilingual edition of the *Hebrew Melodies* to imply a cultural connection between the British poet and Israeli aspirations for a homeland. Given the publication date of 1944, clearly he intended his translation to remind Israelis that the British, despite the White Paper of 1939, were not enemies and, more important, they controlled Jewish immigration during World War II and would be instrumental in determining the status of the area afterward.

Moshe Giyora—Diasporean Zionism

Like Orland, Moshe Giyora was an Ashkenazi Jew who emigrated to mandated Palestine and lived through both the Holocaust and the Israeli War for Independence. Translating more than a decade after statehood, however, Giyora seems to have used Byron to question the efficacy of the extremist attitudes being taken by Israelis in their national identity, especially denigration of the Ashkenazi tradition and diasporean Jewry.

Scant information about Giyora is available. Born in Sophia, Bulgaria, in 1919, he moved with his family to Palestine Israel in 1924, where he received his education, including studies at the Hebrew University.[18] He wrote several books of poetry, including *Be-reshit: shirim ve-sonetot* (In the Beginning: Songs and Sonnets; 1941–42), *Ha-shoshanah ha-kehulah: Shirim* (The Blue Rose; 1959–60), and *Shalhavot ve'efronim* (Flames and Ashes; 1970). Giyora also translated literature from Spanish and English. His Hebrew version of Childe Harold's farewell to England, published in *Ha-shoshanah ha-kehulah*, opens the section of translations that also includes poems by Alfred de Musset, Dorothy Parker, and Boris Pasternak.[19]

While Giyora does not indicate why he translated Harold's farewell, regardless of his intention, the decision is consistent with the national reassessment that occurred during the period between the Sinai campaign of 1956 and the Six Day War in 1967.[20] Historically, Israelis have always been in the self-contradictory position of relying on assistance from the very people they disparage. Considering themselves superior to diasporean Jews, many Israelis are said to have been especially ashamed of the way the central and eastern European Jews passively went to their deaths rather than actively opposing the Nazis. Yet the state required immigration, especially from Holocaust survivors, to increase its population; and equally as important, the economy relied on money donated by western Jews. After the Sinai campaign, some diasporean Jews began to shift their focus from Israel to their own communities, believing that they could implement a spiritual form of Zionism through social activism rather than financial support of Israel.[21] In that context, Giyora's translation of Harold's farewell can be read as a plea that Israelis moderate their attitude toward those Jews who chose to remain in the Diaspora rather than make *aliyah*.

Although written before—and arguably serving as a contributing factor to—the scandalous behavior that would result in Byron's final exile from Great Britain, the first canto of *Childe Harold* provides an early glimpse of the incipient Byronic hero, a man who, rather than be constrained by social restrictions, preferred to leave his homeland. Like the diasporeans, Harold travels away from rather than toward his homeland; and he brings with him a keen sense of personal ethics, from whose perspective he evaluates the ravages of war-torn Europe and judges his own behavior. Also like the diasporeans, Harold is an intellectual elitist who is lionized for his mental and emotional sensitivity, if not for his physical or military prowess.

In contrast to most of the poem, the ten-stanza song, which is inserted between stanzas 13 and 14, is not in the voice of the third-person narrator but is sung by Harold himself, thereby providing a first-person glimpse into the mind of the main character. In the first two stanzas of the song, Harold says his farewell to "my native shore" (1.1) and anticipates the new life he is sailing toward: "And I shall hail the main and skies, / But not my mother Earth" (2.3–4). Although he seems not to regret that "Deserted is my own good hall, / Its hearth is desolate" (2.5–6), the stoicism is contrasted by the other two characters in the song, the page who misses his parents, and the yeoman his wife and children. Harold dismisses the concerns of both, accusing the page of naiveté—"If I thy guileless bosom had

CHAPTER 4

/ Mine own would not be dry" (5.7–8), and contrasting the yeoman's grief with his own good cheer:

> Enough, enough, my yeoman good,
> Thy grief let none gainsay;
> But I, who am of lighter mood,
> Will laugh to flee away.
>
> *(7.5–8)*

Harold grieves because he has no ties with anyone on shore: "My greatest grief is that I leave / No thing that claims a tear" (8.7–8). For that reason, he looks to the sea, ending the last stanza with the same line he used to conclude the first: "My native Land—Good Night!" (10.8), though this time inserting an exclamation point, as opposed to the period he had used earlier. The difference punctuates the transformation from an elegiac mood in the beginning, as Harold mourned the loss of his homeland, to the anticipation of new adventures abroad, the exclamation point severing the emotional ties with the past as he moves on toward Iberia.

As with his use of the Byronic hero, Giyora modulates his language to suggest that modern Hebrew, too, is strengthened by external contributions. From the days of the earliest settlements, Israelis had privileged Hebrew over any other language—completely rejecting Yiddish for its association with the diasporean masses and English for its reminders of colonialism. Yet Hebrew, unlike other languages, had not had the opportunity to evolve organically, but had been wrenched out of what had been its rabbinic home and artificially thrust into the twentieth century. The result was an uneven instrument that could renounce its past only at the expense of full expression. Giyora's Hebrew translation of Harold's song suggests that the Israeli attitude toward its linguistic history, and by extension toward its identity, is shortsighted. Using the first three stanzas as examples, here is Byron's original:

> **1**
>
> Adieu, adieu! my native shore
>   Fades o'er the waters blue;
> The Night-winds sigh, the breakers roar,
>   And shrieks the wild seamew.
> Yon Sun that sets upon the sea
>   We follow in his flight;

Farewell awhile to him and thee,
   My native Land—Good Night.

2

A few short hours and He will rise
   To give the Morrow birth;
And I shall hail the main and skies,
   But not my mother Earth.
Deserted is my own good hall,
   Its hearth is desolate;
Wild weeds are gathering on the wall;
   My dog howls at the gate.

3

Come hither, hither, my little page!
   Why dost thou weep and wail?
Or dost thou dread the billows' rage,
   Or tremble at the gale?
But dash the tear-drop from thine eye;
   Our ship is swift and strong:
Our fleetest falcon scarce can fly
   More merrily along.

In Giyora's translation:

1

Farewell, farewell! shore of my origins
Lost in the blue sea.
Seagull roars, waves call out,
And the night wind howls.
There, on the sea, warmth is extinguished.
There is not there for us release.
Say farewell also to her, also to you,
My land.—Goodnight!

2

A few hours—and she will rage;
He will give birth to the dawn.
And I will bless then the pounding sea,
But not landscape-mother-parent.

There my good palace is deserted,
And desolated is the hearth.
Thorns and thornbushes on the wall.
My dog howls at the threshhold.

3

Come here, my little page!
What do you cry and lament?
Are you afraid of storms,
Beneath the raging gale?
All tears send away—and cut it off
Swift is the boat, strong.
Also the swiftness of every falcon
He is proud he flies.

In several significant respects, my English version "night wind howls" (1. 4) fails to render the full implication of Giyora's "ru'aḥ lel telil," the Hebrew of "The Night-winds sigh" (1.3). The words for "night" and "howl," *leila* and *yalel,* possibly connected by the associations of screeching in the night, create an auditory pun, especially through the reduplicated *l*s in both words. More important, the word for "wind," *ru'aḥ,* brings with it an overlay of religious connotations, it being used, as noted earlier, in Genesis 1:2, for "the *spirit* of God was moving over the face of the waters," as well as meaning "soul." The implication seems to be that the farewell is divinely sanctioned. This interpretation is underscored when in stanza 3, line 4, instead of translating the word "gale," in Byron's "Or tremble at the gale?" Giyora Hebraizes a neologism, *gal,* thus introducing English heteroglossia into his Hebrew version of Byron's description. Similarly, he Hebraizes the word "page," in Byron's "Come hither, hither, my little page!" emphasizing that this particular relationship of servitude is British, not Jewish. Finally, the phrase "landscape-mother-parent" strips away any possibility of interpreting Byron's "mother Earth" (2:4) in anything even remotely resembling Zionist terms.

The inclusion of both religious and English connotations into the Hebrew version of Harold's farewell transforms Byron's song articulating a sardonic choice of self-exile from one's homeland into a subtle warning about the dangers of a rigidly exclusive identity. Regardless of Giyora's intention, the Hebrew translation of Harold's farewell seems to serve as a reminder that if a homeland fails to accommodate all of its citizens, then some—like Harold and diasporean Jews—might choose to sever their ties.

Shmuel Friedman and Michael Desheh —Moral Traditionalism

The war against Lebanon in 1982 produced a marked shift in Israeli public opinion. For the first time in the nation's history, Israelis did not unite behind the military; instead, a significant peace movement consolidated against what many believed to have been a war of choice as opposed to a war for survival.[22] Published in 1983, Shmuel Friedman's bilingual edition of the *Hebrew Melodies* and the accompanying epilogue by Michael Desheh seem to reflect the antiwar movement, presenting the British poet as an intellectual whose moral conflicts with the overt militarism and religiosity of his own country can apply to the excesses wrought by the Israeli national identity in the last decades of the twentieth century.[23] Specifically, instead of what had been interpreted as a collection of poems advocating political Zionism, Friedman's translation and Desheh's essay suggest that the Israelis would do better to return to the spiritual values of Zionism.

Shmuel Friedman—Israeli Translator

I have not found out anything about Shmuel Friedman, though his subtle use of Hebrew, despite the post-1982 publication date, brings the *Hebrew Melodies* back to what had been its original pre-Zionist mode of thought. Before Herzl consolidated the movement, Zionism had been viewed metaphorically, the return to Jerusalem being interpreted as support for social values in the host country. Now, with statehood a fact, the elegiac tone of the *Hebrew Melodies* implies a criticism of Israel itself for having lost its own moral compass, as derived from the spiritual values of Zionism. This shift can be seen in two poems that had previously been used to articulate earlier attitudes toward Zionism: "She Walks in Beauty," and "Oh! Weep for Those."[24]

"She Walks in Beauty," as already mentioned, was completed before Byron's collaboration with Nathan, and, in fact, was written about Anne Beatrix, wife of Byron's second cousin Robert John Wilmot. However, successive generations of Jewish translators transformed the unnamed subject variously into a symbol for the Jewish woman, the Jewish people, or the

Shekhinah, the female symbol of divine immanence. Friedman, however, uses biblical and kabbalistic terminology to transform the poem into a paean of the mystical qualities of God. To consider the first stanza:

> Her beauty perfection perfection shining
>   There is no cloud, stretches out a sea-of-stars
> Light-shadow is met the image of light,
>   Lay bare grace without stain;
> After will be blended in embellished light,
>   Clouds withhold from rainy day.
>
>   (ll. 1–6)

Several things stand out in Friedman's translation. First, the subject of the poem, Byron's "She," is reduced to a modifier of the new subject, the abstract "beauty." There is no stated verb, only the duplicated "perfection," which is followed by the Hebrew *bahir*, defined as "shining" or "brightness," and also, as noted previously, title of a medieval mystical text, *Sefer ha-Bahir*. In the third line, the root for "shadow" is *zel*, and "image" is *demut*, both appearing in Genesis 1:26: "And God said, Let us make man in our image [be-**zal**-menu], after our likeness [ki-**demut**-enu]." Together, the words mystify the subject of the poem, bringing the focus back to the creator whose brightness can be found through his creature, man, who was formed in his image and likeness. The implication seems to be more Kabbalist than Zionist: that the esthetic experience should be the means of reaching God; and by implication, political Zionism should be the basis for a spiritual return to the One, not a physical end in itself.

This view of Zionism comes through even more strongly in "Oh! Weep for Those," Byron's elegy for the lost Zion. While Orland had used the last stanza as a plea for British support in the Israeli struggle for independence, Friedman, who translated after the State of Israel had been criticized for expansionism, transforms Byron's poem into a lament for the loss of Zionist values:

> Oh! Weep for the Weepers
>
> Oh, weep for the weepers on the waters of Babel,
> Their land is a dream, desolate is God's Temple;
> The harp of Zion is broken, they will lament,
> And in their God-less temples they will prostrate themselves!
>
> Where will Israel wash her swollen feet?
> And song of Zion be full of sweetness?

When will the song of Judah make tremble for the second time
The hearts in the heavenly song?

The feet of the tribes wander, weak-breast,
Will there be found refuge for this people?
There is found a nest for the dove, also for the fox shelter,
For all the people their inheritance/property—for Israel only the pit!

Published after statehood, the poem can make sense only in spiritual terms, that the mourning is for those whose "land is a dream," that is, for those who feel that the moral foundation of Zionism is in jeopardy. Friedman differentiates between spiritual and historical Zionism by changing Byron's references to "shrines" in the first stanza:

Oh! weep for those that wept by Babel's stream,
Whose shrines are desolate, whose land a dream;
Weep for the harp of Judah's broken shell;
Mourn—where their God hath dwelt the Godless dwell!
(ll. 1–4)

By translating the "shrines" from Byron's "Whose shrines are desolate," as the singular *mikdash-ha'el,* literally, "the temple of God," and then using *hekhalam,* "their temples," to indicate where "their God hath dwelt," Friedman specifies the Temple as the center of the Jewish spiritual existence, as opposed to the "shrines" where "the Godless dwell." Similarly, by changing Byron's "harp of Judah's broken shell" into the "harp of Zion," he emphasizes both the biblical heritage and moral obligation of contemporary Zionists.

The last line underscores the need to return to spiritual Zionism. In arguing for independence, Orland had retained the literal meaning of Byron's "Mankind their country—Israel but the grave!" In Orland's version: "And land for man, and for Israel—the grave." In contrast, Friedman completely eliminates the word "country," the physical reality of the state no longer being in question. Even more telling, however, in changing the focus from the physical land to the "inheritance," that is, heritage, he uses the neutral term *nahalah* instead of the more suggestive root *yarash,* as already noted etymologically linked to Jerusalem, the focus of Zionism. Similarly, instead of *kever,* the Hebrew word for "grave," he chooses *bor,* "pit," the term, as seen in the earlier discussion of Joseph, that signifies the first move into the Egyptian Diaspora and Jewish slavery. Together, these roots invert the tenor of Byron's line. Instead of lamenting what is already a lost homeland, they warn that the existing state could be jeopardized by the loss of spiritual values.

Michael Desheh—Israeli Commentator

Consistent with Friedman's translation, Michael Desheh's biographical and historical essay presents Byron in the image of those antiwar Israelis who called for a national return to moral integrity. As with so many of the other Jewish Byronists, I have almost no information about Desheh. Born Michael Eisenstadt in Bobruisk, in 1915, Desheh moved with his parents to mandated Palestine in 1925.[25] After completing high school, from 1936 to 1938 he studied at the teachers' college in Jerusalem, and beginning in 1938 held teaching posts in various places; then, from 1954, when he completed his education at the Hebrew University, he taught in Beer Sheva. Desheh's formal literary career began in 1937, and he published collections of poetry, newspaper articles, and occasional pieces.

Desheh's nine-page essay uses Byron as the means of reconnecting Israelis with what had been denigrated as the diasporean identity: intellectual superiority and moral integrity. Introducing Byron as one of the most highly praised poets of his generation, Desheh defines Byronism as what might be considered the equivalent of the Israeli antiwar movement: "The concept 'Byronism' became a symbol for the war against the hypocrisy of enslavement, in conventions that passed in time: the war for truth and freedom of the state and society. He had a great influence, both direct and indirect, on many Hebrew poets, such as: Mikh"l, Maneh, J. L. Gordon, D. Frishman, S. Tchernichowsky, and others" (56).[26] By invoking the names of earlier Hebrew poets, Desheh associates the development of Hebrew literature with Byronism, implying that the true Israeli identity derives from the broader sense of Hebrew culture, as developed not only from the Diaspora but from non-Jewish sources as well. Desheh then establishes his thesis, that the Greek war for independence in which Byron participated was a valid use of militarism:

> In this period Byron was a hero of liberty and righteousness, the weapon used against the shackles imposed by the artificial and counterfeited morality of England, of all Europe. His heart was open and sensitive to the suffering of working and oppressed people, and thus he

made holy his years by wrestling with the Italians to throw off the yoke of the military, and to end his life in the war, actually a participant in the struggle of the Greek rebels against the Turks. (57)

The first section of the essay is a biographical sketch, revolving around the theme of excessive religiosity: "The small orphan grew in a childhood refuge, raised by a woman who possessed distorted ethics, that grew on the blessing of the Calvinistic faith. This woman imposed her fear on the boy in the scary stories about hell. There was created abundant horror for the living wanderer except for her morals, that she turned against English society at another time" (58). Desheh clearly does not blame Calvinism per se, only its distortion by a mother who early on created "abundant horror" in Byron's childhood, though later, its social manifestation caused his permanent exile: "As a result, humiliation hung over Byron like social excommunication. And just as in the years of his glory he received great glory from his social circles, now were closed in his face all of the doors and there remained head-shaking and isolation. In 1815 Byron left England, never to return" (59). In his self-imposed Diaspora, Byron wrote some of his most famous work and fought with the Greeks for their independence: "From the days of his youth Byron admired ancient Greece, its literature, its works of faith and the works of liberty of the ancient Greeks. From the midst of this awe, he identified with the Greek people who were starting a national movement, which strove to oppose the Turkish yoke" (60). The description of Greek culture and the emphasis on liberation together implicitly criticize the 1982 war in Lebanon.

Next, Desheh summarizes the history of Byron's collaboration with Nathan:

> All who read at their first encounter the *Hebrew Melodies* consume the songs in one gulp. And the first perception that dominates is wonder, the wonder of joy and even a bit of national pride. Wonder because a great poet, who is the son of a foreign people, collected a book of poems about the subject of the Jewish people in the midst of the construction and identification of a nation of men and the historical lights that were these peoples'. Pride about the strength of the Book of Books and the wonders in the stories of the Jewish people for the appeal of a great poet and of the greatness of our people and its story. (61)

Through his discussion of the collaboration with Nathan, the brief biographical sketch of Nathan, and the description of the London musical scene

CHAPTER 4

(including references to John Braham), Desheh generates a world republic of culture, if not letters per se, in which the Jews are appreciated for their contributions, and Zion is seen even in songs like "She Walks in Beauty," a lyric celebrating female pulchritude. Moreover, speculates Desheh, Nathan's religiously based music likely inspired Byron: "The voice of these songs burned deep in Byron's soul. Listen to the holy songs with the melodies by Isaac Nathan—perhaps the collaboration between the poet and the composer helped renew his sense of excitement and experience" (63–64).

Desheh's reference to Nathan takes this study full circle, it having begun with Byron and his contemporaries D'Israeli and Nathan. In between, Byronic materials have provided a touchstone for the evolution of Jewish culture, as it developed from the Haskalah, survived the ideological Yiddishists and Zionists, and now confronts the existential needs of the Israelis.

Conclusion
Translation and *Allegoresis*

In its effect, if not its conscious intention, translation is a form of transcultural *allegoresis*.[1] Allegory, most often defined as an extended metaphor in which key figures symbolize abstract concepts, is a notoriously unstable genre, its dominant characteristic being the deliberate disruption of the conventional relationship between signs and their referents, to imply that words do *not* mean what they say. Historically, that instability made possible periods of rampant *allegoresis*, the imposition of unintended allegorical readings on particular texts, a blatant example being the attempt by early church fathers to Christianize what had clearly originated as pagan texts. When, in time, audiences could no longer accept the plethora of what were obviously arbitrary readings, allegory fell out of favor in the West.

Existing in what amounts to a parallel cultural universe, translation constitutes a kind of *allegoresis*. When a translator displaces a text from its original context, he or she disrupts the relationship with external reality, replacing the author's intention with his or her own. Regardless of the translator's diligence, the new language will, inevitably, control the way the text will be both rendered and received; and for its part, the audience will perforce process the new text according to the strictures of its own interpretive community, which can differ radically from that for which the text was intended. The result is a reinterpretation often far beyond the range of anything imagined by the original author. Not surprisingly, this study, in its totality, reveals an allegorical reinterpretation of the conventional Byron: the translators all had their own reasons for rendering their texts; the Jewish culture created its own context; the Hebrew and Yiddish languages introduced their own levels of signification; and the Jewish interpretive community, with its long tradition of *allegoresis*, exposed the possibility of as yet unexplored, if not entirely new, meanings for the texts.

CONCLUSION

Translators' Intentions

Regardless of how they felt about Byron, all of the men surveyed in this study used *allegoresis* as a tool for expanding the communal Jewish identity and for determining their own personal Jewish identities. For contemporaries Isaac D'Israeli and Isaac Nathan, collaboration with Byron was part of a process that yielded opposite results for each of them. D'Israeli used his analysis of the concept of genius to remain, nominally, at least, a Jew, concluding that there was no logical reason to convert. In contrast, after collaborating with Byron on the *Hebrew Melodies,* his only specifically Jewish work, Nathan eventually left the Anglo-Jewish community entirely, moving to Australia, where he devoted himself to indigenous music.

The other Byronists in this study all remained in their own communities, though their choice of language and venue implied a political statement about their attitude toward the Jewish identity. Most obviously, the *maskilim,* all of whom translated Byron into Hebrew, were part of a political movement whose aim was the eventual secularization of the Jewish identity. Yiddishists took a different political stance. Because their language was considered a *jargon,* generated by the uneducated masses for their everyday vernacular, its use in translation implied a rejection of the Hebrew elite, constituting instead the attempt to construct a bridge between the intelligentsia and the lower classes. Finally, the political Zionists adapted Byron for their cause as well. Between 1897 and 1917, in the interim between the time when the First Zionist Congress advocated and the Balfour Declaration guaranteed a Jewish homeland, there was little consensus about the viability of Zionism, and Byronists used translation to stake out different theoretical positions. Then, after Zionism became an existential reality, Jews translated Byron as part of the ongoing dialogue about the direction being taken in Israeli politics.

Cultural and Linguistic Contexts

It might seem to require excessive *allegoresis,* but actually, the specific works that were translated—*Childe Harold,* canto 1, *Hebrew Melodies, The Prisoner of Chillon, Mazeppa, Darkness, Manfred, Cain,* and *Heaven and Earth*—all readily lend themselves to a particularly Jewish reading. In addition to the obvious biblical themes, Byron's rejection of orthodox Christianity in these works yields an archetypal structure that can be adapted to the Jewish cycle of exile and return. Key to that structure is the trope of the "Wandering

Jew."[2] Although it was originally an anti-Semitic construct intended to validate the Christian myth, Byron's inversion transforms the Wandering Jew into a figure that approximates the archetypal Jewish hero.

Historically, the trope of the Wandering Jew developed as a negative representation of Christ. As it crystallized, the legend revolved around a man who refused to permit Jesus to rest while carrying his cross on the road to Calvary. In response to the man's admonition, "Walk faster," Jesus is said to have uttered the curse, "I go, but you will walk until I come again!" Thus doomed, the Wandering Jew would in time represent the inverse of basic Christian doctrine: his initial blasphemy constituted the reprobate's rejection of Christ; his intellect, the forbidden knowledge of original sin; his peripatetic homelessness, the curse of Cain; and his inability to die, the eternal damnation of Satan.

In Europe, the legend was used to help consolidate Christian hegemony, the Wandering Jew's specific ethnicity becoming less important than his ability to provide cohesion for the dominant population. In medieval England, as religion became subordinated to incipient forms of nationalism, he was de-Judaized, chronicler Roger of Wendover transforming the blasphemer into a nonsectarian witness awaiting Christ's return; and with the awakening of learning in the Renaissance, he became the repository of knowledge gained through his manifold experiences. But in the Reformation, he was re-Judaized, as it were, re-presented as an all-purpose Antichrist who could be invoked variously by both Catholics and Protestants to symbolize, by contrast, the truth of their competing versions of Christianity. With the Enlightenment, the Wandering Jew was immortalized into a kind of deus ex machina who devoted his life to performing good deeds; and as culminating in the pre-Romantic period, he was a world traveler whose vast experience produced the social commentary, criticism, and satirical observations of the historian or philosopher. By the turn of the nineteenth century, however, the Wandering Jew had been transformed into a character that would be associated with the Romantic hero. Having been ostracized for rejecting the dominant ethos, his intellectual superiority prevented his assimilating with the majority of people, leaving him a world-weary nomad who identified far more closely with the demonic Satan than with the deified Christ. Not surprisingly, Romantic writers appropriated for themselves this trope that had originated as a symbol of alterity.[3]

For Byron in particular, the "Wandering Jew" provided an archetypal figure through which to explore his own conflict between moral integrity and the hypocrisy of social compromise. As a religious skeptic, he personally rejected much of Christian theology; however, as a father who feared legal restrictions against his being able to see his daughter, he censored himself, refraining from publicizing overtly antithetical views. Instead, he inverted the myth, recasting the "Wandering Jew" as the hero, defined in terms of the independent individual who resists public pressure to conform. By implication, this transforms Christ into the villain, his insistence on passive conformity undermining the personal integrity required for what is now identified as the true means of salvation. Although Byron could never bring himself to articulate the full implications of his renovated myth, nevertheless, his dramatic heroes explore the dimensions of the dilemma within the context of an implicitly Christian world: Cain and Manfred, the men of integrity who accept with dignity punishment for their choices; and Japhet, the compromiser who must live with his regrets.

Byron's inversion of the myth conforms with the self-image of the Jews who see their resistance to Christian pressure heroically, as adherence to their beliefs, regardless of the consequences. The difference is that while Byron's narrative structure is linear, the Jews' is cyclical. Generated around a myth of exile and return, the Jewish Messiah is projected as a fully human being who will lead his people back to their geographical homeland, where they will be free to live according to their own principles, not those of the dominant community in the Diaspora. Within this context, the works discussed in this study are easily allegorized in terms of the Jewish myth: symbolizing the cycle itself, *Darkness* can be read either as completing the old or initiating the new *shemittah*; in the first canto, Childe Harold surveys the geography of Jewish exile; the *Hebrew Melodies* are proto-Zionist; the prisoner Bonivard, like religious Jews, is eventually redeemed for remaining true to his father's faith; Mazeppa, like the diasporean Jew, serves the host country, eventually to become a figure of the new Israeli; and Manfred, Cain, and Japhet exemplify the Jewish hero who is forced to confront the threat to personal integrity by pressure to conform.

In addition to the archetypal parallels, the new languages perforce impose an overlay of Jewish allegory onto what originated as barely Christian texts. As the language of the Bible, Jewish liturgy, and later rabbinic discourses, Hebrew is inextricably connected to Judaism, its syntax and vocabulary inevitably suggesting religious *allegoresis*, even when not intended by the translator, much less by the original author. In contrast, Yiddish, as a fusion language, contains a large component of religiously oriented Hebrew along with a plethora of terms and expressions borrowed from the many cultures with which the Jews interacted over the centuries.

As a result, the choice of a Hebrew, German, Russian, French, or Polish term inevitably introduces figurative dimensions that, again, are not necessarily intended.

Interpretive Communities

When Byron was translated into Hebrew and Yiddish, he was introduced into a culture that had a long tradition of *allegoresis*. The Hebrew root for "translate," *targem,* also means "to interpret," and religious Jews still study the "interpretation" of the most famous "translation," the *Targum Onkelos,* an Aramaic translation of the Bible from the second century. Even before that, conundrums in the Bible were resolved allegorically; and Philo of Alexandria formalized the use of allegory to validate Moses as the source for knowledge. Later exegetes used *allegoresis* to rationalize contradictions, and Kabbalists developed entirely new readings based on elaborate hermeneutical formulas. Religious Jews, believing in the divinity of the Bible, justify *allegoresis* by claiming that their text is fully motivated, that whatever can be found there was intended by the author. Extending that line of thought even further, many Jews believe that the interpretations are also part of the divine intention; after all, they derive from the original text, which comes from God himself. Consequently, the concept of an interpretive community that functions to impose limits on interpretation is, for all practical purposes, nugatory. Although not all Jews are willing to accept all interpretations, each of the various factions within the community inevitably validates its stance through *allegoresis.*

From this perspective, it is not only appropriate, but in some respects essential, to read Byron allegorically. Most of the translated texts are, quite literally, interpretations of the Hebrew Bible, subjects including Cain and Abel, Noah, Jephtha's daughter, Saul, and Herod, to name a few. Even though Byron was a *ger,* a non-Jew, so, too, was Onkelos, the Aramaic translator, before he converted to Judaism. Within the Jewish context, therefore, it could be argued that these nineteenth- and twentieth-century translators were all just incorporating *Targum Byron* into their own exegetical tradition, where he would be allegorized in much the same way all the other Bible commentators had been before him. The only difference is that the Jewish translators secularized Byron's *midrashim.*

In the final analysis, *allegorisis,* and through it translation, represents a leap of faith. Based on the assumption that all signs are fully motivated and possess the potential of signifying a plethora of concepts beyond their conventional meanings, allegorisis places the burden of interpretation on the reader, whose function is to locate possible—though not necessarily intended, accurate, or even unique—meanings for unstable texts. In its totality, translation underscores the unreliability of language, substituting imprecise words for what were often equally imprecise terms in the original language. Yet author, translator, and reader alike all assume that the text will be able to convey something significant to their respective worlds. Comparable to Philo, who used allegory to revivify the Bible for his world, the Jews discussed in this study used translation to adapt Byron for theirs.

Appendix
Transcriptions

Because the Hebrew and Yiddish translations of Byron are fairly inaccessible, this appendix provides a sampling. The transcriptions are arranged in the order in which they are discussed in the text, with sections for chapters 2 through 4. Although I have made every effort to be accurate, it should be noted that these passages are not edited, only transcribed. Also, because many of the publications are in fragile condition, some available only on microfilm, and Yaakov Ẓevi's, in particular, being a hand-written codex that he continued to amend, the copy texts were not always easily decipherable.

For those who want to compare different Hebrew and Yiddish versions of more extended passages, the appendix contains all versions of Cain's first soliloquy leading up to the arrival of Lucifer, the first part of *The Prisoner of Chillon*, and the conclusion of *Darkness*: *Cain* because the play provoked so much discussion among Jewish critics; *The Prisoner of Chillon* because, other than the *Hebrew Melodies*, it was the most frequently translated work by Byron; and *Darkness* because it is the only clear instance in which a later translator, Rabener, might have been responding to an earlier one, Letteris. Finally, because there are so many individual lyrics within the *Hebrew Melodies*, it was impossible to provide typescripts of them all. However, there are multiple versions of a number of them, especially the Hebrew and Yiddish versions of three by Nathan Horowitz, who translated Byron into both languages.

List of Transcriptions

Yaakov Zevi
Cain (I.1.64–82) 180

Meir Halevi Letteris
"Oh! Weep for Those" 181
"The Wild Gazelle" 181
Darkness (ll. 69–83) 182

Matisyahu Simḥah Rabener
The burden of Matisyahu: In praise of Moses Monetfiore (stanzas 1–2) 183
To the composer of the melodies: A poem to Lord Byron: Acrostic 183
"She Walks in Beauty" 184
"The Harp the Monarch Minstrel Swept" 184
Darkness (ll. 69–91) 185

Judah Leib Gordon
"If That High World" 186
"The Wild Gazelle" 186

Ezekiel Bleicher
Harold's farewell (stanzas 1–3) 187

Max (Mordechai) Hershman
The Prisoner of Chillon (part 1) 188

Nathan Horowitz
"She Walks in Beauty" (Yiddish) 189
"The Harp the Monarch Minstrel Swept" (Yiddish) 189
"On Jordan's Banks" (Yiddish) 190
"She Walks in Beauty" (Hebrew) 190
"The Harp the Monarch Minstrel Swept" (Hebrew) 191
"On Jordan's Banks" (Hebrew) 192

Transcriptions

Abraham Asen
The Prisoner of Chillon (part 1) 192
Cain (I.1.64–79) 193

Moisei Khashtshevatski
The Prisoner of Chillon (part 1) 194

Solomon Mandelkern
"She Walks in Beauty" 195

David Frishman
Cain (I.1.64–79) 196

Isaac Loeb Baruch (I. L. Brocowitz)
The Prisoner of Chillon, first version (part 1) 197

Jacob Orland
"If That High World" 198
"Oh! Weep for Those" 198

Moshe Giyora
Harold's farewell (stanzas 1–3) 199

Shmuel Friedman
"She Walks in Beauty" 200
"Oh! Weep for Those" 201

APPENDIX

Yaakov Ẓevi

Cain (I.1.64–82)

Myster nach Lord Byron in 3 Acten, קין, יאקב צבי ברבי אברהם הלוי,
מליצה בת שלש מערכות.

קין (נשאר לבדו)
הכזה תקראו חיים עמל נפש?
ולמה אעמול פה, על מה זאת אֶתְיַגֵּיעָה?
אולי בעד אבי שבי תקהינה?
אם עבד בריתו, אכל, שבע בושׂר היא מצא כדי עֲוֹלָתוֹ מוחר כפילים
כי שלחו אותו חוצה מהסתפח
בנחלות אלהים כָּלָה גֵרֵשׁ גרשוהו,
ואנכי מה? מדוע לא יַנְקֵינִי?
אם פשעתי טרם גוחי מרחם
אן צפיתי כי יקדמוני ברכים,
גידים לבשתי עור עלי רקמתי
אם על יומי לפני אלהים שועתי?
לקול הנחש ולקול אשתו מדוע
למה יקצוץ עליו שדי ליסרהו?
מה יועיל מוסר אב לנפש הילד
האוכל בתאות נפשו מן החרם?
פן תושב הגציבה אחרי הַכָּהוּ?
אכן, למען לא ימעול שנית מעט
לא בעבור כי חָטָא יתן לו בְּקוֹרֶת
פן יאכל אבי שבית מפרי הדעת
היחטוא שבית -- אחרי יגרש מגן מעדן!
אך מה אומר „שבית,? ושם בנאות חֶמֶד
במה חטא? העץ עשה פריהו
מדוע בעד אבי פריו לא יעש?
ואם לא! למה לא הפריד אֵל בֵּינָם!
בין אדם מאדמה איש מלא יצר
ובין עץ גְּבַהּ הקומה, בתוך הגן נְטָעוֹ
תאוה לָעַיִן מֶרמוֹן נָזִית?
אֵל אשר אפנה פי איש לא ישיבני
בלתי: חפץ אלוה הוא רצון אליה
והוא הטוב אל כל טוב לנו יצמיח
מה? יען כי לכח אמיץ הנה!
לכן החכמה לפניו כל עת משחקת
ואם מטוב לַכִּיל עקב ידו נוצחת?

180

Transcriptions

לפני פריו יהלל עף ופרי מצרני
כלענה ויצום עלי ללחם...
מי זה בא? ראה פניו למלאך אליה.
אך בצלם יתהלך קודר שחוח

Meir Halevi Letteris

"Oh! Weep for Those"

מאיר הלוי-מה"ל לעטריס, עפרות זהב, המה שירים יקרים מגדולי משוררי העמים, עשוים בדמותם ונעתקו ללשון עבר.

1

הֵילִילוּ מַר לְעָם אַרְצָם עָזָבוּ
עַל נַהֲרוֹת בָּבֶל בִּכְאֵב לֵב יָשָׁבוּ
עַל כִּנּוֹר קֹדֶשׁ כִּי נֻפַּץ עַל סָלַע
עַל הוֹדָם כִּי נִדָּח אֶל כַּף הַקָּלַע!

אָן תַּדִיחַ עַמִּי מִדַּם רַגְלֶיךָ?
מִי יָנֵעִים עַל עָשׂוֹר נֹעַם שִׁירֶיךָ?
מָתַי בִּיהוּדָה עוֹד יַעַל שָׁמַיִם
קוֹל גִּילַת וָרַנֵּן שִׁיר וּמְצִלְתַּיִם!

הָהּ שִׁבְטֵי יִשְׂרָאֵל עַד דַּכָּא בָאוּ
אֵיפֹה מָנוֹחַ מַרְגֵּעָה תִּמְצָאוּ!
גַּם עוֹרֵב יִמְתָּא קֵן וּמְגוּרוֹ גָּבֶר,
שׁוּעָל נִקְרַת צוּרִים, וִיהוּדָה -- קָבֶר!

"The Wild Gazelle"

2

אַיֶּלֶת בַּשָּׂדֶה קַלָּה מִנֶּשֶׁר
עַל הָרֵי יִשְׂרָאֵל עָפוֹת רַגְלֶיהָ,
עַל יִבְלֵי מַיִם, לָדַעַת פֵּשֶׁר,
שָׁם תַּעֲרוֹג שָׁם תִּתְמַהּ עַל הוֹד מַרְאֶיהָ
רַגְלֶיהָ לֹא רָפוּ אַף לֹא יִיעָפוּ
עֵינֶיהָ כַיּוֹנִים חֵן חֵן נִשְׁקָפוּ.

APPENDIX

קַלָּה מִזֹּאת בִּבְנוֹת צִיּוֹן חָזִיתִי
בָּרָה וִיפֵה־פִיָּה אַיֶּלֶת חֶמֶד
עַל הָרִים, בֶּעָרִים, כָּזֹאת רָאִיתִי
שָׁם בָּחוּר וּבְתוּלָה הָלְכוּ צֶמֶד.
עוֹד שִׂרְיוֹן וּלְבָנוֹן עוֹד עוֹד יִרְעָשׁוּ --
וּבְנוֹת צִיּוֹן נָדוּ אַרְצָם נָטָשׁוּ!

יֶתֶר עֹז לַלְּבָנוֹן נוֹשֵׁן בָּאָרֶץ
מִשִּׁבְטֵי יִשְׂרָאֵל נָעוּ גַם נָדוּ,
לֹא יִשָּׁמַע קוֹל נֹגֵשׂ אוֹ צִוְחַת פֶּרֶץ
אֵין כּשֵׁל בַּאֲרָזָיו אַף בַּל נִלְכָּדוּ;
אֶרֶץ מֹלֶדֶת לֹא יוּכַל לָנוּחַ
עַל אַדְמַת נֵכָר לֹא יֹאבֶה לִפְרוֹחַ!

אַךְ נַחְנוּ נִדָּחִים אֶרֶץ צַלְמָוֶת
עַל אַדְמַת אֵל נֵכָר לָמוּת אִי־כֹּחַ,
בִּמְקוֹם עַצְמוֹת הוֹרַי יֵשְׁנוּ הַמָּוֶת
לֹא לָנוּ קֶבֶר, לֹא לָנוּ מָנוֹחַ!
הָהּ, אֶבֶן לֹא נוֹתַר מִבֵּית קָדְשֵׁנוּ,
עַל כֵּס שָׁלֵם יוֹשֵׁב לַעַג רִישֵׁנוּ!

Darkness (ll. 69–83)

חזיון חשך

כָּל מְלוֹא תֵבֵל שְׁמָמָה! זֹאת הָאָרֶץ
מִשְׁכְּנוֹת מַמְלְכוֹת גּוֹיִם רַבַּת הֶחָיִל
הָיְתָה לְמַטִּיל־תֹּהוּ, עַרְעָר בְּעַרְבוֹת שְׁחָקִים,
שְׁכוּלָה, גַּלְמוּדָה, מְעוֹן בַּלָּהָה, יְוֵן צַלְמָוֶת,
שְׁאִיַּת עוֹלָמִים. הַמַּעְיָנִים בַּנְּחָלִים,
גַּם הַיָּם הַגָּדוֹל רְחַב יָדַיִם דּוּמָם
שָׁכְנוּ כַמָּוֶת, אֵין מָה יַעַר מְצוּלָה בִּתְהוֹם
רַבָּה. אֳנִיּוֹת נְטוּשׁוֹת בְּלֵב יָם הִתְקַלְקָלוּ,
תֹּרֶן וָנֵס הִתְפָּרְדוּ, נָפְלוּ אֶל
הַמַּיִם וְלֹא הִכּוּ גַלִּים. גַּלִּים יָשְׁנוּ
הַמָּוְתָה, סוּפָה וְרוּחַ יִשְׁתֹּקוּן
בְּמוֹ מְרוֹמִים. גַּם עַנְנֵי עָב חָלְפוּ, הָלְכוּ,
נָדוּ; בִּלְעֲדֵיהֶם לְמַדַּי יָמִישׁ חֹשֶׁךְ
עוֹלָמִים. תַּחַת הָאָרֶץ חָשְׁכָה, תַּחַת
מְלֹא תֵבֵל מְעִי אֲפֵלָה מְנֻדָּח סֶלָה.

Matisyahu Simḥah Rabener

The burden of Matisyahu: In praise of Moses Monetfiore (stanzas 1–2)

מתתיהו שמחה ראבענער, נְגִינוֹת עֵבֶר: שירים שונים יסודתם בהררי קדש, אשר העתקתי משירי המליץ האנגלי המפואר בשערים לשם ולתהלה לָאָרד בֵּירָאן.

מַשָּׂא מַתִּתְיָהוּ. מַהֲלָל משֶׁה מָנְטִיפִיּוֹרֶה:

מֵאָז משֶׁה מְחוֹקֵק, מָשׁוּי מִמַּיִם,
מוּרָם מֵעָם, מֵאֱלֹהֵי מָרוֹם מָשִׁיחַ.
מַרְחָם מְשַׁחֵר, מֵהֵיכַל מֶלֶךְ מִצְרַיִם,
מֵאָן מֵהִתְעַלֵּם מֵאֶחָיו, מַצִּיץ מַשְׁגִּיחַ.

מָאַס מוֹשַׁב מַשְׂכִּיתוֹ, מְעוֹנַת מַדְהֵבָה,
מְפַלֵּט מְרֵעֵהוּ מִיַּד מֵצְרֵי מִתְנַקֵּם,
מִפֶּרֶךְ מַתְבֵּן מַלְבֵּן, מַעֲמָסַת מַעֲצֵבָה,
מִתְאָב מְנוּחַת מַעֲדַנּוֹת מִתְבּוֹנֵן מִתְחַכֵּם.

To the composer of the melodies: A poem to Lord Byron: Acrostic

לַמְנַצֵּחַ בִּנְגִינוֹתַי: מִכְתָּם אֶל לָארד בֵּירָאן: Akrostichon

לַמְנַצֵּחַ בִּנְגִינוֹת קֹדֶשׁ בְּסוֹד לַהֲקוֹת שָׁמַיִם,
אוֹבִילָה מִנְחַת זִכָּרוֹן מִמֶּגֶד שְׂפַת עִבְרִיָּה
רַבּוֹת פָּעַלְתָּ, נֶאְדָּרִי! לַתּוּשִׁיָּה כְּפָלַיִם,
דִּבְרֵי שִׁירְךָ מַה מָתְקוּ מֵעֲסִיס גֶּפֶן פּוֹרִיָּה.
בָּרָן יַחַד שִׁבְטֵי יָהּ בִּלְשׁוֹן צִיּוֹן וִירוּשָׁלַיִם,
יַזְכִּירוּ שִׁמְךָ לְתִפְאֶרֶת, מֵלִיץ רַב הָעֲלִילִיָּה!
רָצִיתָ בַּת־יְהוּדָה, שַׂחָה קוֹדֶרֶת שִׁבְעָתַיִם
אָהַבְתָּ אֱמֶת וֶאֱמוּנָה, וַתִּשְׂנָא סְעִפִּים וּרְמִיָּה.
נַפְשְׁךָ בְּצֵל שַׁדַּי תִּתְלוֹנָן צְרוּרָה בִּצְרוֹר הַחַיִּים.

APPENDIX

"She Walks in Beauty"

בַּת יְהוּדָה.

בְּיִפִי תִפְאֶרֶת תִּתְהַלֵּךְ, כְּלִיל דְּמָמָה
בְּהִלָּם כּוֹכְבֵי נֶשֶׁף בְּעֶצֶם שָׁמַיִם;
הוֹד צִלְלֵי אֹפֶל וְזִיו נֹגַהּ הָרָמָה
יַחְדּוּ בְּפָנֶיהָ, בְּיִפְעַת עֵינָיִם:
אוֹר נֶחְמָד וְנָעִים יוֹפִיעַ עֲלֵי אֲדָמָה, --
נֶעְדָּר בַּיּוֹם בָּהִיר לְעֵת הַצָּהֳרָיִם.

הָרַב צֵל אֹפֶל אוֹ הָגָה בְרַק-מְאוֹרוֹת,
חֵין הַיֹּפִי יִצְעַר, יַחֲלוֹף וְאֵינֶנּוּ, --
בֵּין קְוֻצּוֹת תַּלְתַּלִּים, כָּעוֹרֵב שְׁחוֹרוֹת,
יַאְדִּיר הַמֵּצַח בְּחֵן הֲדַר מַרְאֵהוּ, --
בּוֹ הָרוּחַ יַבִּיעַ בַּעֲשָׁתּוֹת טְהוֹרוֹת:
'מַה טּוֹב וּמַה נָּעִים מָקוֹם מְנוּרֵהוּ!

וַעֲלֵי הוֹד מִצְחָהּ, עֲלֵי תַאֲמֵי-לְחָיַיִם,
הֵן יְחַוֶּה דּוּמָם בְּאֵין אֹמֶר וּדְבָרִים,
כְּלִיל יְקוֹד יָפְיָהּ, חֵין שְׂחוֹק שְׂפָתַיִם,
רוּחַ שֶׁקֶט שַׁאֲנָן, הוֹלֵךְ לְמֵישָׁרִים,
לֵב אוֹהֵב שָׁלוֹם, חָפֵץ לִרְאוֹת חַיִּים,
מְעוֹנַת אַהֲבָה בָרָה, זְבוּל תֻּמַּת יְשָׁרִים.

"The Harp the Monarch Minstrel Swept"

כִּנּוֹר דָּוִד.

כִּנּוֹר יְדִיד-יָהּ, הַמּשֵׁל בְּיִרְאַת אֱלֹהִים,
אָז יְדֵי מֶלֶךְ הִשְׁמִיעוּ קוֹל זְמִירָךְ!
הוֹמָה בְהַדְרַת-קֹדֶשׁ אֵל אֵל בַּגְּבֹהִים,
רַחֲשֵׁי-לֵב בַּדֶּמַע יַעֲלוּ שִׁירָיִךְ;
כְּפָלַיִם יְבַכּוּךְ! נִתְּקוּ מֵיתָרָיִךְ!

הוּא הֵמֵס כַּדּוֹנַג לֵב קָשֶׁה כָּאֶבֶן,
הֵעִיר צֶדֶק בְּחֻבּוֹ, לֹא יָדַע בְּחַיָּיהוּ, --
אֵי לֵב נָחוּשׁ, קוֹלוֹ שָׁמַע וַיָּבֶן,
אֵינֶנּוּ אֻכַּל מַלְהֲבוֹת שִׁירֵיהוּ? --
כִּנּוֹרוֹ, יֹאמַר, נַעֲלֶה מִכִּסְאֵהוּ.

Transcriptions

הוּא יִתֵּן עֹז לְמַלְכּוֹ, גֹּדֶל לְאֵל-עוֹלָם,
בִּיעַף עַל הִגָּיוֹן בְּרוּחוֹ פִּי-שְׁנָיִם,
עֲמָקִים יִדֹּדוּן, הָרִים נָשְׂאוּ קוֹלָם.
גַּם אַרְזֵי לְבָנוֹן יִשְׂחוּ אַפָּיִם
בְּהִתְאַבֵּד זִמְרַת -- יָהּ לַעֲלוֹת שָׁמַיִם.

מֵאָז-בְּשֶׁנָם נֶאֱלָם, יָדָם עֲלֵי אֲדָמָה, --
עֲלֵי כַּנְפֵי אַהֲבָה, עֲלֵי רִנָּה וּתְפִלָּה
נֶפֶשׁ נַעֲנָה כִּי תֵדָא לְעַרְבוֹת הָרָמָה,
הֵד לַהֲקַת נְגִינוֹת, צִלְצְלֵי רִנַּת תְּהִלָּה
תַּקְשֵׁב וְתִשְׁמַע בַּחֲלוֹם בְּהָקִיץ סֶלָה.

Darkness (ll. 69–91)

חֶזְיוֹן מַחְשָׁךְ. (שירה בת שש מדות)

אֶבֶן בֹּהוּ תְמוּנָתָהּ, גַּלְמָהּ יְוֵן צַלְמָוֶת! --
פְּלָגִים יִבְלֵי מַיִם, נַהֲרֵי נַחֲלֵי זֶרֶם,
גַּם הַיָּם הַגָּדוֹל הַסּוֹבֵב עַפְרוֹת תֵּבֵל,
שָׁכְנוּ כָּאֶבֶן דּוּמָם, שֶׁקֶט כִּרְפָאִים שָׁאֲנָנוּ,
בְּמַעֲמַקֵּי תְהוֹם רַבָּה נֶאֱסַף נִשְׁמַת חַיִּים.
אֳנִיּוֹת עֲזוּבוֹת חָפְשִׁי, בִּמְצוּלַת מַיִם יִרְקָבוּ,
תָּרְנָם יִתְפָּרֵד לִגְזָרִים וְלֹעַ הַיָּם יִבְלָעֵמוֹ,
תְּשׁוּאוֹת דָּכְיָם יִשְׁתֹּקוּ, וְאֵין קֶצֶף בִּפְנֵיהֶם,
גַּלִּים יְשֵׁנוּ הֲמוֹנָתָהּ, פִּיּוֹת מִשְׁבָּרִים קְבָרִים.
סְעָרוֹת תֵּימָן וְסוּפָתָהּ יְלַחֲצוּ בְּמוֹ-רָמִים,
עָנָן וַעֲרָפֶל נָדֹדוּ, נְשִׂיאִים יִתְהַלְּכוּ לָמוֹ,
בִּלְעָדָם חֹשֶׁךְ לְמַדַּי, שֹׁאָה וְאֵמֶשׁ לְמַכְבִּיר,
אַךְ חֹשֶׁךְ הַשַּׁלִּיט, הוּא הַתֵּבֵל סֶלָה.

185

APPENDIX

Judah Leib Gordon

"If that High World"

כתבי יהודה ליב גורגון. שירה.

א

אִם אֱמֶת הַדָּבָר כִּי בַשָּׁמַיִם
עוֹד בֵּין הָרוּחוֹת הָאַהֲבָה שׁוֹכֶנֶת,
כִּי אֵין שָׁם אָסוֹן, אֵין דִּמְעוֹת עֵינַיִם.
אֵין לֵב מִתְעַצֵּב, נֶפֶשׁ מִתְאוֹנֶנֶת --
אָז שָׁלוֹם לָכֶם, עוֹלָמוֹת אֵין חֵקֶר.
וּבָרוּךְ בֹּאֲךָ, רֶגַע הַמָּוֶת,
עֵת מְאוֹר נֶצַח מִיפְעַת הַבֹּקֶר
יָנוּס לֵיל עָמָל, תָּפוּג כָּל עַצֶּבֶת.

אֱמֶת הַדָּבָר! וּמַה-טּוֹב חֶלְקֵנוּ!
תִּקְוָה זֹאת תָּסִיר מִלִּבֵּנוּ אֲבָל
בְּעָמְדֵי עַל יַרְכְּתֵי בוֹר שַׁחַת רַגְלֵנוּ
וּשְׁנוֹתֵינוּ נִרְאֶה גָזוּ כַהֶבֶל.
כָּל יוֹרְדֵי בוֹר! זִכְרוּ זֹאת הִתְאוֹשָׁשׁוּ;
שָׁם, בִּמְקוֹם כָּל הָרוּחוֹת יִתְאַחֲדוּ,
שָׁם אֵין עוֹד אֵיבָה, הַלְּבָבוֹת נִצְמָדוּ
קָרְבוּ לִפְנֵי אֲדֹנָי וַיִּקְדָשׁוּ.

"The Wild Gazelle"

ג

נְדוּ לַמְיַלֶּלֶת עַל נַהֲרוֹת בָּבֶל,
עַל שִׁירָה כִּי שָׁבַת מִפִּי הַנֵּבֶל,
עַל אַרְצָהּ כִּי עַל יַד חֶרֶב הִגִּירוּ,
עַל אֵל צוּרָהּ בֵּאלֹהֵי זָר הֵמִירוּ.

אָן רַגְלְךָ בְּצֵקָה, גּוֹי אֹבֵד, תָּנוּחַ?
מָתַי עַל צִיּוֹן יַעֲרֶה הָרוּחַ,
וּמִשִּׁירוֹת הֵיכָל כִּי יִתְּנוּ קוֹלָם
יָשׁוּב לֵב עַמָּהּ וִיחִי כִּימֵי עוֹלָם?

Transcriptions

מָתַי הָהּ, גֻּלֶּה אֵל כָּל אַפְסֵי אָרֶץ,
תִּמְצָא מָנוֹחַ מִשֵּׁד וּמִפָּרֶץ?
גַּם יוֹנָה מָצְאָה קֵן, מָעוֹן כָּל גֶּבֶר,
סֶלַע הַשָּׁפָן, וִיהוּדָה -- רַק קָבֶר!!

Ezekiel Bleicher

Harold's farewell (stanzas 1–3)

י. בלייכער, טשיילד האראלד, פֿאעמא פֿון לארד בייראן.

אדיע, אדיע! מיין היים פערשווינדט
אין בלויען ים ווייט, ווייט;
עס רוישט דער ים, עס זיפֿצט דער ווינד,
א וואסערפֿויגעל שרייט.
מיר זעגלען זו דעם גאלדענעם זוים,
וואו ס'זינקט די זון אין פראכט;
איך זעגען מיך מיט זון און היים,
מיין פֿאטערלאנד -- גוט נאכט!

ביז ווידער וועט די זון אויפֿגעהן,
בלויז שעה'ן נאר געווערט;
דאן זעה איך נאר דעם ים אליין,
ניט מעהר די ליעבע ערד.
פֿער'יתומ'ט איז מיין אלטער שלאס,
וויסט אלץ ארום און רונד;
די וועגד בעדעקט א ווילדעס גראז,
ביים טויער קלאגט מיין הונד.

"אהער, אהער, מיין פאזש, טרעט צו,
וואס ווינסט און קלאגסט, דו קינד!
צי פאר די וועלען ציטערסטו?
שרעקט שטורעם דיך און ווינד?
וויש אב די טרעהרען -- זיי נישט באנג,
פֿאר וועלען שרעק דיך ניט:
די שיף איז שטארק -- ס'איז לייכט איהר גאנג,
קיין פֿויגעל האלט איהר מיט!"

APPENDIX

Max (Mordechai) Hershman

The Prisoner of Chillon (part 1)

מאַקס הערשמאַן, דער געפֿאַנגענער פֿון שיליאַן

מײַן קאָפּ איז שוין גרוי, אָבער ניט פֿון קיין יאָהרען,
און גרוי איז ער אויך ניט אין אײן נאַכט געוואָרען,
ווי ס'האָט זיך מיט אַנד'רע פֿון פּחד געטראָפֿען;
און שוואַך מײַנע גלידער -- האָטש ניט פֿון קיין אַרבײט.
זײ זײַנען פֿון ווערטלאָזער רוה בלויז פֿערגלויווערט:
אַ שפּיעל צײג זײ זײַנען געוועזן אין דער תפיסה;
און מײַן איז געוויעזן דער שיקזאַל פֿון יענע,
פֿאַר וועמען די געטליכע ערד און דער הימעל
איז תמיד פֿערשלאָסען, פֿערצוימט און פֿערבאַנען.
געליטען האָב איך פֿאַר מײַן פֿאָטערס בלויז גלויבען,
אין קײטען געשמידט, פֿון אַ לאַנגזאַמער מיתה
געשטאָרבען איז ער בײַ אַ שאַנד-סלופ, מײַן פֿאָטער,
ווײַל ער האָט זײַן גלויבען געוואָלט ניט באַשפּעטען,
און פֿאַר די חטאים די יונגערע דורות
געפֿונין אין פֿינפֿערניש האָבען אַ ישוב . . .
געוועזן זײַנען זיבען -- געבליבען בלויז אײנער --
און זעקס אין דער יוגענד, אין עלטער בלויז אײנער
שוין האָבען מיט שטאָלץ זײַער לעבען פֿערלוירען:
אין פֿײַער האָט אײנער און זווײַ אויף די פֿעלדער
דאָרט האָבען מיט בלוט זײַער גלויבען פֿאַרשטעמפּעלט;
געשטאָרבען ווי העלדען, אַזוי ווי דער פֿאָטער,
פֿאַר גאָט וואָס די פֿײַנד האָבען תמיד פֿאַרלײקענט;
און דרײַ האָבען יאָהרען געשמאַכט אין אַ תפיסה,
פֿון וועמען פֿאַרבליבען איז אָט דיזע רואינע.

188

Transcriptions

Nathan Horowitz

Hebrew Melodies — in Yiddish

נתן האראוויץ, בייראן'ס העברעאישע מעלאדיען

"She Walks in Beauty"

אין שעהנהייט . . .

אין שיהנהייט וואנדעלט זי ווי נאכט:
אין וואלקענלאז שטערענדיגע לופֿט
פֿון גלאנץ און דונקעלהייט דער פראכט
איז אויסגעמישט אין מינע און אויג --
ווי געבוירען פֿאר יענעם מילדען שיין
וואס פֿאלט ניט אויף א מיאוס'ען טאג!

און וועניגער א שטראהל, א שאטען מעהר,
וואלט צוגעבען צום וואונדער-חן
וואס איסגעמישט ז'אין ראבֿ-שווארץ לאק,
און אויף איהר צארט און קלאהר געזיכט,
דער אויסדרוק וואו עס זאגט ווי ריין;
ס'איז דער געדאנק, דער מיין, דער קלעהר! . . .

און אויף די באקען, אויפֿ'ן ברעם,
אזוי ליעבליך שטיל, און דאך בערעדט,
דער שמייכעל נעהמט, קאליר צוציהט,
דאך מיט ערגעבענעם געמיהט --
קיין שלעגטס ניט האב'נדיג אויסגעאבט
א הארץ וואס היים אונשולדיג ליעבט!

"The Harp the Monarch Minstrel Swept"

די הארפע פֿון דוד המלך . . .

די הארפע פֿון דוד המלך,
איהר קלאנג, ווייַלע באנג,
ט'אומעטום איינגעדרונגען,
און אין טרערען זושפרונגען . . .
ס'האט אייזערנע הערצער --
געריהרט און בעצוואואנגען,
יעדער אויער ט'פֿערנומען די שירה --

189

APPENDIX

ביז זיין לירע:
ט'זיין קעניגליכען טראהן איבערשטייגען!
אבגעבען פלעגט'ס א ליב זו דעם בורא
ווער יעדען בעזארגט און בעהיט --
אברופען פלעגען טהאלען זיך פריילך,
און צעדרען און בערגער זיך בויגען און נויגען
ס'האט הימלען דערגרייכט --
זייט דאן כאטש געוויכט,
דאך רייסט אב און נעהמט נאך געפאנגען
דאס הימלישע ליעד:
פון שפל'ע, וואכענדיגע פערלאנגען! . . .

"On Jordan's Banks"

ביים ברעג פון ירדן . . .

ביים ברעג פון ירדן געהען דעם אראבער'ס קעמלען אום;
אויף זיונס בארג מתפלל זיינען די פאלש-גלויבענדע דום;
און אונטער דעם בארג סני בוקט מען זיך זום בעל --
אויך דארט וואו איז זשע, גאט, דיין דונער-קנאל!?
דארט וואו דיין פינגער האט געקריצעט געבאט אין לוח שטיין,
דארט וואו באוויזען דיני קינדער האסטו זיך אליין --
טיעף איינגעהילט אין פייער-פלאמען-קלייד,
ניט זעהנבאר כאטש צו ברוואים לעבעדיגעראהייד!
אין קולות און אין בליצען ווידער, ווידער זיך באוויז! --
צושטעטער דעם בעדריקערס שווערד, פון האנד איהם ארויסרייס!
ווי לאנג וועט ס'לאנד פון אונרעכט זיין געדראהט?
דיין טעמפעל פוסטעוועין ווי לאנג וועט? גאט!

Nathan Horowitz

Hebrew Melodies—in Hebrew

נתן האראוויץ, *שירי ישראל של ביירן*

"She Walks in Beauty"

היא מצניעה לכת ביופי . . .

היא מצניעה לכת ביופי בלילה
באויר לא מעונן וכוכביות הרקיע;
ומיטב האופל וזוהר מגולה

נפגשים בחן מראה ומבטה המניהה;
ובכך תשתלם לעדינות אותו האור
שהשמים מונעים מיום לא יקר! . . .
וביותר קצת צל וחיסור אור אורב:
כמעט שהיה מתקלקל כל נאות חמדתה
המתגוללת בקוצותיה השחורות כעורב
ומהילה ברוך על זכות הוד דמותה,
במקום שם רעננות ההגיון תביע
הביבות הדר התום המשפיע! . . .
ועלי הלחי הצח, ועל המצח הבהיר
כה שוקט כה נוח ועם זה מלא נעימה:
הצחוק מצליח, הנון מאיר ומפאר,
ומספר על סבר טוב מימים ימימה --
על טוב טעם ושכל עם שלומי הנמוכים,
ועל לב מלא אהבה לצדיקי נדחים! . . .

"The Harp the Monarch Minstrel Swept"

המלך המשורר . . .

הכנור שהמלך המשורר הגיע
לפני עבדיו הנאמנים במשיח אלוהי רומה;
אשר זמרתו הללה הקדושה בבכיה,
וכל קרב היה הומה לאדוני בכל נימה:
יכפלו דמעותיו על חיי בושה וכלימה! --
הוא רכה קשי-המזג וברזל כל תכונה,
והעניק מעלות טובות לכל נמבזה ושפל;
ולא נמצא כבד לב נשמה אי-נבונה
שלא יתרגש ולא יתלהב לנגינתו עלי נבל --
עד שזמרתו התגברה על כסאו בתבל!
כלי-שירתו ספרה נצחונות המשיח --
וחניפה לאלוהינו רוממות התפארת;
כל עמק שפלינו בתפילותיו השתמח,
כל הר וגבעה על ידו התנצח בזמירות;
כנורו שאף השמימה עם כל טוהר הדרות;
ובהלכו ואיננו, אף שלא השמע יותר:
הותיקות ותולדתה האהבה הנעלה,
מצוים בחזון נפרץ כבאותו המיתר,
את הרוח לעוף לבת-קולו למעלה
בדמיונות אותם חומריות האור לא תבלה! . . .

APPENDIX

"On Jordan's Banks"

על שפת הירדן . . .

על שפת הירדן שם גמלי הערבים תועים,
על ציון הר הקודש עובדי גילולים מרשיעים:
ומעריצי הבעל משתחוים על שיפוע הר-סני!
גם שם, עוד שם, וקול רעמך מחדיש אדוני!
גם שם במקום אצבעותיך חקקו דברותיך,
במקום שם, רוממותך -- צל שדי, נגלה לעמיך,
ותפארתך התעטפה בלבת אש שמים:
בכבוד הגבורה אשר לא תראה לבשר בחיים!
הה, הבט נא על משנאך בהבהקת ברקים!
והעבר מצוקת החרב בתורת שחקים!
עד מתי תחת רגלי כל אכזר תחולל אדמתך?
עד מתי ישום היבלך בהעדר שכינתך?!

Abraham Asen

The Prisoner of Chillon (part 1)

דר. א. אייסען, לאָרד בײראָן: דער געפאַנגענער פון שילאָן.

איך בין שוין גרוי, -- דאָך ניט די יאָרן
האָבן דאָס געמאַכט,
ניט דורך איין נאַכט
איז ווייס מיין קאָפ פון שרעק געוואָרן;
ס'האָט ניט די אַרבעט מיך פאַרקרימט,
נאָר שלעכטע רו האָט מיך פאַרצערט,
ווייל תפיסה איז געווען באַשטימט
און אויך אַ מזל מיר באַשערט,
ווי די, וואָס פון דער וועלט פאַריאָגט
און פריי צו אָטעמען פאַרזאָגט;
צוליב מיין פאָטער'ס גלויבן געטראָגן קייטן
און אָפט אויף זיך דעם טויט געבעטן;
פאַר'ן גלויבן האָט מיין פאָטער ס'לעבן
צום מאַרטער-סלופ אַוועקגעגעבן
און אויך פאַר דעם האָט מען פאַרשיקט
די זין אין תפיסה, און דערשטיקט.
זיבן זיינען מיר געווען;
איצט -- איך איינער נאָר אַליין!
יאָ, געווען צוזאַמען זיבן,

זעקס נאָך יונג, און איינער אַלט, --
ביז צום לעצטן טאָג פאַרבליבן
שטאָלץ אַנטקעגן שׂונאס געוואַלט.
איינער אין אַ פייער, צוויי
געפאַלן דורך מלחמה-גלוט,
הייס פאַרזיגלט מיט דאָס בלוט
זייער גלויבן האָבן זיי;
אַלע קעמפנדיק פאַר גאָט --
ווען דער שׂונא האָט פאַרשפּאַט;
דריי אין טורמע-גרוב פאַרטריבן,
איך -- אַ חורבה -- בין פאַרבליבן.

Cain (I.1.64–79)

דר. א. אייסען, קין

קין
אַליין

און דאָס איז לעבן! --
בלויז אַרבעטן! -- פאַרוואָס מוז איך דאָס טון?
דערפאַר וואָס סהאָט מיין פאָטער נישט געקענט
אין דעם גן-עדן אויפהאַלטן זיין אָרט.
איז דאָס מיין שולד? כ'בין דאַן אויף דער וועלט
נאָך נישט געווען און נישט פאַרלאַנגט צו זיין;
אויך פרי איך זיך נישט וואָס איך בין שוין דאָ.
פאַרוואָס האָט ער דעם שלאַנג און ווייב געפאָגט?
און אויב שוין יאָ, פאַרוואָס קומט לייד ן מיר?
וווּ ליגט די זינד? -- דער בוים איז דאָך געווען
פאַרפלאַנצט, פאַרוואָס דען עפּעס נישט פאַר אים?
אויב נישט, פאַרוואָס אים צוגעלאָזט צום בוים,
דער שענסטער אין דעם קרייז? -- אויף אַלעם דעם
איך הער נאָר שטענדיק איינס: "עס איז אַזוי
געוואָלן גאָטס ווילן, און ער איז דאָך גוט".
פון וואַנען ווייס איך דאָס? דערפאַר וואָס ער
אַלמעכטיק איז קומט שוין אַלגוטס אַרויס?
איך משפּט לויט די פרוכט -- די פרוכט איז ביטער
און כ'מוז זי עסן פאַר אַ צווייטנס זינד. --
ווען זע איך דאָ -- אַ מלאך אין געשטאַלט,
אין דאָך זיין אויסדרוק איז צו ערנסט, שטרענג
צו זיין אַ גייסט:

APPENDIX

Moisei Khashtshevatski

The Prisoner of Chillon (part 1)

מ. כאשטשעוואצקי, בײראָן - דער געפֿאַנגענער פֿון שיליאָן.

מײַן קאָפּ איז גרוי, נאָר ניט פֿון יאָרן,
ניט גרייַז געוואָרן
פֿאַר איין נאַכט,
ווי פֿון אַ איבערשרעק זיך מאַכט.
מײַן גוף איז ניט פֿון אַרבעט מאַט,
ס'האָט בייזע רו אים אויסגעשעפֿט.
איך האָב אין טפֿיסע לאַנג געלעבט.
דאָס וויסטע מזל כ'האָב געהאַט --
ס'איז מיר דער וועג צו לופֿט, צו ערד
געווען פֿאַרשטעלט, געווען פֿאַרווערט.
כ'האָב פֿאַרן פֿאָטערס פֿרייַען דראַנג
געצאָלט מיט צוואַנג און טויט-פֿאַרלאַנג.
דער פֿאָטער איז געפֿאַלן טויט,
נאָר פֿעסט אין זייַנס געווען פֿאַרגלויבט.
און אונדז -- די קינדער פֿון זייַן שטוב,
האָט מען פֿאַרמוויערט אין אַ גרוב.
פֿון זיבן -- כ'בין אַצינד אַליין.
זעקס יונגע, איינער שוין אַ גרייַז,
האָבן געשטריטן לאַנג און דרייַסט --
די פֿייַן האָט זיי געשטאַרקט נאָך מייַן.
אין פֿייַער -- איינער, צוויי -- אין פֿעלד
האָבן פֿאַרגאָסן זייער בלוט,
און ווי דער פֿאָטער פֿול מיט מוט
דעם פֿייַנט אקעגן זיך געשטעלט.
און דרייַ -- פֿאַרשפּאַרט אין טפֿיסע-שטייַג,
כ'בין פֿון די דרייַ דער לעצטער צווייַג.

194

Solomon Mandelkern

"She Walks in Beauty"

ד"ר שלמה מאנדעלקערן, *שִׁירֵי יְשֻׁרוּן, עַל-פִּי לוֹרְדְּ בַּיְרוֹן.*

שׁוּלַמִּית.

בִּיקָר תִּפְאַרְתָּהּ כְּלִילַת-יֹפִי מִתְהַלֶּכֶת
כְּלֵיל בָּהִיר בַּשְּׁחָקִים, כּוֹכְבֵי-אוֹר כִּי יִנְהָרוּ,
צִלְלֵי נֹעַם וּנְגֹהוֹת יַחְדָּו בַּמַּעֲרֶכֶת
עַל-הוֹד פָּנֶיהָ וְעֵינֶיהָ תֹּאֲמִים חֻבָּרוּ;
מֵחֹם הַיּוֹם, עֵת הַשֶּׁמֶשׁ בָּעֹז דֹּרֶכֶת,
נְעָמוֹת עֵדֶן כָּאֵלֶּה אַף-אֻמְנָם נֶעְדָּרוּ.

בְּעֹדֶף הַצֵּל אוֹ בִּמְעַט הָאוֹר כִּמְלֹא-שַֹעַר
מֵחִין עֶרֶךְ הֲדָרָהּ הַחֲצִי יִגְרָע, --
מִקְוֻצּוֹתֶיהָ הַשְּׁחֹרוֹת כְּעוֹרֵב הַיַּעַר
וּמִזִּיו צַחֲחוֹת עַל-פָּנֶיהָ יִגְרָע;
נֹגַהּ לְרַעְיוֹנֵי טֹהַר מִצְחָהּ אַגַּן הַסַּהַר,
„מַה-נָּעִים שֶׁבֶת פֹּה!" קוֹל דְּמָמָה יִשְׁמָע.

וְעַל-רַקָּתָהּ, אַף עַל-לֶחְיָה כְּגֶפֶן פֹּרַחַת
גַּם-בְּדוּמִיָּה וָשֶׁקֶט דֵּי-בְאֵר יַבִּיעַ --
שְֹחוֹק לֹקֵחַ לֵב, יִפְעָה כְּאֶקְדָּה זוֹרַחַת,
אוֹת כִּי כָל-יָמֶיהָ אַךְ טוֹב נַפְשָׁהּ הַשְֹבִּיעַ;
רוּחָהּ מִכֹּל בָּאָרֶץ יָרְחָה שָׁלוֹם וָנַחַת
וּבְלִבָּהּ אַהֲבָה בָרָה -- כְּזֹהַר הָרָקִיעַ!

APPENDIX

David Frishman

Cain (I.1.64–79)

דוד פרישמן, *קין. שיר-חזיון על-פי כתבי הקדש. מאת לורד בַּיְרוֹן.* תרגם מאנגלית לעברית דוד פרישמן.

קין (לבדו).

וְלָזֹאת יְקָרֵא חַיִּים! -- עֲבוֹדָה! אַךְ לָמָּה אֶעֱבוֹד? --
רַק עֵקֶב לֹא הִתְחַזֵּק אָבִי עַל הַמָּקוֹם
אֲשֶׁר הָיָה לוֹ בְעֵדֶן. אַךְ לִי וְלָזֹאת מָה אֵפֹא?
אֲנִי אָז לֹא-נוֹלַדְתִּי: לֹא שָׁאַלְתִּי כִּי אִוָּלֵד,
וְגַם עֲלֵי לֹא עָלַצְתִּי בְחֶלְקִי כִּי נוֹלַדְתִּי.
מַדּוּעַ לְקוֹל הַנָּחָשׁ שָׁמַע וּלְקוֹל הָאִשָּׁה?
אוֹ לָמָּה זֶּה, אִם שָׁמַע, עַל כָּכָה סָבַל נִסְבֹּל?
וּבַמֶּה עֲוֹנוֹ גָדוֹל? הֵן שָׁתוּל הָיָה הָעֵץ --
וְלָמָּה אֵפֹא אָמַר: לֹא הָיָה הָעֵץ גַּם לוֹ?
וְאִם לֹא גַם לוֹ, עַל מַה-זֶּה נִטַּע קָרוֹב אֵלָיו,
וְכֻלּוֹ יָפֶה וְנֶחְמָד וְתַאֲוָה לָעֵינַיִם?
אַךְ הֵם רַק דָּבָר אֶחָד יַעֲנוּ עַל כָּל הַשְּׁאֵלוֹת:
„הוּא חָפֵץ -- וְהוּא הֵן טוֹב". אַךְ מִי לִי זֹאת יוֹכִיחַ?
הֲבַאֲשֶׁר הוּא כֹל יָכוֹל כִּי לָכֵן טוֹב מִכֹּל הוּא?
וַאֲנִי אַל-פִּי הַפְּרִי רַק אֶשְׁפּוֹט -- וְהוּא מַה מָּר --
אֲשֶׁר נָטַל עָלַי לְאָכְלָה עַל חֵטְא, וְהוּא לֹא חֶטְאִי.
אַךְ מָה הַמַּרְאֶה פִּתְאֹם? -- צֶלֶם מַלְאָךְ צַלְמוֹ,
רַק פָּנָיו לָבְשׁוּ קַדְרוּת וּמַרְאֵהוּ סָר וְזָעֵף
שִׁבְעָתַיִם מִן הָרוּחוֹת:

196

Isaac Loeb Baruch (I. L. Brocowitz)

The Prisoner of Chillon, first version (part 1)

יצחק-לייב ברוך (י"ל ברוכוביץ), אֲסִיר *שִׁילְיָן*. פּוֹאֵמָה מֵאֵת לוֹרְד בַּיְרוֹן.

שְׂעָרִי הִלְבִּין, אַךְ לֹא מֵעֵת,
אַף לֹא בֶּן לֵיל זְוָעָה וּרְתֵת
קָפְצָה עָלָיו שֵׂיבַת-פִּתְאוֹם
כְּשׁוּב שַׁעַר רַבִּים מִשַּׁד בְּלֹא-יוֹם.
גֵּוִי נִדְכֶּה, אַךְ לֹא מֵעָל,
הוּא שַׁח מִבַּטָּלָה בַּת-שְׁאוֹל.
צְמָתַנִי צֹק מַאֲסָר אָיֹם,
מַר גּוֹרָלִי גּוֹרַל קְשִׁי-יוֹם,
שֶׁבְּלִי אֲוִיר וּבְלִי קַו אוֹר
הֻמָּק יָמַקּוּ אַט בַּבּוֹר.
זוּ עַל נָצְרִי אֶת דַּת הָאָב
דֻּכֵּאנִי כְּלוֹא וָעֹנִי רָב.
אָבִי עַל עֵץ מֵת מָוֶת מָר,
עַל כִּי מִדַּת קָדְשׁוֹ לֹא סָר,
בִּגְלַל זֹאת גַּם זַרְעוֹ הָהּ! רָד
בְּלֹא-עֵת לִנְאוֹת צַלְמָוֶת-עַד.
שִׁבְעָה הָיִינוּ, אַךְ כָּעֵת
בִּלְתִּי אֶחָד, שֶׁבַע אַיִר וּשְׂאֵת
עוֹד חַי חַיֵּי צוּקָה וֶעֱנוּת;
שִׁשָּׁה עוֹדָם בַּאֲבִיב שַׁחֲרוּת
מְלֵאֵי גָאוֹן מֵחֲמַת הַצָּר
עָלֵימוֹ בָּא הָהּ! קֵץ אַכְזָר.
אֶחָד בְּלֶבַב לֶהָבוֹת הַיְקוֹד
וּשְׁנַיִם עַל שְׂדֵה קְרָב נָשָׁד.
שָׁפְכוּ דָמָם בְּעַד כְּבוֹד הָאֵל,
אֲשֶׁר הַצָּר נִאֵץ, חִלֵּל.
שְׁלֹשָׁה הֻטְּלוּ אֶל בּוֹר הַשְּׁבִי;
מֵהֶם שָׂרַדְתִּי רַק אֲנִי.

APPENDIX

Jacob Orland

"If that High World"

יעקב אורלנד, לורד ביררון, מנגנות עבריות

אם העולם.

אִם הָעוֹלָם אֲשֶׁר נָתַּו
מֵעֵבֶר לָנוּ, בְּרִית יִשְׁמֹר;
אִם עוֹד הַלֵּב שָׁם יֶאֱהַב
וְעַיִן אֵין-דִּמְעָה תְּאוֹר --
בְּרוּכִים הֵם מֶרְחֲבֵי הַהוֹד
וּשְׁעַת הַמָּוֶת שֶׁהֶנֵּצָה,
עֵת נִתְעוֹפֵף מֵאֲדָמוֹת
וּמוֹרָאָן, אֵלֶיךָ -- נֶצַח.

כֵּן הַדָּבָר: הֵן לֹא בִּכְדִי
כֹּה יִחַתָּנוּ זֵכֶר קֵץ,
עֵת נוֹעָזִים נִפְרָץ הַדִּין
וְאֶל דִּינֵנוּ נֵאָלֵץ.
הוֹ, נַחֲזֶה-נָא יוֹם עֲתִידוֹת,
עֵת לֵב בְּלֵב רֵעוֹ יָצוּד;
עִמָּם מֵימֵי הַנֵּצַח שְׁתוֹת
וְעִמָּהֶם הֱיוֹת אַלְמָוֶת.

"Oh Weep for Those"

הוֹ, בְּכוּ נָא לַבּוֹכִים.

הוֹ, בְּכוּ נָא לַבּוֹכִים עַל נַהֲרוֹת בָּבֶל,
מוֹלַדְתָּם חֲלוֹם וּמִקְדָּשָׁם אָבֵל,
סִפְדוּ לִיהוּדָה וּלְשֶׁבֶר כִּנּוֹרֶיהָ
וּלְבֵית-אֵל סִפְדוּ, אֲשֶׁר אֵין-אֵל הִנֵּה.

וְאֵי תִּרְחַץ צִיּוֹן רַגְלֶיהָ מִן הַדָּם?
וְאֵימָתַי יֵעוֹר שִׁירָה אֲשֶׁר נָדָם?
וְזֶמֶר יְהוּדָה אֲשֶׁר שִׂמַּח לֵבָב,
אֵיכָכָה יִשָּׁמַע וְאֵיךְ עוֹד יֶעֱרַב?

שִׁבְטֵי הַנּוֹדְדִים וִיגִיעֵי הַכֹּחַ,
אֵי-אָן תַּרְחִיקוּ נוֹד וְתִמְצְאוּ מָנוֹחַ!
יֵשׁ קֵן לְיוֹנַת-בָּר וְלַשּׁוּעָל חוֹרֵהוּ
וְאֶרֶץ לָאָדָם, וּלְיִשְׂרָאֵל -- קִבְרֵהוּ.

Moshe Giora

Harold's farewell (stanzas 1–3)

מֹשֶׁה גִּיּוֹרָא, הַשּׁוֹשַׁנָּה הַכְּחֻלָּה, שִׁירִים

שִׁיר הַפְּרֵדָה אֲשֶׁר לְצֶאֱלָד הָרוֹלְד.

א

"שָׁלוֹם, שָׁלוֹם! חוֹף מְכוֹרָה
אוֹבֵד בְּיָם מַכְחִיל.
צוֹרֵחַ שַׁחַף, גַּל יִקְרָא,
וְרוּחַ לֵיל תֵּילִיל.
שָׁם, עַל הַיָּם, חַמָּה תִּדְעַךְ;
עֵינֵנוּ לָךְ שְׁלוּחָה,
אֹמַר שָׁלוֹם גַּם לָהּ, גַּם לָךְ,
אַרְצִי. -- לֵיל מְנוּחָה!

ב

שָׁעוֹת מִזְעָר -- וְהִיא תִּרְעַם;
תֵּלֵד אֶת שַׁחֲרָהּ.
וַאֲבָרֵךְ אָז שְׂחֹק יָם,
אַךְ לֹא נוֹף-אֵם-הוֹרָה.
שָׁם הֵיכָלִי הַטּוֹב עָרִיר,
וְשׁוֹמֵמָה הָאָח.
שָׁמִיר וָשַׁיִת עַל הַקִּיר.
כַּלְבִּי עַל סַף יִנְבַּח.

ג

"גֶּשׁ הֵנָּה, פַּז' קָטָן שֶׁלִּי!
מַה תֵּבְךְ וְתֵאָבַל?

APPENDIX

הַאִם תִּירָא מִנַּחְשׁוֹלִים,
תַּחַת מִצְעַף גַּל?
כָּל דֶּמַע־עַיִן שָׁלַח -- וְגַז.
קַל הָאֲנִי, חָזָק.
גַּם הַמָּהִיר בְּכָל הַבָּז
גֵּא מֶנּוּ לֹא יַסִּק".

Shmuel Friedman

"She Walks in Beauty"

שמואל פרידמן, לורד ביירון, מנגינות עבריות

יָפְיָהּ כָּלִיל כְּלֵיל בָּהִיר.

יָפְיָהּ כָּלִיל כְּלֵיל בָּהִיר
אֵין עָב, זְרוּעַ יָם־כּוֹכָב;
אוֹר־צֵל נִפְגַּשׁ דְּמוּתָהּ יָאִיר,
יַחְשׂף חִנָּהּ לְלֹא רְבָב;
אֲחַר נִמְזַג בְּאוֹר שַׁפְרִיר,
שְׁחָקִים מוֹנְעִים מִיּוֹם שֶׁל סְתָו.

אוֹר־פָּז נֶחְלָשׁ, אוֹ צֵל חוֹלֵף,
כְּלָל לֹא יָעִיב אֶת זִיו־אוֹרָהּ;
תַּלְתַּל גּוֹלֵשׁ כִּשְׁחוֹר עוֹרֵב,
יַקְרִין דְּמוּתָהּ בִּנְהָרָה.
מַחְשֶׁבֶת תֹּם יְרַחֵשׁ הַלֵּב
זַכָּה, וּכְמוֹ גּוּפָהּ טְהוֹרָה.

לְחִי סוֹמֶק וּמֵצַח זַךְ,
כָּל־כַּךְ עָנֹג וְכֹה בָּהִיר;
קַלּוֹת יִסְחַט חִיּוּךְ נִדָּח,
וְנֹעַם חֶסֶד־אֵל יָעִיר;
שַׁלְוָה סָבִיב רוּחָהּ תִּשְׁלַח,
לִבָּהּ אַהֲבַת־תֹּם יַסְתִּיר.

200

Transcriptions

"O Weep for Those"

הוֹי! בְּכוּ לַבּוֹכִים.

הוֹי! בְּכוּ לַבּוֹכִים עַל מֵי בָּבֶל,
אַרְצָם חֲלוֹם, חָרֵב מִקְדַּשׁ-הָאֵל;
כִּנּוֹר-צִיּוֹן שָׁבוּר, הֵם יִסְפְּדוּ,
וּבְהֵיכָלָם חַסְרֵי-אֵל יִסְגְּדוּ!

אֵי יִשְׂרָאֵל יִרְחַץ רַגְלָיו בְּצִקּוֹת?
וְשִׁיר צִיּוֹן יִתְרוֹנֵן מְתוּקוֹת?
שִׁיר יְהוּדָה מָתַי יַרְעִיד שֵׁנִית
אֶת הַלְּבָבוֹת בִּנְגִינָה שְׁמֵימִית?

שְׁבָטִים רַגְלָם זָבָה, תְּשׁוּשֵׁי-חָזֶה,
הֲיִמָּצֵא מִקְלָט לָעָם הַזֶּה?
יֵשׁ קֵן לַתּוֹר, גַּם לַשּׁוּעָל מִסְתּוֹר,
לְכָל עַם נַחֲלָה -- לְיִשְׂרָאֵל רַק בּוֹר!

Notes

INTRODUCTION

1. Spector, "Jewish Translations of British Romantic Literature." As I indicate in that essay, little archival work has been done on Jewish translation. For the bibliography, I looked through whatever bibliographical resources I could find, checked catalogues of collections that might contain Jewish and Byronic materials, followed through on footnote references, and checked whatever archives I knew about, especially those of Abraham Asen at the YIVO Institute for Jewish Research in New York. Still, as I stress in the article's subtitle, the bibliography can be considered only preliminary, for undoubtedly there exist chapbooks that were never catalogued or have been lost, and poems that were issued in periodicals that also remain either uncatalogued or have been lost. Also, it should be noted, this study includes only those who translated enough Byron to base any analysis on; instances of individual lyrics have been omitted.

2. Despite its current pejorative connotations, I deliberately use the word *elitism*, not only because of Byron's aristocratic heritage but because intellectual Jews of the nineteenth and early twentieth centuries were considered part of the intelligentsia. My approach is consistent with that of Gilman in *Multiculturalism and the Jews;* see especially chapter 3, "Jews and the Constitution of the Multicultural Ethnic," where he discusses the transformation of the Jewish identity from a religious to a cultural orientation (45–64). As for the specific qualities of intellectual elitism and moral integrity, Gilman quotes Einstein's assertion that "the pursuit of knowledge for its own sake, an almost fanatical love of justice and the desire for personal independence—these are the features of the Jewish tradition which make me thank my lucky stars that I belong to it" (103; Gilman quotes Tauber, "Einstein and Zionism").

3. The essays in Hirst's collection *Byron, the Bible, and Religion* provide a good overview of the ways that the interests of Byron and the Jews intersected with each other.

4. For an overview of translation theory, see Munday, *Introducing Translation Studies.* Much of this discussion is based on Benjamin's "The Task of the Translator."

NOTES TO INTRODUCTION

5. As Venuti says in *The Scandals of Translation:*

> The selection of foreign texts and the development of translation strategies can establish peculiarly domestic canons for foreign literatures, canons that conform to domestic aesthetic values and therefore reveal exclusions and admissions, centers and peripheries that deviate from those current in the foreign language. Foreign literatures tend to be dehistoricized by the selection of texts for translation, removed from the foreign literary traditions where they draw their significance. And foreign texts are often rewritten to conform to styles and themes that *currently* prevail in domestic literatures, much to the disadvantage of more historicizing translation discourses that recover styles and themes from earlier moments in domestic traditions. (67)

6. Venuti argues that translation redefines the notion of authorship:

> Translation can be considered a form of authorship, but an authorship now redefined as derivative, not self-originating. Authorship is not *sui generis;* writing depends on pre-existing cultural materials, selected by the author, arranged in an order of priority, and rewritten (or elaborated) according to specific values. . . . From this point of view, what distinguishes translation from original composition is mainly the closeness of the mimetic relation to the other text: translation is governed by the goal of imitation, whereas composition is free, relatively speaking, to cultivate a more variable relation to the cultural materials it assimilates. (Ibid., 43–44)

7. According to Casanova, "For an impoverished target language, which is to say a language on the periphery that looks to import major works of literature, translation is a way of gathering literary resources, of acquiring universal texts and thereby enriching an underfunded literature—in short, a way of diverting literary assets" (*World Republic of Letters,* 134).

8. Lecercle's thesis in his book *The Violence of Language* is "the fact that all speakers are 'violently' constrained in their use of language by quite particular social and psychological realities."

9. Again Casanova: "Works of great literary subversiveness, ones that leave a mark in the center, are often translated by writers who themselves are international and polyglot and who, determined to break with the norms of their native literary space, seek to introduce into their language the modernity of the center" (*World Republic of Letters,* 134).

10. Benjamin sees in translation "the great motif of integrating many tongues into one true language" ("The Task of the Translator," 77); Casanova, "the process of unifying literary space" (*World Republic of Letters,* 134). For information about cosmopolitanism during Byron's time, see Scrivener's *Cosmopolitan Ideal.*

11. A very useful overview of Jewish attitudes toward translation can be found in Toury, "Translation and Reflection on Translation." the introduction to Singerman's *Jewish Translation History.* Of particular relevance to this study are the sections "The Enlightenment Period" (xx–xxv), "The Revival Period" (xxvi–xxviii), and "The

'Israeli' Age" (xxviii–xxix). It should be noted that Byron is mentioned only twice in Singerman's bibliography, in both cases his name being included in lists of western writers being translated. The first reference is to a Hebrew work by Menuḥah Gilbo'a, *Ben re'alixm le-romantikah* (Between Realism and Romanticism), and the second is to Prager, *Yiddish Culture in Britain*.

12. The distinction among the types of translation comes from Jakobson, "On Linguistic Aspects of Translation." It should be noted that the Jewish translators seldom indicated their copy text, so there is always the possibility that they used other translations as the basis for their versions of Byron.

13. Macaulay, "Moore's Life of Byron (June 1830)," 159.

14. Writing for a twenty-first-century Anglo-American audience, Douglass, in "Byron's Life and His Biographers," says: "The story of his life has changed as facts have emerged, but it has also changed with changes in culture and in practices of reading. With his ironic distance and skepticism, he appears more and more like our contemporary" (25). The most comprehensive biography is Marchand, *Byron*.

15. Priestman, in *Romantic Atheism*, asserts: "Whatever his philosophical inconsistencies . . . Byron certainly publicized and made glamorous the stance of the solitary individual somehow ennobled by his exclusion from a Christian order in which he may or may not believe" (238).

16. Though far better read than many of the Jewish translators, Ryan comes to virtually the same conclusion about Byron's character: "Byron's idea of reform involved the excoriation of hypocrisy, the unsettlement of complacency, and the redemption of the idea of the holy so that it would become less readily available to sanctify bad government" (*Romantic Reformation*, 150). On Byron, see especially chapter 4, "The Ironies of Belief" (119–51).

17. On Byron's attitude toward the Jews, see Matar, "English Romantic Poets and the Jews," especially 228–31. Like many of his contemporaries, Byron idealized the ancient Israelites but vilified contemporary moneylenders; as Matar puts it, "As symbols, the Jews fulfilled for him a literary function; but as financiers, they provoked his hatred" (231).

18. Unless otherwise indicated, these brief surveys of Byron's works are based on two standard studies: Marchand, *Byron's Poetry;* and Graham, *Lord Byron*.

19. It should be noted that Byron was advised by his publisher John Murray to tone down the satire. For a discussion of the Murray/Byron relationship, see Graham's essay "Byron and the Business of Publishing."

20. Graham, *Lord Byron*, 128. On the Byronic hero, see also Thorslev, *The Byronic Hero*.

21. The second edition was issued in 1818 under the title *The Literary Character, Illustrated by the History of Men of Genius, Drawn from Their Own Feelings and Confessions;* the third edition, considerably enlarged and improved, was published in 1822, and the fourth edition in 1828. Isaac D'Israeli's son Benjamin edited a new edition in 1859.

22. For a survey of the anti-Semitic responses to Byron's participation in the Jewish project, see the introduction to Burwick and Douglass, *A Selection of Hebrew Melodies*, 15–17.

NOTES TO INTRODUCTION

23. Dennis, "Making Death a Victory," 157.
24. This is Dingley's interpretation of the poem in his "I had a Dream."
25. According to Leonard S. Goldberg in "'This gloom . . . which can avail thee nothing'":

> Just as friction over what properly belongs to him makes Cain a useful representation for Byron's own domestic life, his turn from immanence and into a life of uncertainty, confusion, and denial makes him a logical focus for an investigation into the skepticism central to the stances most characteristic of Byron's later writing: the mobility, celebrated in *Don Juan,* through which he negates any center his consciousness might care to hold, and the critical posture which—certainly in the case of received readings of *Cain*—seems the ethical measure of ontological freedom. That in Cain Byron finds an understudy for the roles he has played both as guilty heir and as "idiot questioner" means that his tragedy can serve as a locus for testing the legitimacy of his own skepticism. An undercurrent of the play thus allows it to consider the philosophically respectable way in which denials are able to conceal illusions, and the ease with which the self can become bound to the altar of its own bad faith. The provocations of the play have far less to do with the inviting "mental mode" that Byron dramatizes through Cain, and that through the work he is familiarly read as endorsing, than with his exposure of an epistemic stance that, while it seems wholly congruent with radical freedom and apparently licenses a bold inquiry into religion and morals, distances him from the humanness for which he claims to speak. (208)

26. In "Byron's Cain," Quinones explores the significance of the historical context for reading *Cain:* "[T]he Cain and Abel theme, beginning with Byron, is ideally situated between theology and history, bringing with it, into a world where new values and new forms of being are struggling to be created, some residue adherent to a more fundamental and theological view of the world" (41). Of use in this regard, Looper's *Byron and the Bible* is designed to "provide ready access to the abundance of biblical material in Byron's work. This present study is an attempt to meet this need for a comprehensive reference compendium" (9).
27. Hirst, "Byron's Lapse into Orthodoxy," 152. Hirst expands his analysis in his essay "Byron's Revisionary Struggle with the Bible."
28. Schock, "The 'Satanism' of *Cain* in Context," 187.
29. Graham, *Lord Byron,* 119.
30. Stevens, "Scripture and the Literary Imagination," 119.
31. On Byron's skepticism, see Thorslev, "Byron and Bayle."
32. The standard history is Sachar's *History of the Jews in the Modern World.* On Europe in particular, see Vital, *A People Apart.*
33. On Wessely, see Edward Breuer, "Naphtali Herz Wessely"; and "The Wessely Affair: Threats and Anxieties," the fourth chapter of Feiner, *Jewish Enlightenment,* 87–104.
34. The standard history of Reform Judaism is Meyer, *Response to Modernity.* Gilman associates religious reform with decorum, the attempt to demonstrate that Jews are capable of conforming to western codes of social behavior (see chapter 2, "Jews

and the Culture of Decorum in Enlightenment and Post-Enlightenment Germany," in *Multiculturalism and the Jews,* 23–43).

35. Benedict Anderson, *Imagined Communities,* 6.

36. "Iberblik iber mayn lebn," *Yubileum-bukh* (Warsaw, 1925), 13; translated in Goldsmith's *Modern Yiddish Culture,* 107. Goldsmith discusses Birnbaum in chapter 4 (99–119).

37. The survey of Yiddishism is heavily indebted to Goldsmith's *Modern Yiddish Culture.*

38. For a history of the Hebrew language, see Sáenz-Badillos's *History of the Hebrew Language.* The standard history of Yiddish is Weinreich, *History of the Yiddish Language.* Harshav focuses more closely on the Yiddish identity in *The Meaning of Yiddish.*

39. See chapter 8, "The Czernowitz Conference" in Goldsmith, *Modern Yiddish Culture* (183–221).

40. Ibid., 184.

41. For an overview, see "The Emergence of Yiddishism" and "The Political Impetus," the second and third chapters of Goldsmith, *Modern Yiddish Culture,* 45–97; also see "Yiddish Ideologies," the seventh chapter of Liptzin's *History of Yiddish Literature,* 112–35.

42. On the emergence of the Bund, see Gitelman's *Century of Ambivalence,* 14–17.

43. On Zhitlowsky, see see "Haim Zhitlowski: Language, Political Radicalism, and Modern Jewish Identity," the second chapter of David H. Weinberg's *Between Tradition and Modernity,* 83–144; also see "Chaim Zhitlowsky," chapter 7 of Goldsmith, *Modern Yiddish Culture,* 161–81.

44. Zhitlowsky, "Dos program un di tsielen fun der monatsshrift, *Dos neie leben,*" 14. On the ideology of *Dos neie leben,* see "The Politics of *Yidishe Kultur:* Chaim Zhitlovsky and the Challenge of Jewish Nationalism," the third chapter of Michels' *A Fire in Their Hearts,* especially 144–52.

45. For an overview of Russian Jewry, see Gitelman's *Century of Ambivalence,* as well as his "The Evolution of Jewish Culture and Identity in the Soviet Union."

46. Gitelman, "The Evolution of Jewish Culture and Identity in the Soviet Union," 10–13.

47. For a brief overview, see Schweid's "Aḥad Ha-am." Information about Aḥad-Ha'am as a transitional figure comes from "Ahad Ha-Am: Culture and Modern Jewish Identity," the fourth chapter of Weinberg's *Between Tradition and Modernity,* 217–91.

48. Letter to Y. [Zeev?] Zeitlin dated July 11, 1909, in Asher Ginsberg, *Igrot* Aḥad Ha'Am [The Letters of Aḥad Ha'Am], 6 vols. (Tel Aviv: Dvir, 1956–60), 3:216; quoted in Weinberg, *Between Tradition and Modernity,* 279.

49. The phrase derives from the title of Bauer's book *Die Judenfrage.* For background of the discussion, see Vital, *A People Apart,* 189–98.

50. Sáenz-Badillos discusses the evolution of modern Hebrew in the last chapter of his *History of the Hebrew Language;* see 267–87.

51. Klausner and an unnamed editor, "Ben-Yehuda." More recently, scholars have begun questioning just how influential Ben-Yehuda actually was. For example, see Seidman, "Lawless Attachments."

52. This is Goldberg's thesis in *The Divided Self*. See also Rosenthal's *Irreconcilable Differences?*

53. The turn to militarism was not the introduction of a new characteristic but the recuperation of a postbiblical hero, Judah Maccabee, whose exploits are recounted in 1 and 2 Maccabees.

54. According to Bregman, "[I]n 1982, for the first time in Israel's history, Israelis criticized and also took a stand by refusing to cooperate and fight" (*Israel's Wars*, 176).

55. Such was Einstein's view in 1933, when he asserted that "Palestine is not primarily a place of refuge for the Jews of eastern Europe, but the embodiment of the reawakening of the corporate spirit of the entire Jewish nation," and that "the support for cultural life is of primary concern to the Jewish people. We would not be in existence today as a people without this continued activity in learning" (quoted by Gilman in *Multiculturalism and the Jews*, 108).

56. The latest comprehensive history of American Judaism is Sarna's *American Judaism*.

CHAPTER 1

1. For an overview of Anglo-Jewish history during the period, see Endelman, *The Jews of Georgian England*. Also of interest are his *Radical Assimilation in English Jewish History* and *The Jews of Britain;* Katz's *The Jews in the History of England;* Felsenstein, *Anti-Semitic Stereotypes;* and Ragussis, *Figures of Conversion*. On Jews and British literature, see Cheyette, *Constructions of "the Jew";* Galchinsky, *Origin of the Modern Jewish Woman Writer;* Scheinberg, *Women's Poetry and Religion in Victorian England;* Page, *Imperfect Sympathies;* Valman, *The Jewess in Nineteenth-Century British Literary Culture*. See also my two collections: *British Romanticism and the Jews* and *The Jews and British Romanticism*.

2. Unless otherwise indicated, biographical information on D'Israeli is from Ogden's *Isaac D'Israeli*. For a more recent critique of D'Israeli's oeuvre, see Peterfreund's "Not for 'Antiquaries,' but for 'Philosophers.'"

3. On D'Israeli's attempt to carve out a niche for himself, see Peterfreund's "Identity, Diaspora, and the Secular Voice in the Works of Isaac D'Israeli."

4. Quoted in Ogden, *Isaac D'Israeli*, 195.

5. D'Israeli, *Vaurien*, 203n.

6. Ibid., 202–3.

7. See William Bruce Johnson's introduction to the facsimile edition of Sharpe's *Dissertation upon Genius*, x.

8. Sharpe, *Dissertation upon Genius*, 7.

9. From the nineteenth century to the present, the concept of *genius* has been used as a marker of social outcasts. On the anti-Semitic use of *genius*, see Gilman's *"Smart" Jews;* on homophobic responses, see Elfenbein, *Romantic Genius;* and on pathological manifestations, see Felluga, *The Perversity of Poetry*.

10. For etymologies of the terminology, see Klein, *Comprehensive Etymological Dictionary of the Hebrew Language*. For background information about the Jewish

attitude toward the concept of genius at significant historical periods, see Urbach, "The Talmudic Sage"; Safrai, "Elementary Education."

11. As D'Israeli says in *The Literary Character* (2nd ed.):

> During the long interval which has elapsed since the first publication, the little volume was often recalled to my recollection, by several, and by some who have since obtained celebrity; they imagined that their attachment to literary pursuits had been strengthened even by so weak an effort. An extraordinary circumstance has concurred with these opinions—a copy which has accidentally fallen into my hands formerly belonged to the great poetical genius of our times; and the singular fact that it was twice read by him in two subsequent years, at Athens, in 1810 and 1811, instantly convinced me that the volume deserved my attention. I tell this fact assuredly, not from any little vanity which it may appear to betray, for the truth is, were I not as liberal and as candid in respect to my own productions, as I hope I am to others, I could not have been gratified by the present circumstance; for the marginal notes of the noble writer convey no flattery—but amidst their pungency and sometimes their truth, the circumstance that a man of genius could, and did read, this slight effusion at two different periods of his life, was a sufficient authority, at least for an author, to return it once more to the anvil; more knowledge, and more maturity of thought, I may hope, will now fill up the rude sketch of my youth, its radical defects, those which are inherent in every author, it were unwise for me to hope to remove by suspending the work to a more remote period. (3–5)

12. Douglass, "Byron's Life and His Biographers," 18. The note for the copy in the Pforzheimer Collection reads: "From Teresa Guiccioli-Byron books. Underscored, passages starred, 'LB' [Lord Byron] written in margin at appropriate spots, all probably in TG hand."

13. As D'Israeli explains:

> As everything connected with the reading of a mind like Lord Byron's [is] interesting to the philosophical inquirer, this note may now be preserved. Of that passage of the Preface of the second Edition which I have already quoted, his Lordship was thus pleased to write: "I was wrong, but I was young and petulant, and probably wrote down anything, little thinking that those observations would be betrayed to the author, whose abilities I have always respected, and whose works in general I have read oftener than perhaps those of any English author whatever, except such as treat of Turkey."

The fourth edition was published in 1828. My text for the quotation is the new edition, edited by Benjamin Disraeli (1881), 6–7.

14. D'Israeli's preface to his *Essay on the Manners and Genius of the Literary Character,* vii–viii. Subsequent quotations from this work are cited parenthetically in the text, by both edition and page number.

15. Annotations of the 1822 edition attribute revisions of this chapter to Byron.

16. In a footnote to the previously cited passage from *Vaurien,* D'Israeli compliments the Jewish community of Berlin for, in effect, establishing the kind of academy

he advocates: "This sketch must not be closed without informing the reader, that in literary Berlin the Jews are now enjoying singular honours as men of genius and study.... There are Jewish poets and Jewish artists of eminence; and which, perhaps, exist no where but in Berlin, a Jewish academy of sciences, and a Jewish literary journal, composed in Hebrew" (203).

17. Annotations of the 1822 edition attribute this chapter to Byron.

18. Annotations of the 1822 edition attribute this chapter to Byron.

19. Ogden, *Isaac D'Israeli,* 113.

20. Annotations of the 1822 edition attribute the expansion of this chapter to Byron.

21. D'Israeli concludes, as the contents of chapter 25 indicate, with the picture of genius in terms of the Byronic hero:

> Professions rise or decline in public esteem according to the exigencies of the times—National tastes a source of literary prejudices—True genius always the organ of its nation—Master-writers preserve the distinct national character—Genius the organ of the state of the age—Causes of its suppression in a people—Often invented, but neglected—The natural gradations of genius—Men of genius produce their usefulness in privacy—The public mind is now the creation of the public writer—Politicians affect to deny this principle—Authors stand between the governors and the governed—A view of the solitary author in his study—They create an epoch in history—Influence of popular authors—The immortality of thought—The family of genius illustrated by their genealogy.

22. According to Ogden, D'Israeli's attitude toward his subject remains ambiguous, the speaker claiming to be a Christian while skeptically deconstructing Christianity (*Isaac D'Israeli,* 202).

23. D'Israeli, *Genius of Judaism,* 15. Subsequent references to *The Genius of Judaism* will be indicated parenthetically in the text.

24. As D'Israeli says:

> A third generation were natives. A fourth were purely English. About the time of the first George this foreign race were zealously national; firm adherents to the Protestant succession. A Romanist on the throne for them would have been reviving the terror their relatives had flown from, and even as late as this period fresh fugitives landed on our coasts. It is evident that the Jews, for every protecting government, became the most zealous patriots. I do not know that their patriotism springs from the most elevated source—it lies more level with common feelings, but it will never dry. The Hebrew identifies his interests with those of the country; their wealth is his wealth; their victories secure his prosperity. On several trying occasions, both in England and in Holland, they have laid on the altar of public safety noble sacrifices of their lives and their fortunes. In recent times, faithful to a paternal government, they have marched in the armies of European sovereigns. Prussia has many Jewish officers; France, since her regeneration, has counted numerous Israelites in her *Ecole Polytechnique,* and the blood of Israel profusely flowed in the fields of Waterloo. The King of Holland has a complete regiment of

gallant Hebrews. All this confirms what I have already asserted, that every native Jew, as a political being, becomes distinct from the Jew of any other nation. If the Jewish military under the King of Holland were to encounter the French Israelites, the combat would be between the Dutch and the French. The Hebrew adopts the hostilities and the alliances of the land where he was born—he calls himself by the name of his country. (Ibid., 250–52)

25. An early version of this section appeared under the title "The Liturgical Context of the Byron-Nathan *Hebrew Melodies*," in *Studies in Romanticism* 47 (Fall 2008): 393–412. Little reliable information is available on Nathan, the biography by Phillips, *Isaac Nathan*, having been superseded—and corrected—by that of his granddaughter, Catherine Mackerras, *The Hebrew Melodist*.

26. Mackerras, *The Hebrew Melodist*, 14.

27. Quoted in ibid.

28. For examples, see Burwick and Douglass, *Selection of Hebrew Melodies*, 15–16. The complete reviews are reprinted in Reiman, *The Romantics Reviewed*. On the *Hebrew Melodies*, see also the edition by Ashton. On John Braham (né Abraham), see Roth, "Braham, John"; and Endelman, *Radical Assimilation*, 46–47. In "Byron and Nathan," Pont argues that Braham played a larger role in the composition than is generally acknowledged; in contrast, Bidney, in "'Motsas' for Lord Byron," argues that Nathan's contribution has been undervalued

29. Evans, whose *Essay on the Music of the Hebrews* was originally planned as a preface to the first edition of the *Hebrew Melodies*, affirms Nathan's authenticity:

> Now, I conceive that this question may easily be answered by what the querist himself has just before stated; for it must be evident to all, that if the Persians have derived their manner of singing "from the ancient Oriental Jews," and if such manner accords with that of the Germans, the latter must possess the true harmony of their ancestors; and hence it will follow, that if you have selected your Melodies, as I understand is the fact, from a variety of chaunts which were sung to you by German Jews, those Melodies are justly entitled to the originality they claim. (44–45)

Nathan himself, in his *Essay on the History and Theory of Music*, defends Jewish music by extolling the "beauty and originality of the Hebrew music" (227). Interestingly, later Jewish musicologists would dispute that claim, though Burwick and Douglass defend Nathan's judgment (*Selection of Hebrew Melodies*, 11).

30. In "Identity and Tradition in the *Hebrew Melodies*," Burwick argues that Byron, too, used the collaboration as a means of exploring his own identity: "As a total performance, the Hebrew Melodies reveal not only how well Byron could attune his lyric to the synagogue music which Nathan brought to him, but also how thoroughly he could engage Hebrew identity and tradition. . . . It was precisely this facile assumption of Jewish identity which was immediately noted in the contemporary reviews" (135).

31. On the music, see Douglass's essays "Isaac Nathan's Settings for *Hebrew Melodies*" and "*Hebrew Melodies* as Songs"; and Burwick and Douglass, *Selection of Hebrew Melodies*, 10–14, and their "Notes on the Songs," 240–42.

32. On the Haskalah in England, see Ruderman, *Jewish Enlightenment in an English Key*. Endelman discusses Anglo-Jewish educational reforms in *The Jews of Georgian England*, 154–59.

33. It might also be possible to include "Warriors and Chiefs" here, its melody, according to Douglass, resembling a Kaddish, this one for the New Year. Information about the Kaddish comes from Posner, Kaploun, and Cohen, *Jewish Liturgy*, 112–15.

34. "Mourner's *Kaddish*," in Silverman, *High Holiday Prayer Book*, 23. All translations of prayers are from the Silverman edition of the *High Holiday Prayer Book*.

35. Posner, Kaploun, and Cohen, *Jewish Liturgy*, 115.

36. All Byronic quotations come from McGann, *Lord Byron*. Poems will be cited by line numbers.

37. Nathan, *Fugitive Pieces*, 6. Subsequent references to *Fugitive Pieces* will be cited parenthetically in the text.

38. On Yigdal, see Posner, Kaploun, and Cohen, *Jewish Liturgy*, 111–12.

39. On the Articles of Faith, see Altman, "Articles of Faith."

40. Silverman, *High Holiday Prayer Book*, 25.

41. Posner, Kaploun, and Cohen, *Jewish Liturgy*, 112.

42. Ibid., 195.

43. Burwick and Douglass, *Selection of Hebrew Melodies*, 240.

44. See ibid., 8.

45. Although the lyric has remained consistent, its musical accompaniment has varied from community to community, there being over two thousand versions. Some evolved from the Sephardi tradition, others Ashkenazi, others still from regional differences within the two major divisions. Beyond that, some of the tunes incorporated contemporary musical forms, others borrowed from other parts of the liturgy (see Posner, Kaploun, and Cohen, *Jewish Liturgy*, 131–33). Baron discusses "She Walks in Beauty" as well as "The Destruction of Sennacherib" in "Byron's Passovers and Nathan's Melodies."

46. Multiple sources have been located for "Oh! Weep for Those" and "My Soul Is Dark" In their introduction Burwick and Douglass, citing Cohen ("Isaac Nathan"), identify the source as a northern folk song adapted for the Passover service (*Selection of Hebrew Melodies*, 13), though in the "Notes on the Songs" they discuss the influence of Kol Nidre (240–41). Because my purpose here is only to suggest the possibility that Nathan was influenced by the liturgical sources of his songs, my discussion is necessarily selective, not comprehensive.

47. See Silverman, *High Holiday Prayer Book*, 206–8, for notes on and the text of the Kol Nidre.

48. Nathan's preface is reproduced in the Burwick-Douglass facsimile of the *Hebrew Melodies* (*A Selection of Hebrew Melodies*, 48).

49. Silverman, *High Holiday Prayer Book*, 227.

50. Lipkind, "D'Israeli, Isaac."

51. Roth, *History of the Jews in England*, 241.

52. Fisch, "D'Israeli, Isaac."

53. Endelman, *The Jews of Britain*, 62.

54. Cohen, "Nathan, Isaac."
55. Bayer, "Nathan, Isaac," 853.

CHAPTER 2

1. On Jewish history in eastern Europe, see "Incarceration: The Jews of Tsarist Russia," the fourth chapter of Sachar's *History of the Jews in the Modern World* (51–72); and Vital, *A People Apart*. On the Haskalah in general, see Feiner's *The Jewish Enlightenment*; on the eastern Haskalah, see Zinberg's *History of Jewish Literature*, especially vols. 10, 11, and 12.

2. Werses discusses the difficulties encountered by young eastern *maskilim* in "Portrait of the Maskil as a Young Man."

3. On Wessely, see Breuer, "Naphtali Herz Wessely"; and "The Wessely Affair: Threats and Anxieties," the fourth chapter of Feiner's *The Jewish Enlightenment*, 87–104.

4. Rashi script is a cursive style of Hebrew typography first introduced by Venetian printer Aldus Manutius in 1501 to differentiate the commentary of Solomon ben Isaac (known as Rashi; 1040–1105) from the biblical text. In the nineteenth century, Rashi script, comparable to the popularity of Gothic script in Germany, was commonly used for secular publications. See Spitzer, "Typography."

5. For a transcription of Yaakov Zevi's Hebrew version of *Cain*, I.1.64–82, see appendix. References to Yaakov Zevi's codex will be cited parenthetically in the text.

6. McGann, *Lord Byron*, 6:229–30. The most extensive edition of Byron's *Cain* is that of Steffan, in *Lord Byron's "Cain."*

7. In *Georges Cuvier*, Rudwick places Cuvier's work in its proper historical context.

8. Zinberg, *History of Jewish Literature*, 10:119; Zinberg discusses Letteris on 10:113–19. See also Werner Weinberg, "Letteris, Meir"; Zinberg, *History of Jewish Literature*, 10:113–19; Kressel, *Leksikon ha-sifrut ha-'ivrit be-dorot ha-aharonim*, 2:247–49; and Waxman, *History of Jewish Literature*, 2:198–201.

9. According to Zinberg, "[H]e also received a higher education at the university in Lemberg, and from a *Yeshivah*-student was transformed into Doctor Max Letteris" (*History of Jewish Literature*, 10:114).

10. On the controversy surrounding the translation, see Neiman, *A Century of Modern Hebrew Literary Criticism*, 40–47.

11. This is the analysis of Zinberg, *History of Jewish Literature*, 10:115.

12. Letteris, *'Afrot zahav;* the quotation is from the first page of an unnumbered two-page introduction.

13. As far as I know, the only surviving copy of the volume is in the collection of the Jewish Theological Seminary of America. Transcriptions of Letteris's Hebrew translations of "Oh! Weep for Those," "The Wild Gazelle," and *Darkness* (ll. 69–83) can be found in the appendix.

14. A prayer of joyful thanksgiving, Hallel is the name for Psalms 113–18 when recited as a liturgical unit. On the Hallel, see Posner, Kaploun, and Cohen, *Jewish Liturgy*, 108–9.

15. Marchand, *Byron's Poetry*, 128.

16. I have no external evidence that the verse from Isaiah was a later addition, only the subjective observation that its placement on the title page is asymmetrical. For the Rabener/Igel edition, I used a microfilm owned by the New York Public Library. References to Igel's preface and Rabener's introduction will be made parenthetically in the text.

17. Transcriptions of the first three stanzas of Rabener's "The Burden of Matisyahu: In Praise of Moses Montefiore" and the acrostic "To the Composer of the Melodies: A Poem to Lord Byron," as well as his Hebrew translations of "She Walks in Beauty," "The Harp the Monarch Minstrel Swept" and *Darkness* (ll. 69–83), can be found in the appendix.

18. Chernovtsy in English, Czernowitz in German, Cernăuți in Rumanian. The city was under Austrian rule from 1775 to 1918, in Rumania from 1918 to 1940 and 1941 to 1944, and is now part of modern Ukraine. For a brief introduction to the Jewish community, see Marton and the editorial staff, "Chernovtsy"; and Reifer and the editorial staff, "Bukovina." The most detailed studies are in Gold's collection of essays, *Geschichte der Juden in der Bukowina*. Of particular use for the nineteenth century is Gelber, "Geschichte der Juden in der Bukowina." Because the German name is more familiar, especially as the name for a major Yiddish conference that was held in the city, in this study I shall consistently use the name Czernowitz.

19. Lvov in English, Lemberg in German, Lwów in Polish; Ukranian city. On the history of the Jews in Lvov, see Rubinstein, "Lvov."

20. On Igel, see Gelber, "Geschichte der Juden in der Bukowina," section 3 (48–56).

21. On Rabener, see Gelber, "Geschichte der Juden in der Bukowina," section 4 (56–59).

22. See chapter 1, "Byron and English Jews," for an overview of Maimonides and his influence on Nathan's liturgical choices for *Hebrew Melodies* (40–41).

23. For a brief introduction to Montefiore, see Lipman's entry in *Encyclopaedia Judaica*. The most recent biography is Collard, *Moses*. Page discusses his wife, Judith Montefiore, in the fifth chapter, "Judith Montefiore's *Private Journal* (1827): Jerusalem and Jewish Memory," of her *Imperfect Sympathies* (105–32).

24. *Tiferet* is discussed more fully in the analysis of Rabener's "A Dark Vision (a poem in six stages)," which evinces a much heavier component of Kabbalism (83).

25. That Rabener's interpretation is consistent with Nathan's seems more attributable to a common cultural base than to the possibility that Rabener had ever heard Nathan's melodies.

26. McGann does not include Isaiah in his list of biblical sources: "B's poem is obviously indebted to various apocalyptic passages in the Bible (see particularly Jeremiah 4, Ezekiel 32 and 38, Joel 2:31, Matthew 25, Revelation 6:12)" (*Lord Byron*, 4:459). Similarly, in his *Byron and the Bible*, Looper does not mention *Darkness* at all.

27. Although the spelling of the words is the same, Letteris does not vocalize his title, so the transliteration reflects the usual pronunciation of the word *ḥezayon*; Rabener, on the other hand, does vocalize his, as reflected in the altered translitera-

tion, *ḥezyon*. There is no evidence that either Letteris or Rabener knew, as Gleckner notes, that Byron originally entitled his poem "A Dream" (*Byron and the Ruins of Paradise*, 199).

28. Basic information about Kabbalism can be found in *Kabbalah,* the compilation of articles written by Scholem for the *Encyclopaedia Judaica*. More detailed explanations about the cosmos and divine emanations (Sefirot) can be found in Schaya, *The Universal Meaning of the Kabbalah*.

29. Letteris's translation of the first eight lines of *Darkness*:

> A harsh vision I envisioned, a dream threatening and formidable.
> The sun was dark in his going stars gathered together
> Their brightness, their path they passed in their going, stretched out
> From the travels of the world [eternal travels], their convoluted sunset went astray,
> There is no light, there is no path. The earth in horrible frost
> Vibrates in a rigid/inflexible darkness, the moon does not
> Shine light on the gloomy and woeful earth, the eyes of
> All animals were filled with hope.

30. Schaya, *The Universal Meaning of the Kabbalah,* 109; the discussion of *tiferet* and *raḥamim* is on p. 50.

31. Gordon's works were first collected in *Kol shirei yehudah leib gordon*. These are reprinted in *Kitvei yehudah leib gordon*. All quotations, which come from the 1953 edition, will be cited parenthetically in the text. I have substituted arabic numerals for the Hebrew pagination in the text. I used the New York Public Library copy.

32. The best source for information about Gordon and the eastern Haskalah is Stanislawski's *For Whom Do I Toil?* For a brief overview, see Ben-Yishai's entry in the *Encyclopaedia Judaica*.

33. On the Society for the Promotion of Culture among the Jews of Russia, see the entry by Slutsky and the editorial staff in the *Encyclopaedia Judaica*.

34. On Golus-Nationalism, see chapter 3, "Byron and the Yiddishists"; and on Ḥovevei Ẓion, see chapter 4, "Byron and the Zionists."

35. Stanislawski, *For Whom Do I Toil?* 32, 46.

36. Transcriptions of Gordon's Hebrew versions of "If That High World" and "The Wild Gazelle" can be found in the appendix.

37. Posner, Kaploun, and Cohen, *Jewish Liturgy*, 133–34.

CHAPTER 3

1. Harshav, *Language in Time of Revolution,* 6–7.

2. For a survey of the Russian attitude toward Byron, see Diakonova and Vatsuro, "No Great Mind and Generous Heart Could Avoid Byronism."

3. Bleicher's translation of *Childe Harold,* canto 1, was first published in 1908–9 in Zhitlowsky's periodical *Dos neie leben*. It was then reprinted twice, first in 1910 in *Eyropeische literatur* (European Literature), edited by Abraham Reisen, and again in Bleicher's *Veh un unruh* (Woe and Restlessness) in 1915. The biographical sketch "Lard Beiran: Biagrafishe natiẓen" (Lord Byron: Biographical Notice) also appeared

in Reisen's *Eyropeische literatur*. His translation of *Heaven and Earth*, *Himel un erd*, into whose title he inserts the parenthetical explanation *der mabul*—the flood—was published in 1919. I used the New York Public Library copies of Bleicher's work. Page references to the biographical notice published by Reisen will be included parenthetically in the text.

4. Information about Bleicher's biography is from Niger and Shatski, *Leksikon fun der nayer yidisher literatur*, 1:330–31.

5. The standard history of Spanish Jewry is Gerber's *The Jews of Spain*.

6. A transcription of Bleicher's Yiddish version of Harold's farewell, stanzas 1–3, can be found in the appendix. The copy text for the transcription is the version found in *Veh un unruh*.

7. McGann, *Lord Byron*, 2:6.

8. Watkins notes in conjunction with both *Cain* and *Heaven and Earth* that Byron's "immediate concern, I believe, was to define as far as was possible the connection between politics and religion; he wished to suggest that the religious values accepted unquestionably by a society as being true, universal, and absolute can be used to sanction and justify political authoritarianism" ("Politics and Religion in Byron's *Heaven and Earth*," 30). My discussion of *Heaven and Earth* is heavily indebted to Watkins.

9. Biographical information comes from Niger and Shatski's *Leksikon fun der nayer yidisher literatur*, 3:612.

10. The title page identifies the biography as part of a series "The Life and Work of Great Men." In Yiddish, the title is: *Lard beiran / zein lebn un tetikeit / frei baarbeit leut N. Aleksandrav*. I have been unable to locate Zilberman's source. Nizhni Novgorod, via e-mail correspondence with Peter Cochran, and Charles Robinson of the University of Delaware, hypothesizes that this is a reference to N. Alexandrov's *Lord Byron: His Life and Literary Creativity* (1892), a source derived from Tiulina's bibliography of all the works in Russian connected with Byron. My copy of Zilberman's biography was provided by the National Yiddish Book Center. References to this biography will be included parenthetically in the text.

11. The primary source cited is Elze, *Lord Byron*.

12. While I have not made an exhaustive search, the three copies I checked all lack pages 87–90.

13. Biographical information comes from Niger and Shatski's *Leksikon fun der nayer yidisher literatur*, 3:228–29; and Prager's *Yiddish Culture in Britain*, 313.

14. Information about *Der arbayter fraynd* is from Prager, *Yiddish Culture in Britain*, 124. A transcription of Hershman's Yiddish translation of *The Prisoner of Chillon*, part 1, can be found in the appendix. I used YIVO's copy of *Der arbayter fraynd*.

15. Wood, in "Nature and Narrative in Byron's *The Prisoner of Chillon*," traces the relationship between the shift in narrative voice and Bonivard's contact with nature.

16. For background information about the poem, see McGann, *Lord Byron*, 4:449–50.

17. Quoted in ibid., 4:450.

18. The *Hamlet* quotations, II.2.241–305, are from Willard Farnham's edition in Shakespeare, *The Complete Works*, 946–47.

19. Information is from Woodcock, "Anarchism."

20. Biographical information comes from Niger and Shatski's *Leksikon fun der nayer yidisher literatur,* 3:68–69; and Prager, *Yiddish Culture in Britain,* 322.

21. See Rothkoff, "Slobodka Yeshiva"; and Ben-Sasson, "Musar Movement."

22. I have been unable to locate copies of Horowitz's *Cain* or *Manfred.* He refers to both in the introduction to his *Sabbath and Other Tales;* and the catalogue of the British Library lists both with the notation "Cuttings from a newspaper. With a MS. title," and the publication date 1925. The bilingual title page for the Yiddish version reads: first in Yiddish—*Beirans / hebreishe melawdien /* iberzetzt fun Natan Horovitz / (ferfaser fun "treumen un gedanken") / mit a farvart; then in English—Byron's / Hebrew Melodies / Yiddish Translation / by / Nathan Horowitz. The imprint is London, 1925. The title page for the Hebrew version is also bilingual: first in Hebrew—*Shirei yisrael / shel beiran /* targum ivri shel: / Natan Horowitz; then in English—Byron's / Hebrew Melodies / Hebrew translation / by Nathan Horowitz. The imprint is London, 1930. I used the New York Public Library copies of Horowitz's work. References to Horowitz's Hebrew and Yiddish translations of the *Hebrew Melodies,* as well as his *Sabbath and Other Tales,* will be indicated parenthetically in the text.

23. Actually a late thirteenth-century text written by Moses de Leon, the *Zohar* was pseudepigraphically attributed to the early mystic Simeon b. Yoḥai. Sperling collaborated on his translation with Simon.

24. Transcriptions of both Horowitz's Yiddish and his Hebrew "She Walks in Beauty," "The Harp the Monarch Minstrel Swept" and "On Jordan's Bank" can be found in the appendix.

25. While these irregularities should be noted, they should not be given too much weight for several reasons: Yiddish orthography had not yet been regularized; the apparent anomalies could reflect dialectical differences; and finally, of course, they could have been introduced by an editor or compositor after Horowitz had submitted his manuscript.

26. As noted in the previous chapter, basic information about Kabbalism comes from Scholem's *Kabbalah* and Schaya's *The Universal Meaning of the Kabbalah.*

27. *Sefer ha-Bahir* (The Book of Splendor), an anonymous twelfth-century text considered to be the earliest work of kabbalistic literature; for an English translation, see *The Bahir.*

28. Biographical information comes from Niger and Shatski's *Leksikon fun der nayer yidisher literatur,* 1:79. Asen left his papers to the YIVO Institute for Jewish Research, New York.

29. See Orni, "Yesud Ha-Ma'alah."

30. On the Americanization of *Yiddishkeit,* see "Jewishness without Judaism," in Sarna's *American Judaism,* 223–27.

31. For an overview of the American Yiddish press, see Halkin, "Press." Also see "The Yiddish Press," chapter 16 of Howe and Libo, *World of Our Fathers,* 518–51; Sanders, *The Downtown Jews;* and Soltes, *The Yiddish Press.*

32. Levinthal, *Judaism.*

33. Asen's Byron translations include: *The Prisoner of Chillon—Der gefangener fun Shilon* (1925); *Hebrew Melodies—Idishe melodies* (1928); and *Cain—Kayin,* first

published serially in *Der oyfkum* (1928) and then in book form, with an introduction by Chaim Gutman (1931). I used the New York Public Library copy of the 1931 edition. References to Asen and Gutman will be indicated parenthetically in the text.

34. Transcriptions of Asen's Yiddish *The Prisoner of Chillon* (part 1), and *Cain* (I.1.64–82), can be found in the appendix.

35. Biographical information on Gutman comes from Ravitch, "Gutman, Chaim"; and Niger and Shatski's *Leksikon fun der nayer yidisher literatur*, 2:177–80.

36. I found "Lord Byron: His Life and His Loves" in box 2 of Asen's papers at YIVO. Unfortunately, the title of the publication was not preserved, only the fact that it was included in the section "From Shabbos to Shabbos," July 14, 1934. There are no page numbers.

37. Biographical information comes from Niger and Shatski's *Leksikon fun der nayer yidisher literatur*, 6:413–15.

38. Simon, "Translation and Poetry" (about Dr. Asen's translation of Lord Byron's *Cain*). I located the article among Asen's papers at YIVO, but the copy does not indicate the name of the journal, only the date, July 1, 1932. Subsequent quotations from this work are cited parenthetically in the text.

39. On Frishman's translation, see chapter 4, 142–48.

40. "Beiran un iden: Tsum 150-tn geburtstag fun lard dgarg beiran." This essay was included in box 2 of Asen's YIVO papers. The reference to Asen at the end suggests that he was not the author, though there is no indication of who actually wrote the piece.

41. The reference to Bleicher's *Hebrew Melodies* is puzzling, since, as far as I have been able to discover, the *Golus*-Nationalist did not translate the proto-Zionist collection.

42. Biographical information comes from Niger and Shatski's *Leksikon fun der nayer yidisher literatur*, 4:98–99.

43. I found a copy of Tenenbaum's "Lard beyrans tanus" in box 3 of Asen's papers at YIVO. There is no publication information available for the article, and no page numbers.

44. Biographical information comes from Niger and Shatski's *Leksikon fun der nayer yidisher literatur*, 4:389–90.

45. See Liptzin, "Khaliastre"; also see Liptzin's *The Maturing of Yiddish Literature*, 106–8.

46. Niger is quoted at end of Khashtshevatski's biographical sketch in Niger and Shatski, *Leksikon fun der nayer yidisher literatur*, 4:390.

47. The title page reads: Beiran / der gefangener / fun shilian / ibergezetst fun english—M. Khashtshevatski. A transcription of part 1 can be found in the appendix.

48. Contrast with Asen's overtly religious rendition of the same lines: "For believing my father's life / To the martyr's post was given away."

CHAPTER 4

1. An overview of Mandelkern's life and work can be found in the entry in the *Encyclopaedia Judaica*. More detailed information can be found in the Hebrew

articles Verba, "Dr. Shelomo Mandelkern ha-nishkaḥ"; and Malachi, "Shelomo mandelkern be-amerika."

2. The title page reads: *Shirei yeshurun / al-pi / lord bairon / me'et / d"r shelomo mandelkern.* / Leipzig [1890] / *Hebrew Melodies / of Lord Byron* / translated by / Dr. S. Mandelkern. / Leipzig 1890. I used the New York Public Library's copy of Mandelkern's translation.

3. Waxman, *History of Jewish Literature,* 3:260–61.

4. A transcription of Mandelkern's Hebrew "She Walks in Beauty" can be found in the appendix.

5. Frishman's *Cain: Kayin. / shir-ḥizayon al-pi kitvei ha-kodesh. / . . . / me'et lord bayron. / targum me-anglit le-ivrit / dovid frishman.* His *Manfred: Manfred / po'emah dramatit / tirgem me-anglit / dovid frishman.* Original publication information about Frishman's *Heaven and Earth* is unavailable. I used the Library of Congress's copy of Frishman's *Cain.* Quotations from Frishman's introductory essay will be cited parenthetically in the text.

6. For a brief introduction to Frishman in English, see Aharon Zeev Ben-Yishai's entry in the *Encyclopaedia Judaica.*

7. Frishman's devaluation resulted in large measure from his having sided with the losing faction on the question of Zionism, having "held collective Jewish redemption to be contingent on the spiritual redemption of the Jewish individual" (Hever, *Producing the Modern Hebrew Canon,* 28). This, according to Hever, defined Frishman as a "minor" writer, "minor literature [being] conceived as a literature seeking to contest and to overthrow the canon and its values. Despite its attempts to violate the canon, minor literature can never fully appropriate features that are central to canonical literature; it thus always remains on the edges, or margins" (29). Aberbach delineates the narrative of the "major" position in "The Renascence of Hebrew and Jewish Nationalism in the Tsarist Empire, 1881–1917," the ninth chapter of *Major Turning Points in Jewish Intellectual History,* 159–88. It is worth noting in this context that Aberbach cites Frishman only once in his book, in a list of "important Hebrew writers of the period" (162).

8. Waxman, *History of Jewish Literature,* 4:357, 351. Waxman discusses Frishman's fiction on 4:44–54, poetry on 4:214–19, and essays on 4:350–59.

9. A transcription of Frishman's Hebrew version of *Cain,* I.1.64–82, can be found in the appendix.

10. Steffan, *Lord Byron's "Cain,"* 27–28, 40.

11. Biographical information comes from Niger and Shatski's *Leksikon fun der nayer yidisher literatur,* 1:455; and *Who's Who in World Jewry,* 49.

12. Quotations from the introduction to Baruch's 192[?] translations of *The Prisoner of Chillon* and *Mazeppa* will be indicated parenthetically in the text. A transcription of Baruch's earlier Hebrew version of *The Prisoner of Chillon,* part 1, can be found in the appendix. I located both publications at the New York Public Library.

13. *Mazeppa* is the only sexually suggestive work by Byron that was translated into either Hebrew or Yiddish. For that reason, it should be noted that the period when Baruch both published his version and emigrated to Palestine coincided with the third *aliyah* (1919–24), a movement characterized by what Biale labels "sexual

utopianism." On sexual attitudes among early Zionists, see chapter 8, "Zionism as an Erotic Revolution," in his *Eros and the Jews*. See especially "Sexual Utopianism and the Second and Third Aliyot," 182–92.

14. McGann, *Lord Byron, The Major Works*, 1041.

15. Biographical information comes from *Who's Who in World Jewry*, 586; and the introductory biographical sketch contained in his *Muḥvar ketavim*, 1:11–14.

16. The English title page reads: Lord Byron / *Hebrew Melodies* / DONE INTO HEBREW / BY / JACOB ORLAND. Subsequent quotations from Orland's introduction are cited parenthetically in the text. I used the New York Public Library's copy of Orland's translation.

17. For a transcription of Orland's Hebrew versions of "If That High World" and "Oh! Weep for Those," see the appendix.

18. Kressel, *Leksikon ha-sifrut ha-'ivrit be-dorot ha-aharonim*, 1:466.

19. A transcription of Giyora's Hebrew version of Harold's farewell, stanzas 1–3, can be found in the appendix. I used the New York Public Library's copy of Giyora's translation.

20. In *Israel's Wars*, Bregman notes that after the Sinai campaign of 1956 came "a period in which Israel had the time to devote to producing some order from the chaos of war and social upheaval. Israeli society after the Sinai campaign became much more cohesive and self-assured, and was able to concentrate on consolidating its position in world affairs and at home" (60).

21. According to David J. Goldberg in *The Divided Self*, "When Israel launched its 1956 Sinai campaign in collusion with France and Great Britain, and was forced to withdraw from Sinai by a sharply critical President Eisenhower, American-Jewish lobbying on behalf of Israel was muted; in the election that immediately followed, Eisenhower actually increased his share of the Jewish vote" (141).

22. See "The Lebanon War and Israeli Society," in Bregman, *Israel's Wars*, 176–78.

23. The title page reads: *Lord bayron / manginot ivriot / nosea ivri adash me'et:/ shmuel fridman*. Michael Desheh's epilogue, "Lord bayron u-mazor 'manginot ivri-yot'" (Lord Byron and his Cycle *Hebrew Melodies*), is on pages 56–64; subsequent quotations from this are cited parenthetically in the text. I used the University of Delaware's copy of the book.

24. A transcription of Friedman's Hebrew "She Walks in Beauty" and "Oh! Weep for Those" can be found in the appendix.

25. Biographical information is from Kressel, *Leksikon ha-sifrut ha-'ivrit be-dorot ha-aharonim*, 1:566.

26. Mikh"l is Micah Joseph Lebensohn (1828–52), Mordecai Zevi Maneh (1859–86), and Saul Tchernichowsky (1875–1943).

CONCLUSION

1. In *Allegoresis*, Longxi differentiates between *allegory* and *allegoresis*:

> Given that a literary work tends to mean more than what it literally says, the relationship between what the text says and how one understands it—

say, the tension between the literal and the figurative—always gives rise to complicated hermeneutic problems. This complexity and tension between words and meanings—between text and its reading—may have been deliberately and systematically built into the text itself, in which case we have the text as an *allegory;* or, the tension may be constructed and formulated in the reader's response to the text, in which case we have *allegoresis* as a special mode of interpretation. The opposition between *compositional* and *interpretive* allegories form two distinct traditions. (62–63)

For an introduction to allegory, see Quilligan, *The Language of Allegory;* and the best study of allegory in the Romantic period is Kelley's *Reinventing Allegory.*

2. The most comprehensive study of the Wandering Jew is G. K. Anderson, *The Legend of the Wandering Jew.* On the legend's prevalence in the Romantic period, see the eighth chapter, "Ahasuerus in the Romantic Heyday" (174–211).

3. On the Wandering Jew in English literature, see Stuart Peterfreund, "Enactments of Exile and Diaspora in English Romantic Literature."

Bibliography

PRIMARY SOURCES

Byron in English

Ashton, Thomas L., ed. *Hebrew Melodies.* Austin and London: University of Texas Press, 1972.

Burwick, Frederick, and Paul Douglass, eds. *A Selection of Hebrew Melodies, Ancient and Modern, by Isaac Nathan and Lord Byron.* Tuscaloosa: University of Alabama Press, 1988.

McGann, Jerome J., ed. *Lord Byron: The Complete Poetical Works.* 7 vols. New York: Oxford University Press, 1980–93.

———. *Lord Byron: The Major Works.* Oxford's World Classics. Oxford and New York: Oxford University Press, 2000.

Steffan, Truman Guy, ed. *Lord Byron's "Cain": Twelve Essays and a Text with Variants and Annotations.* Austin and London: University of Texas Press, 1968.

Byron in Translation

CAIN

Asen, Abraham, Yiddish translator. *Kayin.* Serial publication: *Der oyfkum: Khoydesh zhurnal far literatur un kultur-inyonim* [The Rise: Monthly Journal of Literature and Cultural Matters] 3 (June–July 1928): 41–53; 3 (August–September 1928): 38–53; 3 (October 1928): 26–38. In book form, with introduction by Chaim Gutman: Vilna: B. Kletskin, 1931.

Frishman, David, Hebrew translator. *Kayin: Shir-ḥizayon al-pi kitvei ha-kodesh.* Warsaw: Tushiyah, 1900. Reprint, Warsaw: Merkaz, 1914. Reprinted in his *Targumim* [Translations], edited by Eliezer Steinman, 207–42. Tel Aviv: M. Neuman, Hotsa'at sefarim "Keneset," 1953–54.

Horowitz, Nathan, Yiddish translator. London, 1925?

Yaakov Zevi, Hebrew translator. *Kayin: Myster nach Lord Byron in drei Acten.* Unsdorf, 1851–52.

CHILDE HAROLD, CANTO I

Bleicher, Ezekiel, Yiddish translator. *Tcheild harald, paema fun lard beiran. Dos neie leben* [The New Life] 1(1908–9): 155–57, 217–20, 267–69. Reprinted in *Ey-*

ropeische literatur [European Literature], edited by Abraham Reisen (Warsaw: Progres), no. 12 (1910): 27–32; no. 14 (1910): 28–34; no. 15 (1910): 34–38; no. 16 (1910): 35–38; no. 17 (1910): 31–36; no. 20 (1910): 29–36; no. 21 (1910): 30–36. Reprinted in Bleicher's *Veh un unruh* [Woe and Restlessness], 63–101. London: Kunst, 1915.

Giyora, Moshe, Hebrew translator. "Shir ha-peraidah asher le-tchild herold" [Harold's Farewell]. In his *Ha-shoshanah ha-kehulah: Shirim* [The Blue Rose: Poems], 129–32. Tel Aviv: Adit, 1959–60.

DARKNESS

Letteris, Meir Helevi, Hebrew translator. *Hizayon hoshekh*. In *'Afrot zahav: Hemah shirim ye-karim mi-gedole meshorere ha-'amim* [Gold Dust: These Are Precious Poems from the Great Poets of the World, Made in Their Image and Made Proud in the Hebrew Language], 27–31. Wien: Schmidbauer u. Holzwarth, 1852.

Rabener, Matisyahu Simhah, Hebrew translator. *Hezyon mahshakh (shirah bas shesh mazos)* [A Dark Vision (a poem in six stages)]. Appended to Rabener's translation of the *Hebrew Melodies: Neginot ever, shirim shonim yesudatam be-hareri kodesh*, 27–31. Preface by Eliezer Eliyahu Igel. Czernowitz: Eliyahu Igel, 1864.

HEAVEN AND EARTH

Bleicher, Ezekiel, Yiddish translator. *Himel un erd (der mabul), a mistere fun lard beiran*. Kiev: Darum, 1919.

Frishman, David, Hebrew translator. Original publication data unavailable. Reprinted in his *Targumim* [translations], edited by Eliezer Steinman, 243–60. Tel Aviv: M. Neuman, Hotsa'at sefarim "Keneset," 1953–54. Reprinted in his *Kol kitve* [Complete Works], 7:5–81. Jerusalem: M. Neuman, 1964.

HEBREW MELODIES, COMPLETE

Asen, Abraham, Yiddish translator. *Idishe melodies*. New York: Max Yankovitch, 1928.

Friedman, Shmuel, Hebrew translator. *Lord bayron, manginot ivriot*. B'nei Brak: S. Friedman, 1983.

Horowitz, Nathan, Yiddish translator. *Beirans hebreishe melawdien* [Byron's *Hebrew Melodies*]. London: "Express," 1925.

———, Hebrew translator. *Shirei yisrael shel beiran*. London, 1930.

Mandelkern, Solomon, Hebrew translator. *Shirei yeshurun al-pi lord bairon*. Leipzig: W. Drugulin, 1890.

Orland, Jacob, Hebrew translator. *Manginoth ivriyoth*. Jerusalem: Ahiasaf, 1944.

Rabener, Matisyahu Simhah, Hebrew translator. *Neginot ever, shirim shonim yesudatam be-hareri kodesh*. Preface by Eliezer Eliyahu Igel. Czernowitz: Eliyahu Igel, 1864.

HEBREW MELODIES, SELECTIONS

Gordon, Judah Leib, Hebrew translator. In his *Kol shirei yehudah leib gordon: Yeshanim am hadashim be-arba'ah sefarim* [Complete Poems], 1:64–70. St. Petersburg: Bi-defus G. F. Pines vi-Yesha'ahu Tsederboim, 1884. Reprinted in his *Kitvei yehudah leib gordon: Shirah* [Works of Judah Leib Gordon: Poetry], 161–64. Tel Aviv: Dvir, 1953.

Letteris, Meir Helevi, Hebrew translator. In *'Afrot zahav: Hemah shirim ye-karim mi-gedole meshorere ha-'amim* [Gold Dust: These Are Precious Poems from the Great Poets of the World, Made in Their Image and Made Proud in the Hebrew Language], 24–27. Wien: Schmidbauer u. Holzwarth, 1852.

MANFRED

Frishman, David, Hebrew translator. *Manfred: Po'emah dramatit.* Warsaw: Stybel, 1922. Reprinted in his *Targumim* [Translations], edited by Eliezer Steinman, 261–82. Tel Aviv: M. Neuman, Hotsa'at sefarim "Keneset," 1953–54. Reprinted in his *Kol kitve* [Complete Works], 7:83–168. Jerusalem: M. Neuman, 1964.

Horowitz, Nathan, Yiddish translator. London, 1925?

MAZEPPA

Baruch (Brocowitz), Isaac Loeb, Hebrew translator. *Asir shilyan/Mazepah.* Frankfort am Main: Omanut, 192[?].

THE PRISONER OF CHILLON

Asen, Abraham, Yiddish translator. *Der gefangener fun shilan.* New York: Farlag Feder, 1925.

Baruch (Brocowitz), Isaac Loeb, Hebrew translator. *Asir shilyan.* Translated under the name Y. L. Brocowitz. *Ahiasaf* 8 (1900): 87–96. Revised translation, *Asir shilyan/Mazepah.* Translated under the name Y. L. Barukh. Frankfort am Main: Omanut, 192[?].

Hershman, Max, Yiddish translator. *Der gefangener fun shilian. Der arbayter fraynd* [The Worker's Friend], no. 17, August 13, 1921, p. 6, cols. 1 and 2; no. 18, August 27, 1921, p. 6, col. 1; no. 19, September 10, 1921, p. 6, col. 1; no. 20, September 24, 1921, p. 6, col. 1; no. 21, October 8, 1921, p. 6, col. 1; no. 22, October 22, 1921, p. 6, col. 1; no. 23, November 5, 1921, p. 6, col. 1.

Khashtshevatski, Moisei, Yiddish translator. *Der gefangener fun shilian.* Krakow: Kinder-Farlag bam Ts. K. L. K. Yu. P. O., 1937.

SECONDARY SOURCES

Aberbach, David. *Major Turning Points in Jewish Intellectual History.* New York: Palgrave/Macmillan, 2003.

Altman, Alexander. "Articles of Faith." In *Encyclopaedia Judaica,* 3:654–60. Jerusalem: Keter, 1972.

Anderson, Benedict. *Imagined Communities: Reflections on the Origin and Spread of Nationalism.* Rev. ed. London and New York: Verso, 1991.

Anderson, G. K. *The Legend of the Wandering Jew.* Providence, RI: Brown University Press, 1965.

Asen, Abraham. "Lard beiran: zein leben un zeine libes" [Lord Byron: His Life and His Loves]. Title of publication unavailable. The essay is in the section "From shabbos biz shabbos," July 14, 1934.

The Bahir: An Ancient Kabbalistic Text Attributed to Rabbi Nehuniah ben HaKana, First Century C.E. Translated and edited by Aryeh Kaplan. New York: Samuel Weiser, 1979.

Baron, Jeremy Hugh. "Byron's Passovers and Nathan's Melodies." *Judaism* 51 (Winter 2002): 19–29.

Bauer, Bruno. *Die Judenfrage*. Braunschweig: F. Otto, 1843.

Bayer, Bathja. "Nathan, Isaac." In *Encyclopaedia Judaica*, 12:852–53. Jerusalem: Keter, 1972.

"Beiran un iden: Tsum 150-tn geburtstag fun lard dgarg beiran" [Byron and Jews: On the 150th Birthday of Lord George Byron]. *Der spiegel* 27 (1936): 7.

Benjamin, Walter. "The Task of the Translator: An Introduction to the Translation of Baudelaire's *Tableaux Parisiens*." In *Illuminations*, edited by Hannah Arendt, translated by Harry Zohn, 69–82. New York: Schocken, 1969.

Ben-Sasson, Haim Hillel. "Musar Movement." In *Encyclopaedia Judaica*, 12:534–37. Jerusalem: Keter, 1972.

Ben-Sasson, H. H., and S. Ettinger, eds. *Jewish Society through the Ages*. New York: Schocken, 1969.

Ben-Yishai, Aharon Zeev. "Frishman, David." In *Encyclopaedia Judaica*, 7:198–203. Jerusalem: Keter, 1972.

——. "Gordon, Judah Leib." In *Encyclopaedia Judaica*, 7:797–803. Jerusalem: Keter, 1972.

Biale, David. *Eros and the Jews: From Biblical Israel to Contemporary America*. Berkeley: University of California Press, 1997.

Bidney, Martin. "'Motsas' for Lord Byron: The Judeo-British Literary Persona of Isaac Nathan." *Byron Journal* 25 (1997): 60–70.

Bleicher, Ezekiel. "Lard Beiran: Biagrafishe natizen" [Lord Byron: Biographical Notice]. *Eyropeische literatur* [European Literature], edited by Abraham Reisen, 12: 23–26. Warsaw: Progress, 1910.

——. *Der shtumer monakh* [The Dumb Monk]. Kiev: Dorem farlag, 1919.

——. *Veh un unruh* [Woe and Restlessness]. London: Kunst, 1915.

Bone, Drummond, ed. *The Cambridge Companion to Byron*. Cambridge: Cambridge University Press, 2004.

Boyarin, Jonathan, and Daniel Boyarin, eds. *Jews and Other Differences: The New Jewish Cultural Studies*. Minneapolis: University of Minnesota Press, 1997.

Bregman, Ahron. *Israel's Wars: A History since 1947*. 2nd ed. New York and London: Routledge, 2002.

Breuer, Edward. "Naphtali Herz Wessely and the Cultural Dislocations of an Eighteenth-Century Maskil." In *New Perspectives on the "Haskalah,"* edited by Shmuel Feiner and David Sorkin, 27–47. Littman Library of Jewish Civilization, edited by Connie Webber. London and Portland, OR: Littman Library of Jewish Civilization, 2001.

Burwick, Frederick. "Identity and Tradition in the *Hebrew Melodies*." *Studien zur Englischen Romantik* 1 (1985): 123–37.

Cardwell, Richard A., ed. *The Reception of Byron in Europe*. Vol. 1, *Southern Europe, France and Romania;* vol. 2, *Northern, Central and Eastern Europe*. Athlone Critical Traditions Series: The Reception of British Authors in Europe, edited by Elinor Shaffer. London and New York: Continuum, 2004.

Casanova, Pascale. *The World Republic of Letters.* Translated by M. B. DeBevoise. Cambridge, MA: Harvard University Press, 2004.

Cheyette, Bryan. *Constructions of "the Jew" in English Literature and Society: Racial Representations, 1875–1945.* Cambridge: Cambridge University Press, 1993.

Cohen, Francis L. "Nathan, Isaac." In *Jewish Encyclopedia,* 9:179. New York: Funk and Wagnalls, 1925.

Collard, George. *Moses: The Victorian Jew.* Oxford: Kensal, 1990.

Dennis, Ian. "'Making Death a Victory': Victimhood and Power in Byron's *Prometheus* and *The Prisoner of Chillon.*" *Keats-Shelley Journal* 50 (2001): 144–61.

Desheh, Michael. "Lord bayron u-maḥzor 'manginot ivriyot'" [Lord Byron and His Cycle *Hebrew Melodies*]. In *Lord bayron, manginot ivriot,* translated by Shmuel Friedman, 56–64. B'nei Brak: S. Friedman, 1983.

Diakonova, Nina, and Vadim Vatsuro. "'No Great Mind and Generous Heart Could Avoid Byronism': Russia and Byron." In *The Reception of Byron in Europe,* vol. 2, *Northern, Central and Eastern Europe,* ed. Richard A. Cardwell, 333–52. London and New York: Continuum, 2004.

Dingley, R. J. "'I had a Dream . . .': Byron's *Darkness.*" *Byron Journal,* no. 9 (1981): 20–33.

D'Israeli, Isaac. "A Biographical Sketch of the Jewish Socrates." *Monthly Magazine* 6 (1798): 38–44.

———. *An Essay on the Manners and Genius of the Literary Character.* London: T. Cadell, Junr. and W. Davies, 1795. Second edition, under the title *The Literary Character, Illustrated by the History of Men of Genius, Drawn from Their Own Feelings and Confessions.* London: John Murray, 1818. Third edition, considerably enlarged and improved. London: John Murray, 1822. Fourth edition, London: Colburn, 1828. New edition, edited by Benjamin Disraeli. London: Routledge, 1859; London: Frederick Warne, 1881.

———. *The Genius of Judaism.* 2nd ed. London: E. Moxon, 1833.

———. *Vaurien; or, Sketches of the Times.* Edited by Nicola Trott. London: Pickering and Chatto, 2005.

Douglass, Paul. "Byron's Life and His Biographers." In *The Cambridge Companion to Byron,* edited by Drummond Bone, 7–26. Cambridge: Cambridge University Press, 2004.

———. "*Hebrew Melodies* as Songs: Why We Need a New Edition." *Byron Journal* 14(1986): 12–21.

———. "Isaac Nathan's Settings for *Hebrew Melodies.*" *Englischen Romantik* 1(1985): 139–51.

Elfenbein, Andrew. *Romantic Genius: The Prehistory of a Homosexual Role.* New York: Columbia University Press, 1999.

Elze, Karl. *Lord Byron: A Biography with a Critical Essay on His Place in Literature.* Translated by L. Dora Schmitz. London: Murray, 1872. (Original German edition, 1870.)

Endelman, Todd M. *The Jews of Britain, 1656–2000.* Berkeley: University of California Press, 2002.

———. *The Jews of Georgian England, 1714–1830: Tradition and Change in a Liberal Society.* Philadelphia: Jewish Publication Society of America, 1979. Reprint, Ann Arbor: University of Michigan Press, 1999.

———. *Radical Assimilation in English Jewish History, 1656–1945.* Bloomington: University of Indiana Press, 1990.

Evans, Robert Harding. *Essay on the Music of the Hebrews: Originally Intended as a Preliminary Discourse to the Hebrew Melodies Published by Msrrs. Braham and Nathan.* London: John Booth, 1816.

Feiner, Shmuel. *The Jewish Enlightenment.* Translated by Chaya Naor. Philadelphia: University of Pennsylvania Press, 2004.

Feiner, Shmuel, and David Sorkin, eds. *New Perspectives on the "Haskalah."* Littman Library of Jewish Civilization, edited by Connie Webber. London and Portland, OR: Littman Library of Jewish Civilization, 2001.

Felluga, Dino Franco. *The Perversity of Poetry: Romantic Ideology and the Popular Male Poet of Genius.* New York: State University of New York Press, 2005.

Felsenstein, Frank. *Anti-Semitic Stereotypes: A Paradigm of Otherness in English Popular Culture, 1660–1830.* Baltimore: Johns Hopkins University Press, 1995.

Fisch, Harold Harel. "D'Israeli, Isaac." In *Encyclopaedia Judaica,* 6:109. Jerusalem: Keter, 1972.

Galchinsky, Michael. *The Origin of the Modern Jewish Woman Writer: Romance and Reform in Victorian England.* Detroit: Wayne State University Press, 1996.

Gelber, N. M. "Geschichte der Juden in der Bukowina." In *Geschichte der Juden in der Bukowina,* edited by Hugo Gold, 1:11–66. Tel Aviv: Olamenu, 1958.

Gerber, Jane S. *The Jews of Spain: A History of the Sephardic Experience.* New York: Free Press, 1992.

Gilbo'a, Menuḥah. *Ben re'alixm le-romantikah* [Between Realism and Romanticism: A Study of the Critical Work of David Frishman]. Tel Aviv: University of Tel Aviv, 1975.

Gilman, Sander L. *Multiculturalism and the Jews.* New York and London: Routledge, 2006.

———. *"Smart" Jews: The Construction of the Image of Jewish Superior Intelligence.* Lincoln and London: University of Nebraska Press, 1996.

Gitelman, Zvi. *A Century of Ambivalence: The Jews of Russia and the Soviet Union, 1881 to the Present.* 2nd ed. Bloomington: Indiana University Press, published in association with New York: YIVO Institute for Jewish Research, 2001.

———. "The Evolution of Jewish Culture and Identity in the Soviet Union." In *Jewish Culture and Identity in the Soviet Union,* edited by Yaacov Ro'i and Avi Beker, 3–24. New York: New York University Press, 1991.

Gleckner, Robert F. *Byron and the Ruins of Paradise.* Baltimore: Johns Hopkins University Press, 1967.

Gold, Hugo, ed. *Geschichte der Juden in der Bukowina.* 2 vols. Tel Aviv: Olamenu, 1958.

Goldberg, David J. *The Divided Self: Israel and the Jewish Psyche Today.* London and New York: I. B. Tauris, 2006.

Goldberg, Leonard S. "'This gloom... which can avail thee nothing': *Cain* and Skepticism." *Criticism* 41 (Spring 1999): 207–32.

Goldsmith, Emanuel S. *Modern Yiddish Culture: The Story of the Yiddish Language Movement.* Rev. ed. New York: Fordham University Press, 1997.

Graham, Peter W. "Byron and the Business of Publishing." In *The Cambridge Companion to Byron,* edited by Drummond Bone, 27–43. Cambridge: Cambridge University Press, 2004.

———. *Lord Byron.* Twayne's English Authors Series. Edited by Herbert Sussman. New York: Twayne, 1998.

Halkin, Hillel. "Press." In *Encyclopaedia Judaica,* 13:1053–56. Jerusalem: Keter, 1972.

Harshav, Benjamin. *Language in Time of Revolution.* Stanford, CA: Stanford University Press, 1993.

———. *The Meaning of Yiddish.* Stanford, CA: Stanford University Press, 1990.

Hever, Hannan. *Producing the Modern Hebrew Canon: Nation Building and Minority Discourse.* New York: New York University Press, 2002.

Hirst, Wolf Z. "Byron's Lapse into Orthodoxy: An Unorthodox Reading of *Cain.*" *Keats-Shelley Journal* 29 (1980): 151–72.

———. "Byron's Revisionary Struggle with the Bible." In *Byron, the Bible, and Religion: Essays from the Twelfth International Byron Seminar,* edited by Wolf Z. Hirst, 77–100. Newark: University of Delaware Press, 1991.

———, ed. *Byron, the Bible, and Religion: Essays from the Twelfth International Byron Seminar.* Newark: University of Delaware Press, 1991.

Horowitz, Nathan. *Himnen un fantazien* [Hymns and Fantasies: Melodies Founded on Hebrew Liturgy]. London: Chernitsky, 1927.

———. *Idishe tefilos un piyutim: Zeir vezen geshikhte un bedeutung* [Jewish Prayers and Liturgical Poems: Their History and Significance]. English title: *The Hebrew Liturgy (A Study).* London: Chernitsky, 1929.

———. *King Saul: Biblical Play in Seven Acts.* London: manuscript printed by the author, 1933.

———. *Sabbath and Other Tales.* London: I. Narodiczky, 1926.

———. *Souls in Exile: A Play in Four Acts.* London: I. Narodiczky, 1928. Rev. ed., 1928.

———. *Tefilah un shirah* [Prayers and Songs: Poems]. London: Chernitsky, 1926.

———. *Treumen un gedanken: Auservelte lieder.* English title: *Dreams and Thoughts: Poems.* London: Express, 1924.

Howe, Irving, with the assistance of Kenneth Libo. *World of Our Fathers.* New York: Harcourt Brace Jovanovitch, 1976.

Jakobson, Roman. "On Linguistic Aspects of Translation." In *The Translation Studies Reader,* edited by Lawrence Venuti, 113–18. London and New York: Routledge, 2000.

Katz, David S. *The Jews in the History of England, 1485–1850.* Oxford: Clarendon, 1994.

Kelley, Theresa M. *Reinventing Allegory.* Cambridge: Cambridge University Press, 1997.

Klausner, Joseph Gedaliah, and editor. "Ben-Yehuda, Eliezer." In *Encyclopaedia Judaica* 4:564–69. Jerusalem: Keter, 1972.

Klein, Ernest. *A Comprehensive Etymological Dictionary of the Hebrew Language for Readers of English.* New York: Macmillan, 1987.

Kressel, Getzel. *Leksikon ha-sifrut ha-'ivrit be-dorot ha-aharonim* [Lexicon of Modern Hebrew Literature]. 2 vols. Merhavyah: Sifriyat Po'alim, 1965–67.

Lecercle, Jean-Jacques. *The Violence of Language.* London and New York: Routledge, 1990.

Levinthal, Israel Herbert. *Judaism: An Analysis and an Interpretation.* New York: Funk and Wagnalls, 1935. Yiddish translation: *Yahadut.* Translated by Abraham Ansen. New York, 1949.

Lipkind, Goodman. "D'Israeli, Isaac." In *Jewish Encyclopedia,* 4:621–22. New York: Funk and Wagnalls, 1925.

Lipman, Vivian David. "Montefiore, Moses." In *Encyclopaedia Judaica,* 12:270–75. Jerusalem: Keter, 1972.

Liptzin, Sol. *A History of Yiddish Literature.* New York: Jonathan David, 1985.

———. "Khaliastre." In *Encyclopaedia Judaica,* 10:936. Jerusalem: Keter, 1972.

———. *The Maturing of Yiddish Literature.* New York: Jonathan David, 1970.

Longxi, Zhang. *Allegoresis: Reading Canonical Literature East and West.* Ithaca, NY, and London: Cornell University Press, 2005.

Looper, Travis. *Byron and the Bible: A Compendium of Biblical Usage in the Poetry of Lord Byron.* Metuchen, NJ, and London: Scarecrow, 1978.

Macaulay, Thomas Babington. "Moore's Life of Byron (June 1830)." In *Literary Essays Contributed to the Edinburgh Review.* London: Oxford University Press, 1932.

Mackerras, Catherine. *The Hebrew Melodist: A Life of Isaac Nathan.* Sydney: Currawong, 1963.

Malachi, A. R. "Shelomo mandelkern be-amerika" [Shelomo Mandelkern in America]. *Ha-Doar* 36 (1955–56): 93–94, 115.

"Mandelkern, Solomon." In *Encyclopaedia Judaica,* 11:865–66. Jerusalem: Keter, 1972.

Marchand, Leslie A. *Byron: A Biography.* 3 vols. New York: Knopf, 1957.

———. *Byron's Poetry: A Critical Introduction.* Riverside Studies in Literature, edited by Gordon N. Ray. Boston: Houghton Mifflin, 1965.

Marton, Yehouda, and editorial staff. "Chernovtsy." In *Encyclopaedia Judaica,* 5:393–96. Jerusalem: Keter, 1972.

Matar, N. I. "The English Romantic Poets and the Jews." *Jewish Social Studies* 50 (Summer–Fall 1988/93): 223–38.

Meyer, Michael A. *Response to Modernity: A History of the Reform Movement in Judaism.* New York and Oxford: Oxford University Press, 1988.

Michels, Tony. *A Fire in Their Hearts: Yiddish Socialists in New York.* Cambridge, MA: Harvard University Press, 2005.

Munday, Jeremy. *Introducing Translation Studies: Theories and Applications.* 2nd ed. London and New York: Routledge, 2008.

Nathan, Isaac. *An Essay on the History and Theory of Music; and on the Qualities, Capabilities and Management of the Human Voice.* London: G. and W. B. Whittaker, 1823.

———. *Fugitive Pieces and Reminiscences of Lord Byron: Containing an entire new edition of the Hebrew melodies . . . also some original poetry, letters and recollections of Lady Caroline Lamb*. London: Whittaker, Treacher, 1829.

Neiman, Morris. *A Century of Modern Hebrew Literary Criticism, 1784–1884*. New York: Ktav, 1983.

Niger, Shemu'el, and Ya'akov Shatski, eds. *Leksikon fun der nayer yidisher literatur* [Biographical Dictionary of Modern Yiddish Literature]. 8 vols. New York: Alveltlecn Yidishn Kultur-Kangres, 1956–81.

Ogden, James. *Isaac D'Israeli*. Oxford: Clarendon, 1969.

Orland, Jacob. *Muvḥar ketavim* [Selected Writings]. Organization and afterword by Dan Miron. 3 vols. Jerusalem: Mosad Bialik, 1997.

Orni, Efraim. "Yesud Ha-Ma'alah." In *Encyclopaedia Judaica*, 16:773–74. Jerusalem: Keter, 1972.

Page, Judith W. *Imperfect Sympathies: Jews and Judaism in British Romantic Literature and Culture*. New York: Palgrave/Macmillan, 2004.

Peterfreund, Stuart. "Enactments of Exile and Diaspora in English Romantic Literature." In *Romanticism/Judaica: A Convergence of Cultures*, edited by Sheila A. Spector. Farnham, UK: Ashgate, forthcoming.

———. "Identity, Diaspora, and the Secular Voice in the Works of Isaac D'Israeli." In *The Jews and British Romanticism: Politics, Religion, Culture*, edited by Sheila A. Spector, 127–47. New York: Palgrave/Macmillan, 2005.

———. "Not for 'Antiquaries,' but for 'Philosophers': Isaac D'Israeli's Talmudic Critique and His Talmudical Way with Literature." In *British Romanticism and the Jews: History, Culture, Literature*, edited by Sheila A. Spector, 179–96. New York: Palgrave/Macmillan, 2002.

Phillips, Olga Somech. *Isaac Nathan: Friend of Byron*. London: Minerva, 1940.

Pont, Graham. "Byron and Nathan: A Musical Collaboration." *Byron Journal* 27(1999): 51–65.

Posner, Raphael, Uri Kaploun, and Shalom Cohen, eds. *Jewish Liturgy: Prayer and Synagogue Service through the Ages*. Jerusalem: Keter, 1975.

Prager, Leonard. *Yiddish Culture in Britain: A Guide*. New York: Peter Lang, 1990.

Priestman, Martin. *Romantic Atheism: Poetry and Freethought, 1780–1830*. Cambridge: Cambridge University Press, 1999.

Quilligan, Maureen. *The Language of Allegory: Defining the Genre*. Ithaca, NY, and London: Cornell University Press, 1979.

Quinones, Ricardo J. "Byron's Cain: Between History and Theology." In *Byron, the Bible, and Religion: Essays from the Twelfth International Byron Seminar*, edited by Wolf Z. Hirst. 39–57. Newark: University of Delaware Press, 1991.

Rabener, Matisyahu Simḥah. *Shulamit*. Jassy: H. Goldner, 1880.

Ragussis, Michael. *Figures of Conversion: "The Jewish Question" and English National Identity*. Durham, NC: Duke University Press, 1995.

Ravitch, Melech. "Gutman, Chaim." In *Encyclopaedia Judaica*, 7:987. Jerusalem: Keter, 1972.

Reifer, Manfred, and editorial staff. "Bukovina." In *Encyclopaedia Judaica*, 4:1476–77. Jerusalem: Keter, 1972.

Reiman, Donald, ed. *The Romantics Reviewed: Contemporary Reviews of British Romantic Writers.* 5 vols. New York: Garland, 1972.
Rosenthal, Steven T. *Irreconcilable Differences? The Waning of the American Jewish Love Affair with Israel.* Hanover, NH, and London: Brandeis University Press, 2001.
Roth, Cecil. "Braham, John." In *Encyclopaedia Judaica,* 4:1289–90. Jerusalem: Keter, 1972.
———. *A History of the Jews in England.* 3rd ed. Oxford: Oxford University Press, 1964.
Rothkoff, Aaron. "Slobodka Yeshiva." In *Encyclopaedia Judaica,* 14:1668–69. Jerusalem: Keter, 1972.
Rubinstein, Avraham. "Lvov." In *Encyclopaedia Judaica,* 11:608–13. Jerusalem: Keter, 1972.
Ruderman, David B. *Jewish Enlightenment in an English Key: Anglo-Jewry's Construction of Modern Jewish Thought.* Princeton, NJ: Princeton University Press, 2000.
Rudwick, Martin J. S. *Georges Cuvier, Fossil Bones, and Geological Catastrophes: New Translations and Interpretations of the Primary Texts.* Chicago: University of Chicago Press, 1997.
Ryan, Robert M. *The Romantic Reformation: Religious Politics in English Literature, 1789–1824.* Cambridge: Cambridge University Press, 1997.
Sachar, Howard M. *A History of the Jews in the Modern World.* New York: Vintage, 2005.
Sáenz-Badillos, Angel. *A History of the Hebrew Language.* Translated by John Elwolde. Cambridge and New York: Cambridge University Press, 1993.
Safrai, Shmuel. "Elementary Education: Its Religious and Social Significance in the Talmudic Period." In *Jewish Society through the Ages,* edited by H. H. Ben-Sasson and S. Ettinger, 148–69. New York: Schocken, 1969.
Sanders, Ronald. *The Downtown Jews: Portraits of an Immigrant Generation.* New York: Harper and Row, 1969.
Sarna, Jonathan D. *American Judaism: A History.* New Haven, CT, and London: Yale University Press, 2004.
Schaya, Leo. *The Universal Meaning of the Kabbalah.* Translated by Nancy Pearson. London: George Allen and Unwin, 1971.
Scheinberg, Cynthia. *Women's Poetry and Religion in Victorian England: Jewish Identity and Christian Culture.* Cambridge: Cambridge University Press, 2002.
Schock, Peter A. "The 'Satanism' of *Cain* in Context: Byron's Lucifer and the War against Blasphemy." *Keats-Shelley Journal* 44 (1995): 182–215.
Scholem, Gershom G. *Kabbalah.* Library of Jewish Knowledge, edited by Geoffrey Wigoder. New York: Quadrangle / New York Times, 1974.
Schoville, Keith N. "Shulammite." In *Encyclopaedia Judaica,* 14:1475. Jerusalem: Keter, 1972.
Schweid, Eliezer. "Aḥad Ha-am." In *Encyclopaedia Judaica,* 2:440–48. Jerusalem: Keter, 1972.
Scrivener, Michael. *The Cosmopolitan Ideal in the Age of Revolution and Reaction, 1776–1832.* London: Pickering and Chatto, 2007.

Seidman, Naomi. "Lawless Attachments, One-Night Stands: The Sexual Politics of the Hebrew-Yiddish Language War." In *Jews and Other Differences: The New Jewish Cultural Studies,* edited by Jonathan Boyarin and Daniel Boyarin, 279–305. Minneapolis: University of Minnesota Press, 1997.

Shakespeare, William. *The Complete Works.* Edited by Alfred Harbage. Baltimore: Penguin, 1969.

Sharpe, William. *A Dissertation upon Genius.* 1755. Reprint, edited by William Bruce Johnson. Delmar, NY: Scholars' Facsimiles and Reprints, 1973.

Silverman, Morris, ed. *High Holiday Prayer Book: Rosh Hashanah—New Year's Day, Yom Kippur—Day of Atonement, with a New Translation and Explanatory Notes, Together with Supplementary Prayers, Meditations, and Readings in Prose and Verse.* Bridgeport, CT: Prayer Book Press, 1951.

Simon, Sh. "Iberzeẓung un dikhtung (vegn dr. eisens iberzeẓung fun lard beirans kayin)" [Translation and Poetry (about Dr. Asen's Translation of Lord Byron's *Cain*)]. Publication title unavailable. July 1, 1932, 11–12.

Singerman, Robert. *Jewish Translation History: A Bibliography of Bibliographies and Studies.* Amsterdam and Philadelphia: John Benjamins, 2002.

Slutsky, Yehuda, and editorial staff. "Society for the Promotion of Culture among the Jews of Russia." In *Encyclopaedia Judaica,* 15:58–62. Jerusalem: Keter, 1972.

Soltes, Mordecai. *The Yiddish Press: An Americanizing Agency.* New York: Columbia University, Teachers College, 1924. Reprint, New York: Arno / New York Times, 1969.

Spector, Sheila A., ed. *British Romanticism and the Jews: History, Culture, Literature.* New York: Palgrave/Macmillan, 2002.

———. "Jewish Translations of British Romantic Literature (1753–1858): A Preliminary Bibliography." In *The Jews and British Romanticism: Politics, Religion, Culture,* edited by Sheila A. Spector, 195–210. New York: Palgrave/Macmillan, 2005.

———, ed. *The Jews and British Romanticism: Politics, Religion, Culture.* New York: Palgrave/Macmillan, 2005.

———. "The Liturgical Context of the Byron-Nathan *Hebrew Melodies.*" *Studies in Romanticism* 47 (Fall 2008): 393–412.

Spitzer, Maurice Moshe. "Typography." In *Encyclopaedia Judaica,* 15:1480–88. Jerusalem: Keter, 1972.

Stanislawski, Michael. *For Whom Do I Toil? Judah Leib Gordon and the Crisis of Russian Jewry.* New York: Oxford University Press, 1988.

Stevens, Ray. "Scripture and the Literary Imagination: Biblical Allusions in Byron's *Heaven and Earth.*" In *Byron, the Bible, and Religion: Essays from the Twelfth International Byron Seminar,* edited by Wolf Z. Hirst, 118–35. Newark: University of Delaware Press, 1991.

Tauber, Gerald E. "Einstein and Zionism." In *Einstein: A Centenary Volume,* edited by A. P. French, 199–207. London: Heinemann, 1979.

Tenenbaum, Sh. "Lard beyrans tanus" [Lord Byron's Pretensions/Arguments]. No publication information available.

Thorslev, Peter L., Jr. "Byron and Bayle: Biblical Skepticism and Romantic Irony." In *Byron, the Bible, and Religion: Essays from the Twelfth International Byron*

Seminar, edited by Wolf Z. Hirst, 58–76. Newark: University of Delaware Press, 1991.

———. *The Byronic Hero: Types and Prototypes.* Minneapolis: University of Minnesota Press, 1962.

Toury, Gideon. "Translation and Reflection on Translation: A Skeletal History for the Uninitiated." Introduction to *Jewish Translation History: A Bibliography of Bibliographies and Studies,* by Robert Singerman, ix–xxxi. Amsterdam and Philadelphia: John Benjamins, 2002.

Urbach, E. E. "The Talmudic Sage—Character and Authority." In *Jewish Society through the Ages,* edited by H. H. Ben-Sasson and S. Ettinger, 116–47. New York: Schocken, 1969.

Valman, Nadia. *The Jewess in Nineteenth-Century British Literary Culture.* Cambridge: Cambridge University Press, 2007.

Venuti, Lawrence. *The Scandals of Translation: Towards an Ethics of Difference.* London and New York: Routledge, 1998.

———, ed. *The Translation Studies Reader.* London and New York: Routledge, 2000.

———. *The Translator's Invisibility: A History of Translation.* 2nd ed. London and New York: Routledge, 2008.

Verba, S. "Dr. Shelomo Mandelkern ha-nishkaḥ" [Dr. Shelomo Mandelkern, the Forgotten One]. *Ha-Doar* 33(1953): 524–25.

Vital, David. *A People Apart: The Jews in Europe, 1789–1939.* Oxford History of Modern Europe, edited by Lord Bullock and Sir William Deakin. Oxford: Oxford University Press, 1999.

Watkins, Daniel P. "Politics and Religion in Byron's *Heaven and Earth.*" *Byron Journal* 11(1983): 30–39.

Waxman, Meyer. *A History of Jewish Literature.* 5 vols. New York: Thomas Yoseloff, 1936, 1960.

Weinberg, David H. *Between Tradition and Modernity: Haim Zhitlowski, Simon Dubnow, Ahad Ha-Am and the Shaping of Modern Jewish Identity.* New York and London: Holmes and Meier, 1996.

Weinberg, Werner. "Letteris, Meir." In *Encyclopaedia Judaica,* 11:54–55. Jerusalem: Keter, 1972.

Weinreich, Max. *History of the Yiddish Language.* 2 vols. Translated by Shlomo Noble. Chicago: University of Chicago Press, 1980.

Werses, Shmuel. "Portrait of the Maskil as a Young Man." In *New Perspectives on the "Haskalah,"* edited by Shmuel Feiner and David Sorkin, 128–43. Littman Library of Jewish Civilization, edited by Connie Webber. London and Portland, OR: Littman Library of Jewish Civilization, 2001.

Who's Who in World Jewry: A Biographical Dictionary of Outstanding Jews. Edited by Igal Segal. New York: Who's Who in World Jewry, 1981.

Wood, Gerald C. "Nature and Narrative in Byron's *The Prisoner of Chillon.*" *Keats-Shelley Journal* 24 (1975): 108–17.

Woodcock, George. "Anarchism." In *The Encyclopedia of Philosophy,* 1:111–15. New York: Macmillan / Free Press, 1967.

Zhitlowsky, Chaim. "Dos program un di tsielen fun der monatshrift *Dos neie leben*" [The Program and Goals of the Monthly *The New Life*]. *Dos neie leben* (The New Life) 1 (1908): 3–16.

Zilberman, A. *Lard beiran: Zein lebn un tetikeit* [Lord Byron: His Life and Work]. Free adaptation according to N. Aleksandrav. Biographical Library: The Life and Work of Great Men. Warsaw: "Orient," 192[?].

Zinberg, Israel. *A History of Jewish Literature.* Translated and edited by Bernard Martin. Vol. 10, *The Science of Judaism and Galician Haskalah;* vol. 11, *The Haskalah Movement in Russia;* and vol. 12, *Haskalah at Its Zenith.* Cincinnati: Hebrew Union College Press/New York: Ktav, 1978.

Zohar. Translated by Maurice Simon and Harry Sperling. Introduction by J. Abelson. 5 vols. New York: Soncino, 1933.

Index

NOTE: Page numbers for the most important discussions of main headings and subheadings are given in boldface. Page numbers given in italics indicate pages containing typescripts of Hebrew or Yiddish materials.

Aberbach, David, 219n7
Abuyha, Elisha ben, 61
Aḥad Ha'Am, 19, 138, 143, 149; biography, **15–16**
Aḥiasaf, 16, 148, 149
Aleksandrav, N., 106, 107, 216n10
Alexandrov, N., 216n10
alienation, **23–24**, 101, 147; Byron's, 128; Cain's, 144–47; genius's, 32; Jewish, 156; Wandering Jew as symbol of, 173
aliyah, **17**, 21, 139, 157–58, 161, 219n13
Alkabez, Solomon ha-Levi, 45–46
allegoresis and translation, **171–76**, 220–21n1
allegory, 22, 101, 105, 171, 220–21n1
  in Byron: *Childe Harold,* 101–5; *Heaven and Earth,* 105–6; *Hebrew Melodies,* 141; *Mazeppa,* 156–57; "On Jordan's Banks," 121–22; *Prisoner of Chillon, The,* 110–15, 150–56; "She Walks in Beauty," 141–42; Song of Songs, 47–48; "The Wild Gazelle," 64–65
alterity. *See* alienation
America. *See under* Jewish communities
anarchism, 112
Anderson, Benedict, 10

anti-Semitism, 10, 14, 17, 99; and genius, 208–9; and *Hebrew Melodies,* 7, 37, 97–98; Byron as symbolic victim, 5; Byron's, 6; D'Israeli on, 34; Inquisition, 101; modern, 10, 17, 85, 99, 135; Nazi, 13, 16, 20, 126–27; Soviet, 13, 94–95; Wandering Jew as symbol, 173
Arbayter fraynd (periodical), 20, 109–10
Arbeiter (periodical), 125
Articles of Faith, Thirteen, 40–41
Asen, Abraham, 20, 109, **122–24, 126–30**, 132, *192–93,* 203n1; biography, 122–23; Simon's review of, 129–31
Ashmoret (periodical), 157
Austria. *See under* Jewish communities

Bahir. See Sefer ha-Bahir
Balfour Declaration, 12, **15–17**, 21, 94, 137, 148, 149, 172. *See also* Zionism, political
Baruch, Isaac Loeb (born Brocowitz), 21, 138, **148–57**, *197,* 219–20n13; biography, 148–49
Bayer, Bathja, 52
Benjamin, Walter, 204n10
Ben-Yehudah, Eliezer, **17–18**
Bible, 8, 206n26
  Byron and, 8

237

Bible (*continued*)
  individual books: Ecclesiastes, 82; Esther, 43; Exodus, 43, 119; Ezekiel, 214n26; Genesis, 8, 60, 77, 80–83, 119, 120, 142, 150, 151, 164, 166; Isaiah, 66, 69, 71, 79, 214n16, 214n26; Jeremiah, 214n26; Job, 58, 59, 146; Joel, 214n26; Judges, 47, 90, 91; Kings, 141; Maccabees, 34, 43–44, 208n53; Matthew, 214n26; Numbers, 88; Psalms, 50, 67, 89, 118, 213n14; Revelation, 214n26; Samuel, 49; Song of Songs, 46, 47–48, 70, 141, 142
  language of, xii
Birnbaum, Nathan, 10, 13
Bleicher, Ezekiel, 20, 95, **96–106**, 109, 132, 134, *187,* 215n3, 218n41; biography, 96
B'nei Moshe (Sons of Moses), 16
Bonivard, François (historical), 7, 110, 112
Braham, John, 37, 170
Bregman, Ahron, 220n20
Brocowitz. *See* Baruch, Isaac Loeb
Bund, the General League of Jewish Workingmen in Russia and Poland, **13–14,** 96, 100, 105–6, 135
Burwick, Frederick, 211n30, 212n46
Byron, George Gordon, biography, 4–8
  in Hebrew: Baruch, 153; Desheh, 169; Frishman, 144–45; Orland, 158
  in Yiddish: anonymous, 131–32; Asen, 123–25, 126–28; Bleicher, 97–98; Zilberman, 106–9
Byron, George Gordon, and Jews
  as symbol for, 5–6, 205n17
  with contemporaries, **23–53**: D'Israeli, 24–35, Nathan, 35–52
  specific symbols: Bundist, 96–98; Israeli antiwar movement, 168; Jewish activist, 126; Jewish everyman, 143–48; Joseph, 150; King David, 98; labor Zionist, 125; *maskil,* 58–59; messianic figure, 86; Nazi *Übermensch,* 133; Nazi victim, 127; righteous man, 71, 131; Wandering Jew, 145, 173–74; Yiddishist, 106–9
Byron, George Gordon, works in English
  Cain, 8, 109, 153, 172, 177, 206n25, 206n26
  Childe Harold, canto 1, 6, 109, 172
  Darkness, 8, 172, *17*
  Heaven and Earth, 8, 109, 142, 153, 172
  Hebrew Melodies, 2, 6–7, 19, 23, 52, 83, 108, 109, 153, 172, 177
    collaboration with Nathan, 35–52
    individual lyrics: "The Harp the Monarch Minstrel Swept," 50–51; "If That High World," 38, 39–40; "Jephtha's Daughter," 46–48, 90–91; "My Soul is Dark," 49, 212n46; "Oh! Weep for Those," 50, 212n46; "On Jordan's Banks," 42, 43–45; "O Snatch'd Away in Beauty's Bloom," 42–43; "She Walks in Beauty," 45–46, 170; "Warriors and Chiefs," 212n33; "The Wild Gazelle," 38, 41–42, *186*
  Manfred, 8, 21, 172
  Mazeppa, 7, 172; as allegory of new Jewish identity, 156–5
  Prisoner of Chillon, The, 7, 109, 172, 177; as allegory of anarchy, 112–15; as allegory of new Jewish identity, 150–56
Byron, George Gordon, works in Hebrew:
  Cain, 19, 21, 55, 138, 142; Frishman, 142–48, *196;* Yaakov Zevi, 56–61, *180–81*
  Childe Harold, canto 1, 21, 138, 160; Giyora, 161–65, *199*
  Darkness, 19, 55–56, 68, 121; Letteris, 66–67, 215n29, *182;* Rabener, 79–83, *185*
  Heaven and Earth, 21, 138, 148
  Hebrew Melodies, 19, 20, 21, 55–56, 68, 115, 116, 138
    Friedman, 165–68, *200–1*
    Gordon, 86–93, *186*

INDEX

Horowitz, 119–22, *190–92*
individual lyrics: "The Harp the Monarch Minstrel Swept," 77–78, 120–21, *184–85, 191;* "Herod's Lament for Mariamne," 92; "If That High World," 87–88, 159–60, *186, 198;* "Oh! Weep for Those," 63–64, 67, 89, 159, 166–68, *181, 198, 201;* "On Jordan's Banks," 66, 89–90, 121–22, *192;* "On the Day of the Destruction of Jerusalem by Titus," 92–93; "She Walks in Beauty," 76–77, 120, 141–42, 165–66, *184, 190–91, 195, 200;* "Song of Saul Before His Last Battle," 65–66, 67; "The Wild Gazelle," 64–65, 88–89, *181–82*
Letteris, 63–66, *181–82*
Mandelkern, 139–42, *195*
Orland, 158–60, *198*
Rabener, 76–79, *184–85*
Manfred, 138, 142, 148
Mazeppa, 21, 138, 149; Baruch, 156–57
Prisoner of Chillon, The, 21, 138, 149; Baruch's first version, 150–52, *197;* Baruch's second version, 153–56
Byron, George Gordon, works in Yiddish
Cain, 20, 116, 125, 217n22; Asen, *193;* Gutman, 126–28; Simon, 129–31; Tenenbaum, 132–34
Childe Harold, canto 1, 20, 96; Bleicher, 98–104, *187,* 215n3
Heaven and Earth, 20, 96; Bleicher, 105–6, 216n3
Hebrew Melodies, 20, 115, 116, 131–32, 218n41
Horowitz, 118–19, *189–90*
individual lyrics: "The Harp the Monarch Minstrel Swept," 118, *189–90;* "On Jordan's Banks," 119, *190;* "She Walks in Beauty," 118, *189*
Manfred, 20, 116, 217n22

Prisoner of Chillon, The, 20; Asen, 124–25, *192–93;* Hershman, 110–15, *188;* Khashtshevatski, 135–36, *194*
Byronic hero, 6, 8, 35; and Asen, 124; and Baruch, 150–57; and Bleicher, 96; and D'Israeli, 19, 24–35, 210n21; and Frishman, 142–48; and Giyora, 161–65; as Jewish everyman, 142–48; and Jewish identity, 2, 6; and Khashtshevatski, 134; and Tenenbaum, 132–33

Casanova, Pascale, 31, 204n7, 204n9, 204n10
Chernovtsy. *See* Czernowitz
Cicero, Marcus Tullius, 63
Cochran, Peter, 216n10
Cohen, Francis L., 52, 212n46
Communist Party, 14, 20, 94, 95; Bleicher, 105; Khashtshevatski, 134–35
cosmopolitanism, 3; D'Israeli, 31; Zilberman on Byron's, 108
Cuvier, Georges, 8, 59
Czernowitz (city), **69–70**, 83, 214n18
Czernowitz Conference, 12–13

David (biblical), 45, 49, 51, 67, 77, 86, 97, 118, 120, 121, 140, 141
Delaware, University of, 220n23
Dennis, Ian, 7
Desheh, Michael, 21, 138, **168–70**; biography, 168
Disraeli, Benjamin, 25, 205n21
D'Israeli, Isaac, 2, 4, 19, 23–24, 52–53, 172
biography, 24–25
and Byron, **24–35**
works: *An Essay on the Manners and Genius of the Literary Character,* 6, 16, 23, 27–28, 29–30; *The Genius of Judaism,* 25, 33–35, 52, 210n24; *The Literary Character, Illustrated by the History of Men of Genius, Drawn from Their Own Feelings and Confessions,* 23, 28, 30–33, 209n11, 209n13, 210n21; *Vaurien,* 25, 209–10n16

239

INDEX

Douce, Francis, 25
Douglass, Paul, 28, 205n14, 212n33, 212n46
Drum Africa (periodical), 109
Duff, William, 26

Einstein, Albert, 203n2, 208n55
Eisenstadt, Michael. *See* Desheh, Michael
elitism, 1, 6, 8, 23, 203n2; Byron's, 161; D'Israeli's, 23–35; Frishman's, 143; Jewish, 15, 17–19, 131, 172. *See also* genius
"Eli Zion ve-Areha," 42
emanation. *See* Sefirah/Sefirot
Endelman, Todd M., 52
England. *See under* Jewish communities
Enlightenment. *See* Haskalah
Epicurianism, 6, 108, 116, 130, 131
eshet ḥayil, 77
Evans, Robert Harding, 211n29

Feder (periodical), 123
First Zionist Congress. *See* Zionism, political
Fisch, Harold Harel, 52
Forvarts (periodical), 123, 125
France. *See under* Jewish communities
Frei arbiter shtime (periodical), 125
Freiheit (periodical), 123
Frei yidishe tribune un lashon un leben (periodical), 109
Friedman, Shmuel, 21, 138, **165–68**, *200–1*
Frishman, David, 21, 109, 129, 138, **142–48**, 168, *196,* 219n7; on alienation, 144–47; biography, 142–43
Funk, Y. *See* Horowitz, Nathan

Geiger, Abraham, 9
Gelber, N. M., 71
genius, 23, **25–27**, 208n9; and D'Israeli, **24–35**
Gerard, Alexander, 26
Germany. *See under* Jewish communities
Gilman, Sander L., 203n2, 206n34
Ginsberg, Asher Hirsch. *See* Aḥad Ha'Am

Giyora, Moshe, 21, 138, **160–65**, *199;* biography, 160
Godwin, William, 112
Goethe, Johann Wolfgang von, 61, 96, 127, 146, 149
Goldberg, David J., 220n21
Goldberg, Leonard S., 206n25
Golus-Nationalism, 9, **10–14**, 85, 94–95, 115, 118, 124, 128, 135, 137; and Bleicher, **96–106**, 218n41; and Byron, **96–109**; and Zilberman, **106–9**. *See also* Yiddishism; Zhitlowsky, Chaim
Gordon, Judah Leib, 19, 56, **83–93**, 168, *186;* biography, 83–85
Graham, Peter, 6, 8
Guiccioli, Teresa, 28
Gutman, Chaim, 20, **125–26**; biography, 125

Haganah, 157–58
Hallel, 67, 213n14
Harshav, Benjamin, 94
Ḥasidism, 11, 69, 138–39, 141–42
Haskalah, 1–2, **9–10**, 142, 143, 170; and Byron, **54–93**; in Czernowitz, **69–70**; in the East, 9–10, 19, **54–61**, 69; and Gordon, **83–93**; and Igel, **69–70**; and Letteris, **61–67**; and Mandelkern, **138–39**; and Nathan, 37–38, 41; rabbinic opposition, 1–2, 9–10, 19–20, 57, 84–85; and Rabener, 69–70, **72–83**; and Yaakov Ẓevi, **56–61**
Hebrew (language), xii, 10, 21, 142, 171, 172, 174–75; and Baruch, 154–55; and Giyora, 162; and Gordon, 85, 88; and Horowitz, 118–19; and Igel, 71–72; language controversy, 11, 16, 17–18, 55, 69, 93, 100; and Mandelkern, 142; and Rabener, 72–73, 75–77; and Simon, 129–30; and Yaakov Ẓevi, 60–61
Hershman, Max (Mordechai), 20, 106, **109–15**, *188;* biography, 109–10
Herzl, Theodor, 2, 15, **16–17**, 85, 138, 165

INDEX

Hever, Hannan, 219n7
Hilf (periodical), 148
Hirst, Wolf Z., 8
Holocaust: Israeli attitude towards, 18, 161; and Israeli statehood, 15, 16, 137, 138, **157–60**; and Yiddishism, 10, 12, 13, 20, 95, **128–36**
Horace (Quintus Horatius Flaccus), 63
Horowitz, Nathan, 20, 109, **115–22**, 124, 141, 177, *189–92;* and Kabbalism, 117–18; attitude towards translation, 116–17; biography, 115–16
Ḥovevei Zion (Lovers of Zion), **15**, 85, 139
Humarist (periodical), 123

identity and translation, **1–22**
identity, national, 3, 23–24, 26; Israeli, 18, 137–38, 142, 157, 165, 208n53; Jewish, 1–2, 6, 7, **8–19**, 20–21, 27, 71, 93, 172, 203n2; Nathan, 37, 48; Orland, 158; Rabener, 73, 75; Simon, 128; Yiddishist, 94–95, 101, 106, 109, 115, 135–36
identity, personal: Baruch, 150, 152–53, 156; Bleicher, 101; Byron, 1, **4–8**, 19, 97–98, 106–9, 135, 211n30; Desheh, 168; D'Israeli, 28, 32, 33, 34, 35; Frishman, 143, 149; Giyora, 160, 162, 164; Gordon, 85; Horowitz, 116
Igel, Eliezer Eliyahu, 19, 56; biography, 69–70; preface to *Hebrew Melodies,* 71–72
illuy, 4, 19, 23, 22, **27**, 30, 31, 53. *See also* genius
integrity: and Byron's identity, 1, 5, 7–8, 128, 143, 173–74; Baruch, 150, 153; Desheh, 168; Einstein, 203n2; Israel; and Jewish identity, 1, 6, 18, 19, 23, 52. *See under* Jewish communities

Jakobson, Roman, 205n12
Jewish communities
American, 13–14, 19, 20, 95, **122–34**, 140, 220n21

Austrian, 9, 10, 19, 54, 69, 73, 214n18
English, 6, 20, **23–53**, 74, 95, **115–22**, 140, 157–60, 172, 210–11n24
French, 6
German, 35, 43
Israeli, 17, 21, **137–70**; British mandate, **148–57**; Palestinian period, 16, **138–48**; statehood, 15, 18–19, **157–70**
Russian, 6, 13–14, 54–55, 104–5, 115, 135–36; and anti-Semitic purges, 13, 94–95, 135; Empire, 6, 9–10, 13–14, 19, 54–55, 83–93, 95; pogroms, 6, 10, 15, 20, 21, 85, 93, 96, 101, 115, 137, 143, 149; post-Soviet, 18; Revolution, 12, 20, 98–104, 106, 115, 149
Spanish, 6, 52, 99–100; Inquisition, 99, 102
Jewish education: Asen, 123; Bund, 100, 105; D'Israeli, 25, 34–35; Gordon, 84–85; Haskalah, 9–10, 11, 54–56; Maimonides, 74; Rabener, 72–73; Russian state-sponsored schools, 9–10, 54–55, 84; Yaakov Zevi, 57, 58; Yiddishist, 14, 124
Jewish Theological Seminary of America, 57, 213n13
Johnson, William Bruce, 26
Joseph (biblical), **150–56**
Josephus, Flavius, 92

Kabbalism, and: Alkabez, 45–46; *allegoresis,* 175; Friedman, 166; Horowitz, 117–22; Rabener, 77, 79, 82, 83; Yaakov Zevi, 59
Kaddish, 38–39, 212n33
Khashtshevatski, Moisei, 20, **134–35**, *194;* biography, 134–35
Kibitzer (periodical), 125
Kinah, 42
Kinder zhournal (periodical), 129
Kinnaird, Douglas, 37, 158
Kol Nidre, 48–50, 212n46
Krochmal, Naḥman, 61

INDEX

language controversy, 11–13, 20. *See also* Hebrew (language); Yiddish (language)
Lebediker, Der. *See* Gutman, Chaim
Lecercle, Jean-Jacques, 204n8
"Lekha Dodi," 45–46, 212n45
Lemberg. *See* Lvov
Letteris, Meir Halevi, 19, 55–56, **61–70**, 79, 83, 177, *181–82,* 215n29; biography, 61
Library of Congress, 219n5
Lipkind, Goodman, 52
Longxi, Zhang, 220–21n1
Looper, Travis, 206n26, 214n26
Lovers of Zion. *See* Ḥovevei Ẓion
luftmenshen, 11, 15
Lvov, 61, 69, 70, 74, 213n9, 214n19

Macaulay, Thomas Babington, 4–5, 107
Maccabee, Judah, 34, 208n53
Maggid (periodical), 84
Maimonides, Moses, 40–41, 74
Mandelkern, Solomon, 21, **138–42**, *195;* biography, 138–39
"Ma'oz Ẓur," 43–44, 52
Marchand, Leslie, 66
maskil/maskilim, definition, 9. *See also* Haskalah
Matar, N. I., 205n17
McGann, Jerome J., 156–57, 214n26
Meliẓ (periodical), 85, 139
Mendelssohn, Moses, 9, 25, 35, 52, 55, 56, 73, 74
Messianism, 15, 174; and Gordon, 85–89; and Horowitz, 118–21; and Letteris, 67
Milton, John, 73, 111, 146
minor literature, 3, 219n7
Montefiore, Moses, 69, 73, 74–75, *183*
Moses (biblical), 74, 175
Murray, John, 28, 205n19
Musar movement, **115–16**

Nathan, Isaac, 2, 4, 7, 19, 23–24, **35–53**, 172, 211n29; biography, 35–36; and Byron, **35–52**, 169–70; *Fugitive Pieces,* 40, 43, 47, 49, 51; and Jewish identity, 48–52

National Yiddish Book Center, 216n10
Neie leben (periodical), 13–14, 20, 96, 215n3
New York Public Library, 214n16, 215n31, 216n3, 217n22, 218n33, 219n2, 219n12, 220n16, 220n19
Niger, Samuel, 134
Nishmat Kol Ḥai, 88
Novgorod, Nizhni, 216n10

Ogden, James, 31, 210n22
Omar Khayyam, 116, 123, 124
Orient (periodical), 106
Orland, Jacob, 21, 138, **157–60**, *198;* biography, 157–58
Oyfkum (periodical), 123, 218n33

Perelman, Eliezer Yiẓḥak. *See* Ben-Yehudah, Eliezer
Philo of Alexandria, 175, 176
Plato, 113
Post (periodical), 109
Priestman, Martin, 205n15

Quinones, Ricardo J., 206n26

Rabener, Matisyahu Simḥah, 19, 56, 68–69, **70–83**, 118, 121, 141, 177, *183–85;* acrostic to Byron, 75, *183;* biography, 70; encomium to Montefiore, 75, *183*
raḥamim, 83
Rahlin, N. *See* Horowitz, Nathan
Rashi script, 57, 62, 213n4
Reisen, Abraham, 96, 215n3
Robinson, Charles, 216n10
Roth, Cecil, 52
Russia. *See under* Jewish communities
Ryan, Robert M., 205n16

sabra, 137, 156
Sáenz-Badillos, Angel, xii
Saul (biblical), 49, 65–66, 67, 116, 175
Schiller, Friedrich, 62, 70, 72, 79, 86
Schock, Peter A., 8
Sefer ha-Bahir, 120, 141, 166
Sefirah/Sefirot, 77, 83, 120–22

242

INDEX

Shakespeare, William, 110–11, 123, 151
Sharpe, William, 26–27
Shekhinah, 45–46; in "On Jordan's Banks," 121–22; in "She Walks in Beauty," 45–46, 77, 118, 120, 141, 166
Shelley, Percy Bysshe, 8, 110, 112, 157
shemittah/shemittot, 79, 83, 122, 174
Shulamit (biblical), 70, 141
Simon, Shelomo, 20, **128–32**; biography, 128–29
skepticism, 1, 2, 19, 53, 55; and: Byron, 7–8, 107, 148, 173–74, 205n14, 206n25; Frishman, 143–44, 146; Letteris, 56, 61, 64, 67; Nathan, 23, **35–52;** Rabener, 83; Simon, 129
Slobodka Yeshiva, 115–16
Society for the Promotion of Culture among the Jews of Russia, 84, 139
Soviet Union. *See under* Jewish communities
Spain. *See under* Jewish communities
Spenser, Edmund, 6, 100–101, 103
Sperling, Harry, 116, 117
Spinoza, Baruch, 2, 8, 61, 73, 148
Stanislawski, Michael, 86
Steffan, Truman Guy, 148
Stevens, Ray, 8

Tag (periodical), 129
Targum, 175
Tenenbaum, Shea, 20, **132–34**; biography, 132
tevel, 67, 82–83, 121
tiferet, 77, 83, 121, 122
translation and allegory, 22; and *allegoresis,* **171–76**
translation theory, xi–xii, 2–4; cultural and linguistic contexts, 172–75; interlingual, 4; interpretive communities, 175–76; intersemiotic, 4, 24, 35; intralingual, 4, 23; translator's intention, 172
Tseit (periodical), 109

United States. *See under* Jewish Communities, American

Venuti, Lawrence, xi, 204n5, 204n6
Voltaire, François Marie Arouet, 7, 149, 156

Wandering Jew, 67, 99, 101, 104, 145, **172–74**
Watkins, Daniel P., 105, 216n8
Waxman, Meyer, 139
Wesseley, Naphtali Herz, 9, 35, 57, 58
Winstanley, Gerrard, 112
Wood, Gerald C., 216n15
World War I, 132, 134, 143, 149
World War II. *See* Holocaust
Wordsworth, William, 111

Ya'aleh taḥanun, 50–51
Yaakov Zevi, 19, 55, **56–61**, 62, 93, 109, 177, *180–81*
Yid (periodical), 148
Yiddishkeit, **12**, 131, 217n30
Yiddish (language), xii, 93, 94–95, 171, 174–5; Bleicher, 100; Giyora, 162; Horowitz, 118, 119, 217n25; language controversy, **11–14**, 20; Simon, **129–30;** Zilberman, 109
Yiddishe familie (periodical), 148
Yiddishism, 9, **10–14**, 20–21, 93, **94–95**, 137, 170, 172; Asen, 122–24, 126–32; Bleicher, 96–106; Byron, 94–136; Gutman, 125–26; Hershman, 109–15; the Holocaust, 128–35; Horowitz, 115–19; Khashtshevatski, 134–35; Simon, 128–32; Tenenbam, 132–34; western, 115–28, 130–31, 217n30; Zilberman, 106–9. *See also Golus*-Nationalism
Yidishe folk (periodical), 148
Yidishe presse (periodical), 132
Yidisher arbeter. See Yidisher kemfer
Yidisher kemfer (periodical), 123
Yigdal, 40–41
YIVO Institute for Jewish Research, 203n1, 216n14, 218n36, 218n40, 218n43

Zederbaum, Alexander, 85, 139
Zekunft (periodical), 123

INDEX

Zhitlowsky, Chaim, **13–14**, 16, 20, 94, 95, 96, 137, 215n3

Zilberman, Elkana, 20, 95, **106–9**; biography, 106

Zimrat ha'arez. (periodical), 70

Zinberg, Israel, 61

Zionism, 9, 11, 12, **14–19**, 38, 54, 93, **137–38**, 172, 174; Asen, 123, 124, 125; Baruch, 148–57; Byron, 6–7, 21, 137–70; Desheh, 168–70; Friedman, 165–68; Frishman, 142–48; Giyora, 160–65; Gordon, 56, 84–92; Horowitz, 119, 121; Igel, 71–72; Mandelkern, 138–42; Nathan, 42–45, 53; Orland, 157–60; Rabener, 77; and Yiddishism, 94–95, 125–26

Zionism, political, 2, 7, 12, 16–17, **148–57**

Zionism, spiritual, 15–16, 21, 139, **142–48**, 167

Zionist Congress, First, 15, 17, 139, 172

Zohar, 117, 120, 217n23